BUILDING A BETTER WORLD

Errol Black & Jim Silver

BUILDING A BETTER WORLD

An Introduction to Trade Unionism in Canada

SECOND EDITION

Fernwood Publishing • Halifax & Winnipeg

to our families
Margaret, Sean, Dennis, and Thomas Black
and Loa Henry and Zoe Silver

Editing: Robert Clarke
Cover design: John van der Woude
Cover art: Pulling Together, The Builders of the Rideau Canal, 1826–1832, by Canadian artist Laurie Swim is a fabric mural 7.5' x 16', (2m x 5m) that now hangs in the main lobby of the Hotel Dieu Hospital in Kingston, Ontario. The work, sponsored by the Kingston District Labour Council and the Ontario Arts Council, was sewn in 1995 by the artist and volunteers from the KDLC and the Kingston community.
Printed and bound in Canada by Thistle Printing Ltd.

Published in Canada by Fernwood Publishing
Site 2A, Box 5, 32 Oceanvista Lane
Black Point, Nova Scotia, B0J 1B0
and #8 - 222 Osborne Street, Winnipeg, Manitoba, R3L 1Z3
www.fernwoodpublishing.ca

Fernwood Publishing Company Limited gratefully acknowledges the financial support of the Government of Canada through the Book Publishing Industry Development Program (BPDIP), the Canada Council for the Arts and the Nova Scotia Department of Tourism and Culture for our publishing program.

Library and Archives Canada Cataloguing in Publication

Black, Errol
Building a better world: an introduction to trade unionism in Canada / Errol Black and Jim Silver. -- 2nd ed.

Includes bibliographical references.
ISBN 978-1-55266-260-1

1. Labor unions--Canada--Textbooks. I. Silver, Jim II. Title.

HD6524.B62 2008 331.880971 C2007-906986-X

CONTENTS

ACKNOWLEDGMENTS

For their contributions to the second edition of this book we are grateful to: Wayne Antony, David Camfield, and Robert Clarke. As well, we thank the many trade unionists in Manitoba and elsewhere in Canada who, over the years, have shared with us their ideas and insights about the role of the labour movement in society and supported our efforts to clarify and explain that role in our research and writing. Similarly, thanks to the many trade unions that acquired the book for use in their educational programs and to all the teachers in universities and colleges who used the first edition of the book in their courses. Finally, thanks to the production folks at Fernwood Publishing: Beverley Rach, Brenda Conroy, and Debbie Mathers.

We trust readers will find in this new edition a perspective that will encourage their own research initiatives and inspire lively debates in trade union workshops and educational programs, and in universities, colleges and high schools.

CHAPTER 1

INTRODUCTION

At around 5:30 p.m. on May 1, 2000, in the prairie city of Brandon, Manitoba, about two hundred trade unionists and labour supporters gathered in a Safeway store parking lot. They were there not just to celebrate another "May Day" but also to witness the unveiling of a new banner commemorating a century and a half of labour struggles and gains. The banner, created by local artist Curt Shoultz for the Brandon and District Labour Council, held a particular significance for the assembled workers and their families. Its theme, "Strength in Solidarity," reflected a key element in labour's long history: the recognition that advances can only come "when workers join together and act collectively."

As unionist Jan Chaboyer told the assembled crowd that day, the banner was meant to highlight "the core values and principles of the labour movement, namely, Democracy, Freedom, Social Justice and Equality." Its individual panels, she said, depicted the union members' "historical struggles for `bread, and roses too,' health and safety in the workplace, schools instead of sweatshops for our children, and protection of our natural resources and environment" (Chaboyer and Black 2000).

Chaboyer, the president of a Manitoba Government Employees' Union local of support staff and food workers at Brandon University, and president of the Brandon and District Labour Council, was herself an emblem of labour's particular brand of solidarity. When offered an out-of-scope job at Brandon University, she said she would only accept it if she could remain in the union. The university accommodated her; she went on to do the job at a union rate, considerably below the previous job holder's pay level.

That day Chaboyer went on to tell the gathering that labour's legacy is to be found in the many reforms labour had fought for and achieved: the right to join unions and bargain collectively with employers, the eight-hour day, public libraries and public education, the elimination of restrictions on the rights of citizens to vote and run for office, unemployment insurance, Medicare, the Canada Pension Plan, employment standards legislation, workers' compensation, health and safety legislation, and pay equity and anti-discrimination laws. "Can there be any doubt," Chaboyer said, "that these reforms, and others, have improved the lives of all workers and made our communities better places to live in."

That particular day marked a time when gains made by working people were under threat across Canada — "in danger," as Chaboyer put it, "of being rolled back or eliminated by governments and corporations intent on driving down labour costs and reducing the size of the public sector in the name of enhancing our global competitiveness." In Manitoba, at least one encouraging development had taken place: the election in September 1999 of a New Democratic Party government in the province. Still, Chaboyer cautioned, that victory would not bring automatic changes in legislation and programs for the better. Although the NDP was known as being more sympathetic to labour than other political parties were, there was still a danger that business interests in the province would push the government to the right. Unions would still have to mobilize their resources and apply constant pressure for progressive change (see chapter 5 for a discussion of the complex relationship between unions and the NDP). "We must resolve to do this," Chaboyer said, "in the months and years ahead." Labour would have to defend its historical gains and, even more, add to its rich legacy:

> We must work together to protect the programs and institutional arrangements that enrich our lives... and we must strive to improve conditions for the victims of our changing economy — the homeless, the hungry, the poor and the disadvantaged. And we must support all workers around the world who are engaged in struggles for the rights and benefits we value as workers and citizens in Canada.

After the unveiling and the speeches the participants formed into a lively "Solidarity Banner March" that wound its way along city streets to a rally at the East End Community Centre. The march followed a route that had been walked many times by workers since the early decades of the twentieth century.

Meanwhile, similar events were taking place that day in towns and cities across the country, as affiliates of the Canadian Labour Congress (trade unions, local labour councils, and federations of labour) joined with workers around the world to celebrate May Day — the International Workers' Holiday (see Foner 1986). The ideas and principles expressed by Jan Chaboyer in her passionate statement were echoed that day in the speeches of hundreds of other union activists. A Canadian Labour Congress (CLC) pamphlet explained that the events were organized "to show our communities who we are, as workers and union activists [and] to let people know we're proud to be working people and union members" (CLC 2000).

Typically, the media paid only slight notice to the labour celebrations. In Brandon the coverage consisted of a ninety-second clip on the local television news and a single photograph of a CUPE banner in the *Brandon Sun*. Given that most of the media in Canada are owned by a small number of large corporations, and that those companies in turn derive most of their revenue from advertising purchased by other large corporations, the low mainstream profile should come as no surprise. Media coverage of union activities tends to focus on strikes, picket-line battles, confrontations with governments, attacks on unions by corporate leaders and politicians, and conflict within and between unions. More often than not, media coverage of such incidents obscures both the issues involved and the significance of the issues. The result is that media reports tend to convey the impression that all unions and their members do is strike, demonstrate, and fight amongst themselves. Reports also often misrepresent the position and objectives of trade unions and create an impression that their activities and actions are invariably contrary to the "public interest." (For a general discussion of the union/media issue, see Hackett and Gruneau 1999.)

Wages or Profits?

Unions are, generally speaking, advantageous to workers; but employers tend to oppose unions on the grounds that a unionized workforce brings higher wages and benefit costs and places limits on the ability arbitrarily to impose conditions of work and employment. For these reasons relations between capital and labour, between employers and unions, have always been full of conflict, and union gains have always come as the result of bitter and hard-fought struggles.

A Canadian Centre for Policy Alternatives study, *Rising Profit Shares, Falling Wage Shares,* demonstrates that the struggles of recent decades have shifted wealth from workers to owners.

"The study finds that Canadian workers' wage share of national income is the lowest it's been in 40 years. If workers' real wages had increased to reflect improved productivity and growth, they could be earning an average of $10,000 more each year on their paycheques (in 2005 dollars). [In contrast] corporate profit shares are the highest they've been in 40 years.... In 2005, corporations banked $130 billion more in gross profits than they would have if the profit share had remained at 1991 levels."

Source: Canadian Centre for Policy Alternatives, 2007.

Certainly, strikes, demonstrations, and battles with governments are an important part of what trade unions do; and those events should be covered. They represent tactics that unions must use to advance and defend the interests of working people. Then too, conflict does exist within and between unions — but this is something to be expected and welcomed in democratic organizations. Clashes between rank-and-file members and union leadership over collective bargaining agendas, the handling of grievances, and the conduct of strikes, for instance, are commonplace within unions. National and international unions also experience numerous disagreements at conventions, not only over nitty-gritty issues, such as how a union is being run and the perks that union leaders receive, but also over bigger issues relating to union philosophy and vision. Rank-

and-file members frequently rebel against union leaderships when they feel those leaders have lost touch with their concerns and interests.

The trade union centrals, which seek to bring unions together in common cause, also experience internal strife and upheavals. These problems can arise from differences in philosophy, vision, and politics or from attempts to resolve disputes (usually related to raiding) between affiliated unions. The disputes sometimes result in significant ruptures within the trade union central.

While all of this is going on, though, the things that unions do day in and day out for their members, workers in general, and the marginalized in society tend to pass unnoticed.

For example, each and every year in Canada:

- unions negotiate thousands of collective agreements without incident, thousands of workers obtain redress and justice through grievance procedures, and tens of thousands of union members participate in union-organized training and educational programs;
- unions make representations to governments and their agencies calling for increases in minimum wages, tougher health and safety measures in workplaces, more resources for day care, health, education, and affordable housing, improvements in unemployment insurance and social assistance, more resources for training and education, and expanded opportunities for people with disabilities and young people in trouble;
- unions initiate campaigns in opposition to racism and other forms of discrimination and actions by corporations and governments that damage or undermine the living conditions and rights of working people and their families;
- the Canadian Labour Congress and its affiliates contribute to and participate in the New Democratic Party, the United Way, and numerous coalitions involving women's, anti-poverty, Aboriginal, and other organizations seeking to correct inequities in our society; and
- trade union leaders and activists connect with their counterparts in other countries around the world, providing, for instance, aid and expertise to workers in developing countries who are seeking to build a trade union movement and working within international labour organizations to expand worker and trade union rights.

Trade unions and their members are a major force in our society. They may be the one force that consistently stands up for the interests and rights of all people as workers, as family members, and as citizens and community members. Their actions are, moreover, shaped and guided by a vision of a better society: one in which everyone shares in the benefits of economic

> The International Erosion of Unionization Rates since 1992: Unionization rates have been declining in most advanced industrial countries since 1980. Of the twenty countries for which data are available, unionization rates declined in all but four: Republic of Korea (14.7% to 17.6%), Finland (69.4% to 72.5%), Sweden (78.0% to 80.8%), and Norway (58.3% to 58.5%). Between 1980 and 1990 the unionization rate in Canada slipped from 34.7% to 32.9%.
>
> Since 1992 the rates have held their own in two countries (Belgium and Spain). In all others the rates have declined. The proportionate declines were particularly significant in Australia (39.6% to 22.9%), New Zealand (37.1% to 22.1%), Germany (33.9% to 22.6%), Ireland (49.8% to 35.3%), and the United Kingdom (37.2% to 29.3%). The rate for all countries in the European Union combined declined by 21.3% (33.4% to 26.3%). The countries with the smallest proportionate declines were Finland (78.4% to 74.1%), Sweden (83.3% to 78.0%), and Denmark (75.8% to 70.4%).
>
> The unionization rates for Canada were 34.7% in 1980, 33.1% in 1992, and 28.4% in 2003. These declines were below average so that Canada's standing in terms of the unionization rate went from 14 in 1980 to 13 in 1992 and 10 in 2003.
>
> *Source: Visser 2006*

and social progress; which has no soup lines and people living in the streets, no poverty, and no discrimination; and which is based on solidarity, sharing, and collective action. That vision, though, is at odds with the view promoted by Canada's corporate leaders through organizations such as the Canadian Council of Chief Executives, chambers of commerce, right-wing think tanks such as the Fraser Institute, and the national media. These players favour a society that frees business from restrictions or regulations and subordinates all interests to the operations of markets and monopoly elements and the power of employers.

In recent decades corporations and governments have been waging a concerted and long-term campaign to curtail workers' rights and undermine the power of trade unions. Employers justify this campaign by arguing that worker rights and trade unions impede flexibility in labour and workplaces and impair Canada's ability to compete in international markets. Despite resistance from trade unions, the attack by corporations and employers has met with considerable success. The curtailment of union rights is especially evident in Ontario and Alberta, where changes to labour relations legislation have created greater obstacles to unionization and weakened the capacity of workers to conduct effective and successful strikes. It is also reflected in changes to some collective agreements — changes that have reduced unions' and workers' control over practices such as contracting out and the allocation of opportunities (access to training, or promotions, for instance) within internal labour markets.

In the 1990s the impact of the anti-union campaign was reflected in declining unionization rates. Trade union membership in Canada in 1992 stood at 4,089,000 members representing 28.4 percent of the civilian workforce and 35.7 percent of non-agricultural paid workers. In 2006 the number of union members was 4,441,000, representing 25.6 percent of the civilian workforce and 30.8 percent of non-agricultural paid workers (HRDC 2006). The declining rate of union membership and the erosion of worker rights and union power pose serious threats to the well-being of working people and their communities. They also undermine the very institutional arrangements that are designed to make Canada a democratic, inclusive, and equitable society.

Surely, a robust and forward-looking labour movement is an essential part of a democracy. A corollary of that point is that it is equally essential that Canadians everywhere not just recognize the key issues and concerns that surround union work but also become willing to take up a discussion of the role of trade unions in our lives, in our country. With this in mind we intend, in the following pages, to explore a number of basic questions.

- How are unions structured and how do they work, in union locals and in trade union centrals (local labour councils, provincial federations of labour, and the Canadian Labour Congress)?
- What do unions do and what have they achieved, for their members, for workers in general, and for all of us?
- Where did unions come from, how have they developed historically, and how do they relate to capital and the state?
- What are the politics of unions, and how have they attempted to advance their politics through partisan political activity, extra-parliamentary politics, and participation in coalitions?
- What are the factors that have emerged in Canada in recent decades to stall the forward momentum of unions, place them on the defensive, and weaken their capacity to shape and influence the course of events in the economy and in society?
- Why is it important to all of us that unions rejuvenate and move forward? What are the critical challenges (both internal and external) that must be met so that this can happen?

Our aim, overall, is not just to provide a richer and deeper understanding of the role and impact of trade unions and the labour movement in Canada but also to emphasize, through the evidence of past and present struggles, the absolutely crucial contribution of unionism to the shaping of a more just and humane society.

CHAPTER 2

WORKPLACE CITIZENSHIP

Union Roles and Structures

From their very beginnings trade unions evolved simultaneously with capitalism as workers were driven to organize themselves in unions to defend and promote their economic and political interests. Today they still emerge in opposition to, and provide an ongoing critique of, capital and the state: their agenda calls for institutional change, which they seek to advance through collective action, and their vision calls for a different society in which working people have better lives and more control over conditions in their workplaces and communities (Black 1990: 2).

Since the mid-1850s the working class has grown larger and larger. This growth has occurred through both immigration and the movement of large segments of the population into the wage-labour sector of the economy. In the past half-century women have been a large part of this growth. Since the beginning of the Second World War, the labour-force participation rates of men and women have converged as increasing numbers of women have been pushed or pulled into the labour market in search of paid employment. More recent years have seen a significant increase in the proportion of the paid labour force of non-European descent — immigrants and visa workers from Latin America, the Caribbean, Asia, and Africa. Recent decades have also seen significant changes in the industrial and occupational composition of wage employment. One particularly noteworthy trend has been the growth in service-sector employment (retail trade, personal services, business services, health, education, social services) relative to employment in the goods-producing sector (manufacturing, construction, forestry, agriculture, fishing, trapping). Another has been the growth in contingent employment — part-time, casual, and contract jobs that have low wages and few benefits and rights, and are non-unionized.

Despite these changes, the relationship between workers and employers has remained essentially unchanged. Workers sell their labour-power to employers in exchange for wages; they fill positions in the workplace, under the direction of employers. In what is still one of the most apt descriptions of this relationship, Karl Marx observed that in the labour market, worker and employer ostensibly appear to meet as equals and to enter freely into a bargain that establishes a rate at which workers will be paid while they are in the place of work. But the appearance of equality and freedom is an illusion because the employers own the means of production and the workers' livelihood is therefore dependent upon employers agreeing to hire them. The workers' dependence is deepened all the more because normally there are more workers looking for jobs than there are jobs looking for workers. Employers are therefore able to defer hiring workers if the price is too high — an option denied workers when the price is too low.

> Karl Marx, using powerful imagery, observes that once the deal is done, and the worker has sold his ability to work to the capitalist, "We can perceive a change in the physiognomy of our **dramatis personae**. He who before was the money-owner, now strides in front as capitalist; the possessor of labour-power follows as his labourer. The one with an air of importance, smirking, intent on business; the other timid and holding back, like one who is bringing his own hide to market and has nothing to expect but — a hiding."
>
> *Source: Marx 1965: 176.*

These inequities in the labour market and workplace have always motivated workers to form trade unions. The ability of trade unions to mitigate the inequities depends on trade union power: the capacity to compel employers and/or the state to make concessions that would not be attainable in the absence of trade unions. This power in turn depends on the activism, militancy, combativeness, and solidarity of the members.

THE MOVEMENT IN THEORY

All theories of the trade union movement trace its origins to the conditions experienced by the majority of the population during the transition to industrial capitalism. Trade unions began as an essential response to capitalism. All union theories agree, as well, that workers form unions to give themselves some power in their dealings with employers and the state.

From this common starting point, the theories diverge into two main groups: those that ascribe a revolutionary purpose and role to the union movement; and those that see unions primarily as a means by which workers improve their circumstances within society.

Revolutionary Theories

For Karl Marx, workers formed trade unions and bargained with their employers over wages and working conditions as a means of improving their lot — the lot of the members of a particular union — within the capitalist system. Marx argued that this was a mug's game doomed to failure, because the best that unions could do under capitalism was to try to prevent wage cuts when the economy slumped and the ranks of the unemployed increased, and to extract wage gains from employers when economic times were good. Those efforts would come to nought, he reasoned, because

"A key to the nature of Marx's conception of proletarian socialism is a seldom noted fact: Marx was the first leading figure in the history of socialism to adopt a position of support to trade unions and trade unionism, on principle.

This position was not difficult to take in later decades, after the trade-union movement had entrenched itself; its success was not hard to recognize by that time. What Marx recognized in advance was the basic relationship of trade unions as an institution to the proletariat as a class and to the social revolution as a goal."

Source: Draper 1978: 81.

the general tendency in capitalism was to increase the exploitation of workers and drive down wages. He counselled workers to recognize that while their fights with individual employers might slow down the decline of wages, during bad times the wages would nevertheless continue to decline. More importantly, Marx argued that even if workers did achieve wage gains, the nature of the employer-worker relationship made workers — the majority of the population — subordinate to capitalists. This subordination, structured into the wage-labour relationship, meant that democracy and freedom were not possible within capitalism. The solution in Marxist theory was for workers and their unions to move beyond these never-ending battles with employers to challenge the wage-labour system in its entirety. Workers, Marx (1947: 55) said:

> ought to understand that, with all the miseries it imposes upon them, the present system simultaneously engenders the material conditions and the social forms necessary for the… reconstruction of society. Instead of the conservative motto, "A fair day's wage for a fair day's work!" they ought to inscribe on their banner the revolutionary watchword, "Abolition of the wages system!"

Marx believed that the lessons workers learned in their formation of unions and participation in the labour movement created the conditions required for them to challenge the very existence of capitalism. What lessons did workers learn? For one thing, their early initiatives to establish unions and improve their conditions were an assertion of their rejection as human beings of the oppressive and dehumanizing conditions they faced in capitalist production. For another, the struggles for better wages and conditions clarified their understanding of the limits of their potential to improve conditions in their relationships with particular employers. The inability to gain ground in their isolated conflicts also motivated workers to unite with other workers to build a labour movement based on collective interests and a common vision. Finally, worker involvement in the labour movement and struggles with employers and the state equipped workers with the insights, knowledge, and skills required to achieve social revolution (Draper 1978: 92–98).

Socialist thinkers in Europe and North America subsequently expanded and/or modified Marx's ideas on trade unions. V.I. Lenin, leader of the 1917 Bolshevik Revolution in Russia, saw the spontaneous formation of trade unions as the first step in a process that would see workers outgrow their preoccupations with conditions in their own trade or enterprise or with sectional interests; they would move away from their immediate struggles with particular employers over quite limited objectives and forge a united force that took aim at social revolution. Trade union activities, organization, collective bargaining, and, in particular, strikes, would provide workers with practical schooling:

> A strike teaches workers to understand what the strength of the employers and what the strength of the workers consists in; it teaches them not to think of their own employer alone and not of their own immediate workmates alone but of all the class of employers and the whole class of workers.... A strike, moreover, opens the eyes of workers to the nature, not only of the capitalists, but of the government and the laws as well.... Strikes, therefore, teach the workers to unite; they show them that they can struggle against the capitalists only when they are united; strikes teach the workers to think of the struggle of the whole working class against the whole class of factory owners and against the arbitrary, police government. (Lenin 1970: 63–64)

For Lenin, though, a revolutionary vanguard party was a key ingredient for concrete change. Such a party, he argued, would help workers discover and build their revolutionary potential and ultimately lead them to revolutionary social change.

North American refinements and modifications of Marxian ideas originated primarily with radicals who either had leadership roles in labour organizations outside the mainstream of trade unionism — for example, in the Industrial Workers of the World (IWW) — and/or in socialist political parties (Chamberlain 1965: 263–64).

The IWW, in contrast to Lenin, downplayed the importance of the party and emphasized instead the syndicalist view that revolution could be achieved through direct industrial action in the workplace. If workers took control of capitalist production through creation of one big union and the general strike, control of the state would follow.

Most socialists, however, envisioned distinctive roles being played by unions and parties. Unions had as their primary purpose the struggle for improved conditions for workers in their jobs within the existing capitalist system. But unlike the syndicalists, socialists believed that the broader aim of social revolution and the elimination of the wages system could only be achieved by means of the revolutionary socialist party. This was the approach taken up in Canada by the Communist Party. A variant of this classical Marxist approach sees the party not as the vehicle for the revolutionary overthrow of capitalism and the wage-labour system, but rather as a means for promoting the broader political interests of labour within a reformed capitalist system. In Canada, this approach was taken up by the Co-operative Commonwealth Federation (CCF), forerunner of today's New Democratic Party (NDP).

Accommodationist Theories

The ideas of U.S. accommodationist theorists were more limited still in scope. John R. Commons based his thinking about unions on a careful study of the shoemaking industry in the United States (Chamberlain 1965: 256–62). Unions, he said, had developed after the geographical extension of markets and competition had destroyed the skills and status of craft workers. Originally the production of shoes had taken place in small shops, with owners working alongside skilled shoemakers to produce for the local market. The interests of shop owners and workers coincided: a good price for shoes meant a good wage for workers.

With the increase in the size of markets, local establishments were forced to compete on a wider scale. That development placed pressure on the owners of shoemaking shops to reduce labour costs by holding down wages, mechanizing aspects of production, and replacing skilled workers with less-skilled workers. Eventually the geographical extension of the market promoted mass production and the obliteration of the craft.

According to Commons, unions were initially formed, then, on a local basis to defend traditional craft-based production. They eventually grew into regional and national organizations, and as that happened they became part of the power structure, working jointly with business and the state to establish a "web of rules" to govern the allocation of resources and opportunities in society. Within this framework, unions are simply another special-interest group seeking to use their power to secure benefits for their members.

Selig Perlman theorized that it was workers' concerns about the scarcity of job opportunities and the insecurities of the workplace that motivated them to form trade unions (Chamberlain 1965: 262–66). Their objective in forming unions was to alleviate these problems by gaining more control over decisions in the workplace. Perlman acknowledges in his analysis that the objectives and aspirations of workers are at odds with the mentality and values of business people and entrepreneurs, who resist the imposition of any encumbrances on their ability to exploit opportunities for greater profits. This contest between the interests of workers and entrepreneurs, a contest usually resolved in favour of the entrepreneurs, made workers vulnerable to influence by people outside the labour movement — intellectuals dissatisfied for one reason or another with the workings of the capitalist system. Perlman argued that it was outside intellectuals, not workers themselves, who advocated the more revolutionary approach to trade unionism. He therefore condemned the intrusion of intellectuals into trade union activities and favoured instead the American Federation of Labor (AFL) and its emphasis on pragmatic business unionism — the securing of acceptable contracts from capitalist employers.

A number of theories impute a moral content to the origins and role of trade unions. Frank Tannenbaum, for example, attributed the emergence of unions to the rise of individualism and the destruction of community that accompanied the growth of capitalism (Chamberlain 1965: 266–69). Unions restored community ties and brought renewed social content to the lives of workers. But Tannenbaum feared that as unions grew in size and scope to counter the growth in the size of firms in monopoly capitalism, union leaders would become entrenched and lose contact with the social and moral needs of their members.

Similarly, the Catholic Church, through its popes, attempted to situate trade unions within its own moral precepts. *Rerum Novarum,* a papal encyclical issued by Pope Leo XIII in 1891, rejected the idea of class struggle, condemned socialism as a dead end for workers, and insisted that the way forward for unions was through collaboration and harmony between capital and labour (Black 1984: 11–14).

In *Laborems Exercens*, a papal encyclical issued a century later in 1981, Pope John Paul II set out an analysis of labour that was intended to clarify the Church's understanding of the rights of workers and the role of trade unions for the late twentieth century. John Paul adhered to the core ideas advanced in *Rerum Novarum*. Unions are simply one organization among many established to ensure the rights of their members in capitalist society. Their struggle for social justice for their members "is not a struggle against others" (Pope John Paul II 1981: 40). On the contrary, the struggle is for social harmony with

The views of John Paul II on unions subsequently figured prominently in a document, *Ethical Reflections on the Economic Crisis,* issued by the Canadian Conference of Catholic Bishops (CCCB) in 1983. In particular the CCCB condemned the policies adopted by employers and the federal government to deal with the economic crisis of the early 1980s. As an alternative the Bishops proposed "economic policies which realize that the needs of the poor have priority over the wants of the rich; that the rights of workers are more important than the maximization of profits; that the participation of marginalized groups takes precedence over the preservation of a system that excludes them." As well, the Bishops called for the protection of trade union rights and "a decisive and responsible role [for unions] in developing strategies for economic recovery and development."

the owners and managers of capital. John Paul also rejected the notion of trade unions having a role in politics:

> Unions do not have the character of political parties struggling for power; they should not be subjected to the decision of political parties or have too close a link with them. In fact, in such a situation they easily lose contact with their specific role, which is to secure the just rights of workers within the framework of the common good of the whole of society. (Pope John Paul II 1981: 41)

John Paul cautioned that strikes, while a legitimate tool of workers in their struggle for rights, must not be used in a manner at odds with the interests of society and "must not be abused especially for political purposes" (Pope John Paul II 1981: 42).

A Multiplicity of Roles

Clearly, the various theories advanced to explain the role of trade unions under capitalism show considerable diversity. If there is one conclusion that we can draw, it is that trade unions and the trade union movement play multiple roles in both the lives of their members and the life of society. The question of which roles loom largest in their activities and actions at any given time seems, moreover, to be dictated by economic and social conditions and the nature of the concrete demands made by trade union members.

> Solidarity Forever:
> A central idea in all theories of trade unions is that the key to workers advancing their interests is through collective action based on solidarity. The importance of solidarity to labour is reflected in the song "Solidarity Forever," written by Ralph Chaplin in 1915 as a result of his experiences in the coal-field wars of West Virginia. This song is recognized as the anthem for labour in North America. The first verse and chorus are:
>
> "When the union's inspiration through the workers' blood shall run,
> There can be no power greater anywhere beneath the sun,
> Yet what force on earth is weaker than the feeble strength of one,
> But the union makes us strong.
> Solidarity forever,
> Solidarity forever,
> Solidarity forever,
> For the union makes us strong."

ROLES AND FUNCTIONS

The issue of what it is that unions do — the roles and/or functions of unions — is still a contested terrain. Nevertheless, general agreement does exist in a nucleus of ideas on the specific question of what it is they do for their members (see Freeman and Medoff 1984; Goddard 1994, 1997). These ideas can be combined into three main roles: unions as agents, as promoters of industrial citizenship, and as political voice.[1]

Unions as Agents for their Members

One of the most familiar roles of trade unions is as an agent of their members. Workers form unions to achieve certain objectives relating to "bread and butter issues": higher wages, improved fringe benefits (such as pension plans and life and disability insurance), better and safer working conditions, greater security in their jobs, and fair treatment. It then falls to the union to negotiate a **collective agreement** with employers, establishing a contract that specifies terms and conditions of employment and the rights of unions and employers, and that addresses the concerns and interests of members.

> Most strikes occur in unionized establishments when negotiations to establish a first collective agreement or renew an existing collective agreement stall or fail. Most of these strikes are sanctioned by the union leadership. However, in some situations strikes are spontaneous and not approved by the leadership both during the term of a collective agreement and when negotiations are underway. As well, workers in both unionized and non-unionized establishments may withdraw their labour to protest actions of employers and/or governments that undermine or damage their conditions of work and/or their rights.

The members play a central role in this process: they articulate the issues that they want addressed in **collective bargaining**, a process of formal negotiations between a union and employer to establish a collective agreement; they give guidance to their negotiators during negotiations; they demonstrate the extent of their support of the bargaining position through their willingness to engage in **strike action**, a withdrawal of their labour intended to stop production until a collective agreement is achieved; and they ultimately approve or ratify the terms of settlement. As well, members expect the union leadership and staff to ensure that the employer complies with the letter and the spirit of the collective agreement.

Establishing Industrial Citizenship in the Workplace

Individually workers are relatively powerless in their dealings with employers in the workplace. Unless they have knowledge or skills vital to the enterprise and cannot easily be replaced, they are dispensable. If they confront their employers over some aspect of their job, they can be and often are fired. But in forming a union, workers implicitly enter into an agreement that they will look out for and stand by one another if one or more of them become subject to unfair or arbitrary actions by employers.

Prior to the 1944 establishment of legislation that explicitly guaranteed trade unions as agents of employees and compelled employers to deal with them (see chapter 4), the only method workers had of demonstrating mutual support was through strikes or other actions designed to disrupt production and force employers to reverse their actions. Under existing legislation workers gain protection from employers' arbitrary actions and unfair treatment through grievance procedures entrenched in collective agreements.

As members of unions, individual workers also have the right to participate both directly and indirectly (through their delegates) in the deliberations and debates that take place both within their own unions and within the trade union movement as a whole. They get to vote on the selection of their leaders, on whether or not to strike in support of union demands, on the ratification of collective agreements, on the selection of delegates to union conventions, and on other issues discussed at union conventions. They can seek election to union office as shop stewards or table officers and put their names forward to serve as delegates to conventions or other trade union bodies.

One of the things workers gain by their participation in trade unions, then, is industrial citizenship: the right to a say in the decisions that determine the terms and conditions of their employment in the workplace. Another way of saying this is that unions, and the collective agreements they negotiate, place limits on the otherwise arbitrary power of employers, and therefore make the workplace more democratic than it would otherwise be.

Giving Workers a Political Voice

Unions also provide workers with a way of strengthening their collective voice in the political sphere through both traditional electoral politics and extra-parliamentary activities.

In **electoral politics** — the process through which governments are elected at the federal, provincial, and local levels — unions provide educational programs designed to make their members aware of the benefits or disadvantages of government actions and policies, and to encourage them to be politically active. Many unions also promote support for the New Democratic Party and commit resources, both personnel and money, to the party's electoral efforts (for a further discussion see chapter 5).

Unions also play their political role in **extra-parliamentary activities**, which are designed to challenge and influence government policies and actions independently of electoral politics. In recent decades, governments in Ottawa and in provinces that have adopted policies favouring big (and small) business over workers have shunted the trade union movement in Canada off to the sidelines. In response, the Canadian Labour Congress, provincial federations, and other trade union organizations have attempted to develop a coherent campaign to counter this "corporate agenda." Increasingly, this campaign has involved working with various social movements. Two important examples of this activity are the Pro-Canada Network (later called the Action Canada Network) in the fight against the Canada–U.S. Free

Trade Agreement in 1987 and 1988, and alternative federal budgets and (in some provinces) provincial budgets initiated originally by CHO!CES (a social justice coalition based in Winnipeg) and now co-ordinated by the Canadian Centre for Policy Alternatives in Ottawa and some provinces. While labour in Canada has worked with both the NDP and various extra-parliamentary social movements, the question of how labour should advance its political interests is now very much the subject of debate (see chapter 5).

LABOUR LEGISLATION AND LAW

Prior to 1872, the formation of unions and the sorts of activities that unions now perform on behalf of their members were, for all intents and purposes, outlawed.

This changed in 1872 when a strike of Toronto printers for the nine-hour day gained the support of other workers and escalated into a major confrontation between employers and unionized workers in the city. In response the federal government passed the *Trade Unions Act* and a companion bill, *the Criminal Law Amendment Act*. The *Trade Unions Act* decreed that the formation of a union for the purpose of collective bargaining was neither a conspiracy nor unlawful. The *Criminal Law Amendment Act*, by way of compensation, severely restricted the actions of unions in organizing drives and strikes (Lipton 1978: 28–41).

> The common law of conspiracy (two or more individuals consorting for illegal purposes) could be applied to trade union organizations, making them subject to criminal prosecution. "In addition, because trade unions were regarded as operating in restraint of trade (by interfering with the normal course of business transactions through strikes), they were refused access to the courts and were thus unable to enforce any rights that they might otherwise have had."
>
> *Source: Carter 1995: 58.*

Further changes in legislation occurred over the period 1900 to 1907 as the federal government sought to contain growing conflict in the railway, coal-mining, and streetcar railway (urban transit) industries. These innovations culminated in 1907 in the *Industrial Disputes Investigation Act* (IDIA), designed to curb strikes in key industries. The Act imposed, before any strike or lockout could occur, compulsory conciliation by a tripartite board, composed of representatives named by the union and the employer and a neutral chairperson, in the railway and mining industries and public utilities.[2]

Another significant change in trade union law came in February 1944. Confronted with an unprecedented increase in the incidence of strikes and a marked shift to the left in the politics of working people, as reflected in rising support for the CCF, the Liberal government proclaimed, under the authority of the *War Measures Act*, Privy Council Order PC 1003. The order-in-council, which conceded many of the reforms in industrial relations law that the union movement had previously demanded but been denied, was a major turning point in the legislation covering labour relations in Canada. It created the basis of the framework that would govern industrial relations in Canada during the second half of the twentieth century.

PC 1003 established a process to allow workers to **certify** a union, providing a legal and exclusive right for their union to represent them in the workplace, if 50 percent of the employees in that workplace voted for unionization. Once a union was certified, the law obligated employers to recognize the union as a legitimate agent of their workers and to bargain in good faith with the union on terms and conditions of employment. PC 1003 also cited certain actions by employers to thwart unions and avoid collective bargaining as **unfair labour practices** subject to penalties. Finally, it established **grievance-arbitration** procedures, which prescribe a mechanism for the resolution of grievances without resort to strike action, to resolve worker and union grievances over the life of a collective agreement. These represented important, indeed historic, gains for Canadian workers. They were the product of decades of often prolonged and bitter struggles (see chapter 4).

Still, the government carefully crafted PC 1003 to limit the potential impact of the new rights conceded to labour. The legislation prohibited strikes during the life of a collective agreement, which meant, among other things, that workers could not strike to resolve grievances or challenge employer initiatives during the life of a collective agreement, or engage in **sympathy** or **solidarity strikes** — that is, strikes by workers not directly involved in a dispute in support of other striking workers. It restricted collective bargaining to particular employers and workplaces and to a limited range of issues, namely, terms and conditions of employment, which constrained initiatives by workers to challenge employer control over workplace and production decisions, such as the role of supervisory staff and the ratio of supervisors to workers.

As well, PC 1003 retained the compulsory intervention provisions of the *Industrial Disputes Investigation Act* and defined a list of union actions that would be treated as unfair labour practices.

Some critics of PC 1003 argue that the legislation's main impact was to shift power from workers to trade union leaders and union bureaucrats and from unions to **labour relations boards** (bodies established by governments to administer industrial relations), and to entrench the power of employers vis-à-vis unions (Panitch and Swartz 1993: 7–20; Haiven 1995: 215–35). Other critics maintain that PC 1003 benefited male industrial workers and failed to address the needs of women workers in the retail and service sectors (for example, Forrest 1995).

For its part, labour was concerned about the lack of security provided for unions under the legislation. While unions had the right to negotiate security provisions into collective agreements, they recognized that employers would oppose their inclusion. Nevertheless, labour accepted PC 1003 as a useful reform that established a legitimate role for trade unions within the political economy of Canada.

The most important unfair labour practices involved the use of coercion and intimidation against employees by employers and/or unions. Employers were expressly prohibited from interfering in the internal affairs of unions and discriminating against or firing employees because of their involvement in a union. Unions were similarly prohibited from using coercion or intimidation to induce or compel employees to join unions.

The issue of union security came to a head in September 1945, when 11,000 Ford workers in Windsor went on strike. A major demand of the striking workers was a union shop provision that would require all workers in the plant bargaining unit to become union members. One element missing from PC 1003 was a **check-off system** for union dues — a clause in a collective agreement authorizing the employer to deduct union dues from the pay packets of employees and to submit those dues directly to the union. Unions saw a check-off system as a necessary element in financial security.

The six-week Windsor strike ended with both sides agreeing to binding arbitration after workers had completely closed off access to the plant with a massive blockade of cars. The matter was referred to Justice Ivan Rand for resolution, and his decision included what came to be known as the **Rand formula**: an agency shop provision recognizing that the union represents all members of the bargaining unit and requiring all members of the bargaining unit, whether union members or not, to pay the dues levied by the union to finance its activities; and with the union dues to be paid automatically by check-off, thereby giving financial security to certified unions. Rand justified his decision on the grounds that there should be no **free riders**; all individuals who benefit from union activities should contribute to the union's finances.

Rand's award also included another part, which he presumably believed was necessary to balance the ledger and ensure that workers and unions did not gain power as a result of his ruling on union security. As an offset to the automatic check-off, Rand established penalties for employees and unions engaging in and/or supporting strikes during the life of a collective agreement. Under the award, employees involved in illegal strikes could be fined and lose seniority, while unions could be faced with a suspension of dues transfers by employers. Moreover, the sanctions against unions could be applied in strike situations if unions failed to condemn and discipline members involved in an illegal strike. Critics of Rand's award have argued that the net result was a reinforcement of the provisions of PC 1003, because

Union Rights Are Human Rights
(card-based vs. vote-based certification):

In 1998 the International Labour Organization (ILO) issued a document titled *Declaration on Fundamental Principles and Rights at Work*. All members of the ILO are obliged "to 'respect, to promote and to realize in good faith' five core rights [in the Declaration] that are deemed to be fundamental human rights." These rights include "freedom of association" and "effective recognition of the right to collective bargaining."

Canada is a member of the ILO, yet many of the provinces are reluctant to respect and promote the principle of freedom of association. At a most basic level the procedures established for certification reflect this reluctance. At present, five Canadian provinces (Newfoundland, Nova Scotia, Ontario, Alberta, British Columbia) require a mandatory vote by all employees in a workplace seeking certification, while five provinces (Prince Edward Island, New Brunswick, Quebec, Saskatchewan, Manitoba) and the federal jurisdiction allow automatic certification based on the completion of membership cards by a majority of employees. The threshold ranges from 50 percent plus one in the federal jurisdiction and some provinces to 65 percent in Manitoba.

Research evidence confirms that workers are more likely to unionize and achieve certification in jurisdictions that have card-based certification systems. A recent issue of the *Fraser Alert* (August 2005), published by the Fraser Institute, an anti-union organization based in British Columbia, cites a number of studies that conclude that mandatory voting has a significant negative impact on the success of certification applications.

It is probably also the case that in jurisdictions with card-based certification procedures the success of unionization drives is likely to decline as the threshold for automatic certification increases. Moreover, in a jurisdiction like Manitoba, where the threshold is 65 percent, the capacity of the union movement to initiate and sustain organization drives is impaired by the significant increase in resources required to increase the sign-up rate from 50 per cent plus one to 65 percent.

Sources: Adams 2003; Clemens, Veldhuis, and Karabegovic 2005.

it promoted bureaucratization of unions and made them responsible for guaranteeing industrial peace during the life of a collective agreement. This in turn undermined union democracy and inhibited the development of combativeness and solidarity within the labour movement.

In the late 1940s the main provisions of PC 1003 were entrenched in federal and provincial industrial relations laws. Moreover, the central provisions in PC 1003 remain at the core of such laws. But significant variations exist in the precise content of the laws across provinces. On the matter of certification, for example, Alberta, Nova Scotia, and Ontario require votes in all situations. Newfoundland requires a vote but can waive the requirement if both the union and employer request the granting of certification. In other jurisdictions the labour relations board can grant certification when it is satisfied that a majority of members have signed membership cards indicating their support for a union. The threshold for card-based certification varies, ranging from more than 50 percent in the federal jurisdiction and Prince Edward Island and Quebec to 65 percent in Manitoba.

Some jurisdictions have mandated compulsory check-off of dues for members of a bargaining unit whether they are in the union or not, whereas in other jurisdictions a dues check-off must be negotiated between unions and employers.

The Rand formula (or variations on it) is now an entrenched feature of most collective agreements; indeed, in six jurisdictions — federal, Newfoundland, Quebec, Ontario, Manitoba, Saskatchewan — the compulsory check-off of dues is required by law. About half of all workers in unionized workplaces are covered by the Rand formula, and another 45 percent by other forms of check-off clauses. As well, about 21 percent of collective agreements have a union shop article and another 21 percent a **modified union shop** article, which exempts from membership only those employees who did not join the union at the time of organization. In contrast, the much maligned **closed shop** provision, which requires union membership as a condition of employment (you must be a member to get a job), is confined for the most part to situations in which unions perform a hiring hall function such as in construction and on the docks.

Sources: Craig and Solomon 1993: 304; Giles and Starkman 1995: 347.

Quebec and British Columbia have legislated **anti-scab laws**, which prohibit employers from recruiting workers called **scabs** — people who continue to work during a strike, or whom management brings in to replace workers on strike. In the early 1990s the Ontario NDP government passed similar legislation, but it was subsequently repealed by a Conservative government led by Mike Harris. Other jurisdictions have restricted the use of professional strikebreakers and/or required employers, before hiring additional workers, to take back workers who were on strike.

All jurisdictions except for Alberta, New Brunswick, and Nova Scotia have established **first contract arbitration** procedures to provide for the imposition of a collective agreement when negotiations for an initial collective agreement fail. The jurisdictions without such laws simply leave it to the parties to fight it out through a strike or lockout. The variations can have a significant impact on how unions fare in organizing and collective bargaining.

Moreover, the laws governing the relations between unions and employers are not static. On the contrary, they are constantly being revised as governments at all levels respond to changing economic conditions and

The Push for Anti-Scab Legislation in the Federal Jurisdiction:
In 2002 and again in 2005, the Bloc Québécois introduced private members' bills (Bill C-328 and Bill C-263) that would have curtailed the employment of replacement workers (scabs) in the federal jurisdiction. The NDP joined the Bloc in supporting the bills, but a majority of Conservative MPs and a significant minority of Liberal MPs voted to defeat both of them. By 2007 another private members' bill proposing such restrictions (Bill C-257) was progressing through the minority Conservative parliament. The bill passed second reading in October 2006 by a margin of 167 to 101 (with the support of NDP and Bloc members and a majority of Liberal members). The bill was read for a third time on March 21, 2007. It was defeated in the ensuing vote because 29 members of the Liberal caucus switched their votes from yeas to nays.

During the debate on Bill C-257, opponents claimed that the law would give unions too much power and disrupt the balance that now exists in federal legislation. Proponents of the legislation argued that those were the same arguments that are made every time a change is proposed that is of potential benefit to working people and their families. They justified the legislation on the grounds that: (i) it would eliminate the violence that leads to property damage and injury and death on picket lines that results when employers recruit replacement workers to undermine the bargaining power of unionized workers; and (ii) it would enhance the ability of workers who are vulnerable to replacement in industrial disputes (primarily workers of limited skills and workers in depressed industries or regions of the country) to improve their wages and working conditions through collective bargaining.

Apparently, the 29 Liberal MPs who switched their vote on March 21 were persuaded that a vote for the bill would give workers and unions too much power and disrupt the balance in the federal jurisdiction.

Source: <canadianlabour.ca/index.php/reality_check_antisc>.

shifts in the character of employer-union relations, and as governments with varying ideologies are elected and defeated. In the first couple of decades after the Second World War, the general trend in many jurisdictions involved changes to the law that, for the most part, were favourable to unions. These included changes that made it easier for workers to form unions, provided greater protection for workers engaging in strike action, explicitly expanded the range of issues subject to collective bargaining (for example, technological change), and mandated the inclusion of articles in the collective agreement advantageous to unions and union members (for example, the inclusion of a requirement that the employer administer the collective agreement in a fair and equitable fashion and with due regard for the rights of workers).

After the end of the long post-war boom in the early 1970s, this relatively progressive trend was reversed, and most governments demonstrated a willingness to amend the laws to accommodate concerns raised by employers and employer organizations. A "favourable" industrial relations climate — favourable to employers — combined with low labour costs became one of the key bargaining chips (along with low taxes, lax regulations regarding business conduct and environmental issues, and the celebration of entrepreneurial and business virtues) that governments used to attract investment. Some governments, most notably the government of Alberta in 1995, have even flirted with the idea of adopting so-called **right-to-work laws** (overtly anti-union laws), which exist in twenty-one U.S. states.

The system of labour law entrenched by the state over the period 1872 to 1950 was established primarily to manage class conflict between workers and employers in the private sector. In many jurisdictions these laws covered workers in local government and the parapublic sector (organizations dependent on government funding, such as schools, hospitals, and Crown enterprises). Public-sector workers proper (that is, civil servants) in all federal and provincial jurisdictions were either denied trade union rights or saddled with restrictions that severely limited their bargaining power. An exception was Saskatchewan, where a CCF government, the first social-democratic government in North America, included public-sector workers under the *Trade Union Act* in 1944. The prevailing restraints were justified on the grounds that governments could not compromise their sovereign power by allowing government workers a voice in the determination of their wages and conditions of employment.[3]

In the United States unions are certified by the federal government through the National Labor Relations Board. However, individual states have the right to pass laws that prevent unions from negotiating union security articles in collective agreements that would require non-members to either join a union or pay union dues. Such laws promote free-ridership: they allow/encourage workers in a unionized workplace, who are guaranteed the benefits of unionization and collective bargaining, to avoid contributing to the costs of union activity. Some twenty-one states (mainly the old slave states in the South and the agrarian states in the Midwest) have right-to-work laws. In 1995 Stockwell Day, then Alberta minister of labour, commissioned a review by the Alberta Economic Development Authority on the feasibility of establishing a right-to-work law in Alberta. The Authority recommended against such a law (Alberta Economic Development Authority 1995). In 2006 the unionization rate for the United States was 13.5 percent.

The rates for right-to-work states ranged from North Carolina (4.1 percent) through Texas (5.9 percent) and North Dakota (8.0 percent) to Iowa (14.0 percent) and Nevada (17.0 percent). Eighteen of these states had unionization rates of less than 10 percent.

All of this changed in the 1960s. A wave of unionization and illegal strikes in Quebec in the early 1960s forced the Quebec government to extend trade union rights, including the right to strike (albeit a right subject to restrictions not imposed on private-sector workers) to all public-sector workers, including civil servants. An illegal strike by militant postal workers across the country in 1965 and growing discontent amongst civil servants forced the federal government in 1967 to extend trade union rights to its workers. *The Public Service Staff Relations Act* entrenched the rights of federal government employees to unionize and bargain collectively with the government and established two options for settlement of collective bargaining disputes. A collective bargaining impasse could be submitted to **arbitration**, in which an independent third party attempted to resolve issues in dispute. Alternatively, to overcome differences in collective bargaining, as a prelude to strike action, a union could opt for a two-stage **conciliation** procedure involving assistance from a single conciliator and then a conciliation board. This option was qualified, however, through a requirement that some employees remain on the job during a strike to provide **essential services** — work deemed vital to the public interest; for example, air traffic control.

Other provinces subsequently followed the examples of Quebec and Ottawa and extended trade union rights to their employees. There were, however, marked differences in how various jurisdictions accommodated these rights. In Manitoba and Prince Edward Island they were incorporated in existing legislation (*Civil Service Act*), while in other provinces new acts were created to accommodate bargaining rights for civil servants (in Newfoundland, for example, it was the *Public Service Collective Bargaining Act*).

Until very recently, a major conundrum existed in the collective bargaining regime established in the public sector, where the state not only is the employer but also retains the power to unilaterally suspend collective bargaining, impose changes in the terms and conditions of employment, and legislate an end to strikes. Governments have invoked this power in an increasing number of situations in the last three decades — in some jurisdictions so much so that the trade union rights of public-sector workers have in practice been nullified (see Panitch and Swartz 2003).

This conundrum was resolved (in part at least) on June 8, 2007, when the Supreme Court of Canada ruled by a vote of six to one that collective bargaining is protected by the Charter of Rights and Freedoms. The decision came in a case involving a challenge by the B.C. Hospital Employees' Union and other health-care unions of Bill 29, a law authorizing the government to repudiate its collective agreement with the unions. The government used Bill 29 to institute the mass layoff of 8,000 workers and contract out their work to private (some of them international) companies. Chief Justice

Labour Reactions to Supreme Court Decision on Collective Bargaining: *B.C. Hospital Employees Union* — Judy Darcy, president: "This is a huge victory for both health care and health-care workers because the Supreme Court of Canada said that Bill 29 violates freedom of association protection in the charter, which cover the right to free collective bargaining."

Canadian Labour Congress — Ken Georgetti, president: "This is a great day for workers because this decision means that the Canadian Charter of Rights and Freedoms does protect workers' rights including the process of collective bargaining.... Finally, workers' freedom of association includes the right to bargain a collective agreement that cannot be ripped apart at the government's convenience."

National Union of Public and General Employees — James Clancy, president: "The court... stated that collective bargaining complements, promotes and enhances fundamental Canadian values such as equality, dignity and democracy. It noted that collective bargaining is a fundamental aspect of Canadian society which predates the establishment of labour relations regimes and that it existed well before the Charter recognized the right to association."

United Food and Commercial Workers (UFCW) Canada — Wayne Hanley, national president: "There was an especially good reason to celebrate Labour Day [in 2007] in the wake of a recent decision by Canada's Supreme Court.... In 1894 when Labour Day was first enshrined as a Canadian national holiday, people understood how precious and how powerful these rights could be if they got together and used them. They also understood that rights can be a responsibility."

Canadian Association of University Teachers — James Turk, executive director, said he's hopeful the judgment will result in a similar outcome for the 8,000-member Federation of Post-Secondary Educators, which launched a challenge of a parallel B.C. law that permitted the refusal of college employers to negotiate key terms of employment with [employee unions]. Turk said, "The Public Education Flexibility and Choice Act undercuts the fundamental nature of the employment contract for academic staff, including the clear adverse impact on academic freedom."

Beverley McLachlin and Justice Louis LeBel wrote in their ruling: "The right to bargain collectively with an employer enhances human dignity, liberty and autonomy of workers by giving them the opportunity to influence the establishment of workplace rules and thereby gain some control over a major aspect of their lives, namely their work." It has been predicted that this ruling will fundamentally alter the nature of collective bargaining in Canada.

While laws governing industrial relations are designed for the express purpose of regulating relations between unions and employers, other laws also impinge on and shape the actions of trade unions and employers and influence the issues that arise in collective bargaining. These laws include:

- employment standards laws, which establish minimum wages, hours of work, vacation entitlements, and other minimum terms and conditions of employment;
- workplace health and safety laws, designed to protect workers from conditions that could damage their health or result in injuries;
- pay equity laws, intended to ensure equal pay for work of equal value in particular sectors of the economy;
- workers' compensation laws, which provide income replacement for workers who are prevented from working because of injuries and/or ill health contracted in the workplace; and
- human rights laws, designed to protect individuals against discrimination in all spheres of activity, including places of employment.

Then, too, other state institutions play a part in managing conflict between labour and capital. Labour relations boards and other bodies created specifically for these purposes administer and enforce the laws passed by governments. The police, and sometimes the military, are often called upon to suppress the picket-line confrontations that often erupt when employers bring in replacement workers to maintain production. Their role in these situations is to protect the property of owners and ensure the safe passage of replacement workers through picket lines. The courts also become involved in interpreting labour laws, dealing with petitions from employers seeking restraints on the picketing activities of workers or demanding compensation resulting from the actions of unions and union members, and hearing cases in which workers are charged for strike-related misconduct or union leaders and unions are cited for various transgressions — for example, defying back-to-work laws, conducting illegal strikes, or occupying workplaces.

Legislation governing industrial relations is, then, contested terrain, and subject to frequent changes (major or minor). The historical record suggests that the development of the laws in Canada has been mediated by two main factors: employers and the state have consistently opposed trade unions and have only conceded rights to workers and their organizations in response to worker militancy; and in all cases the resulting legislation has been designed to ensure that the exercise of workers' rights does not unduly disrupt or interfere with business activity, that is, with the accumulation of capital and the generation of profits. These factors will almost certainly continue to play a decisive role in the future evolution of labour laws in Canada.

The capacity of trade unions to carry out the roles that their members expect them to play is shaped by the laws that not only define their rights and obligations but also impose constraints on how they can work to achieve their goals. The laws also influence to some extent the structure of the trade union movement.

THE MOVEMENT STRUCTURE

The foundation or building blocks of the trade union movement are local unions, which represent workers in a particular workplace or location. Individual workers first become involved in union activity at the local level. Sometimes they are directly involved in an organization drive that results in the certification of a local at their place of work. More often they find employment at workplaces that are already unionized, and they either become members voluntarily or are compelled to join because of union security articles in collective agreements. In 2006, 4,441,000 workers — 30.8 percent of non-agricultural paid workers — belonged to 15,479 locals in 827 unions (HRDC 2006). Between 1998, when union membership was 3,937,790, and 2006, the number of union members increased by 13 percent, though the number of unions declined (from 1,031 to 827) as did the number of union locals (from 16,631 to 15,479). This change was reflected in increases in the average number of members per union (from 3,819 to 5,370) and per union local (from 237 to 287).

Usually local unions are established at a particular workplace with their own executives and governing structures, but some unions have much broader regional locals that bring together workers in many establishments under a centralized executive. For example, the United Food and Commercial Workers (UFCW) members are, for the most part, concentrated in large locals that cover workers across industries and occupations within provinces. In Manitoba 94 percent of UFCW members are in Local 832, while in British Columbia 37,000 UFCW members are in locals 247 and 1518. Workplaces in which unionization is based on a particular craft or occupation may have multiple locals — which was true of railways, for instance, until the many craft unions in that sector were brought together in a Canadian Auto Workers local. University campuses typically have at least four locals involving faculty members, clerical and related support staff, food and service personnel, and maintenance workers.

Whatever the precise nature of the local, membership provides opportunities for workers to gain a voice in the workplace and in their union. Members have the right to attend meetings, voice their opinions and participate in votes on union matters, volunteer for union committees, take part in union education programs, and attend union-organized social func-

Men and Women in Unions — Equal Numbers, Equal Rates:
The latest union membership data for 2006 confirm that the numbers and unionization rates for men and women are almost equal. Canadian unions in that year had 2,051,826 male members and 2,054,325 female members. Moreover, the unionization rates for men and women were 29.4 and 30.1 percent, respectively.

Unfortunately, this convergence is a result of a sharp decline in the unionization rate for men, from 42.1 percent in 1981, and relative constancy in the rate for women, 31.4 percent in 1981. If the 1981 rates for both men and women had held strong through 2006, the country would have had roughly 5.1 million workers in unions (one million more than the actual number of 4.4 million), and almost 90 percent of these members would have been men.

The shifts in the composition of trade union membership mean that women have gained more power and influence in the labour movement, a development reflected in increasing numbers of women in executive and paid positions in trade unions.

Sources: Morissette, Schellenberg, and Johnson 2005; Statistics Canada 2006.

tions. They can participate both as candidates and voters in elections of **shop stewards** (the individuals who police the collective agreement on behalf of union members and carry forward complaints and grievances from members) and of the **union executive** (which manages the affairs of the local). Moreover, if the local is part of a national or international union, members also get the right to seek election as a local delegate to union conventions and other labour bodies that their union is affiliated with (usually **local labour councils**, which represent labour in a particular city or region, and **trade union centrals**, which are associations of unions at the national or provincial level).

Not all union members become active in their local organization. In fact, a common complaint from people active in local unions is that most of the membership is apathetic and the turnout at meetings is low — as low as 5 or 10 percent (Craig and Solomon 1993: 102). The exceptions are meetings at which issues that affect everyone, such as the progress of collective bargaining or employer initiatives that will alter conditions in the workplace, are on the agenda. Member participation in union activities also increases in crisis situations involving layoffs and plant closures or widespread dissatisfaction with the conduct of either the local or the parent union.

Yet low attendance at union meetings and low participation in union-organized functions does not necessarily indicate apathy or a lack of interest. Members can keep abreast of union activities by checking with union activists to find out what happens at meetings or by reading the meeting minutes. They can relay their concerns to shop stewards and others in the union who do attend meetings on a regular basis. As well, many local unions and all parent unions produce regular newsletters that keep members posted on the key developments, and union websites have become common.

The conduct of local unions is prescribed by a union constitution and bylaws that set out the rights and responsibilities of members and define the roles of elected officials in the locals. All locals have an elected executive. The key positions on the executive are the **table officers** (a president, a treasurer, and a recording secretary).

UFCW Local 832 covers workers throughout Manitoba. Its executive consists of a full-time president and a full-time secretary-treasurer elected every four years, and a board of fourteen vice-presidents elected from the rank-and-file membership for two-year terms. Western and Northern Manitoba are guaranteed at least one position on the board. As well, an advisory board includes representatives from all communities that have UFCW members but are not represented on the executive. Representation in particular workplaces is provided by appointed and/or elected shop stewards. The roles and rights of shop stewards are defined in the collective agreements negotiated with employers.

Most locals also have elected **shop stewards**, who are responsible for representing workers in particular occupations or departments. Shop stewards play a key role in local unions. They are responsible for ensuring that the employer complies with the collective agreement. They do the initial processing of member grievances (writing up the grievance and attempting to get it resolved). They raise members' concerns at union meetings and inform them of events and issues within both the local and the parent union, and they help to mobilize members in support of union initiatives at the bargaining table and in strike action. Shop stewards (along with members of the local executive) may also provide members with assistance in the filing of unemployment insurance, workers' compensation, disability insurance, and other claims.

In recognition of the vital role played by shop stewards (in most cases on a voluntary basis), shop steward training is an important component of union training activities.

In addition, in recent years many unions have attempted to lighten the load of shop stewards by creating other voluntary positions within locals that deal with specific programs. A number of unions have established union counsellor positions, for example. These people identify and provide advice and guidance to members who are having problems with alcohol or drugs or personal problems that are undermining their performance on the job. As well, unions that actively engage in political activities encourage local members to run political action campaigns aimed at persuading members to support labour-friendly political parties, usually the NDP, in national and provincial elections and labour-friendly candidates in local elections.

A critical, but often neglected or obscured, point in discussions of union locals is that these local unions and their members ultimately determine the character of the trade union movement. How these levels

The president of a local is responsible for administering the affairs of the local union, which includes chairing local meetings, ensuring that decisions of the local are carried out, keeping members of the local informed on activities in the parent union, and representing the local in the community. The treasurer is responsible for managing the funds of the local and maintaining complete and accurate records of all financial transactions. The recording secretary compiles minutes (a written record of the business conducted) at meetings and handles much of the correspondence. As well, many locals have trustees or directors representing various components of the local membership. Such positions are particularly important in large locals with a diverse membership.

operate, however, is influenced to a large extent by the policies and practices of parent unions. If the parent unions conceptualize their role as primarily that of delivering services to their members, it is most likely that members will become passive. Members in such unions will probably come to see themselves as merely the consumers of union-provided services — the benefits they get from collective agreements and the processing of grievances — which is how they tend to be characterized in neoclassical economics. As a result, members in such unions are likely to perceive the union as something separate from them — a supplier of services in exchange for dues payments. Such unions tend to become stagnant and dominated by careerist trade union leaders whose main preoccupation is to perpetuate themselves in office. Without pressure from an informed and active membership, inertia sets in and the union goes into decline. This was the experience of many international unions and the entire American Federation of Labor–Congress of Industrial Organizations (AFL-CIO) in the United States (Davis 1980; Goldfield 1987: 231–45).

An alternative approach by parent unions starts from a basic assumption: that a union derives its vigour and creativity from an active and involved membership at the local level. The objective of such unions is to nurture the growth of local "cultures of solidarity" (Fantasia 1988) by articulating a vision that links the struggles of local memberships to a broader struggle involving all members of the union, other unions in the labour movement, and workers in general. To this end, the union encourages its members to become involved in and contribute their efforts and ideas to building the organization. Members are not treated as passive recipients of services, but as active agents playing a role in constructing both the union and the larger labour movement. Members are mobilized to take job action not just to get a better deal for themselves (more wages in their pockets, a better pension plan, shorter hours) — although that is part of it — but also because a victory will provide an impetus for similar gains by other locals in the union and members of other unions. They are encouraged as well to get involved in political struggles and align themselves with other progressive organizations in the community.

The feedback effects generated by this dynamic relationship (pressure from the members, positive responses from the leadership, more pressure from the members) create a virtuous cycle that drives the union forward and enhances the prospects for growth and improved outcomes in collective bargaining. This sort of behaviour — sometimes characterized as class or social unionism — was typical of early industrial unions (the Knights of Labour and One Big Union, for example) and of the industrial unions established in the 1930s and 1940s. Contemporary examples are more difficult to find, although within the Canadian labour movement the vision and principles of social unionism remain rooted in many industrial unions and tend to reassert themselves when unions are under siege, as they have been for much of the past thirty years.

Parent Unions

Almost all local unions are affiliated with a national or international union (a parent union) and therefore subject to the constitution and bylaws of these organizations. Some of the parent unions are very large. In 2006 in Canada, nine unions (two international and seven national) had memberships of over 100,000, which taken all together accounted for 49.7 percent of total union membership. Another ten unions (three international and seven national) had memberships of between 50,000 and 99,999, ac-

A distinction is sometimes drawn between the philosophies of **business unionism** and **social unionism**. Business unions are said to be preoccupied with advancing the interests solely of their own immediate members and not at all interested in broader social or economic goals. Social unions are characterized as inspired by social-democratic values and committed to advancing the interests not just of their immediate memberships but of workers in general. This distinction had considerable validity in the first seventy-five years of the twentieth century, but the changing composition of the workforce (most notably the increase in numbers of women) and the growing hostility of employers and governments to unions have blurred the lines. In practice, most unions now reflect the influence of both philosophies. The main exceptions are some international unions that seem trapped in the old and obsolete traditions of AFL craft unions.

Professor David Camfield (2006) has developed a four-part categorization: business unionism endorses the status quo, focuses on collective bargaining within the limits established by employers and the state, and believes in a top-down structure of control dominated by incumbent leaderships and bureaucrats; social unionism may be critical of aspects of the status quo but backs away from confrontation, militancy, and internal democracy; mobilization unionism promotes solidarity and militancy in struggles to protect and advance workers' rights, but maintains top-down control; and social movement unionism seeks to build unions based on democratic practices, militancy, and collective action and is inspired by a vision of a better society.

counting for another 14.2 percent of total membership.

Of the nine unions with 100,000 or more members, four (Canadian Union of Public Employees, National Union of Public and General Employees, Public Service Alliance of Canada, and Fédération de la santé et des services sociaux) are public-sector unions, with a combined membership of 1,161,000. The other five predominantly private-sector unions — United Steel, Paper and Forestry, Rubber, Manufacturing, Energy, Allied Industrial and Service Workers International Union; National Automobile, Aerospace, Transportation and General Workers Union of Canada, more commonly known as the Canadian Auto Workers (CAW); United Food and Commercial Workers Canada; Communications, Energy and Paperworkers Union of Canada (CEP); and International Brotherhood of Teamsters — have a combined membership of 1,048,000. Still, of the 256 national and international unions active in Canada, 188 (73 percent) had memberships of less than 10,000 (HRDC 2006).

Local unions pay the bulk of the dues levied to the parent union. In exchange for these dues, the parent union provides locals with the expertise necessary to negotiate collective agreements, carry grievances forward to a successful resolution, lobby governments for legislation and programs beneficial to their members, and represent the interests of members in trade union centrals. In most unions, as well, the parent unions maintain a strike fund that members can draw on when they are on strike or locked out.

The main link between the parent union and the local is provided by paid union employees who are responsible for providing services to the locals (they are referred to as either **business agents,** which is typical of international unions, or **union representatives**, who are often recruited from the union's membership). As well, large unions either employ or retain lawyers, economists, journalists, and other staff with other sorts of expertise to provide specialized services for the membership.

In most conventional interpretations, unions exist to serve their members' interests. As Neil Chamberlain (1965: 92) noted, however, "Once a union comes into existence, it becomes an ongoing institution which of necessity develops its own organizational interests and requirements, and these in some respects might differ from the interests and objectives of its members." Although that assertion has a certain validity, the extent to which the institutional needs of the union collide and conflict with the needs of members depends to a large extent on how member interests are defined and the extent to which members are engaged in their unions. Unions must be disciplined to advance collective objectives, and this discipline may require strong leadership; but at the same time unions are democratic organizations. Union leaders are, after all, elected. They will need to recognize that actions by the union that go against the wishes of members could not just undermine their positions in the union but also compromise the union's very future. Trying to force a strike by a union local on an issue that may be of great importance to the union but is opposed by the local members — for example, when an employer is demanding wage concessions under threat of plant closure — could generate serious rank-and-file opposition. When outright conflicts emerge the impact on the local and parent unions will depend on the mechanisms that exist to mediate and resolve such conflicts.

Union Centrals

Parent unions also seek to promote both their institutional interests and the interests of their members by forming federations of trade unions or union centrals to advance their common goals and interests.

Unions created centrals to perform functions that they could not carry out effectively on their own. Since 1956, when the Trades and Labour Congress and the Canadian Congress of Labour merged, the dominant trade union central has been the Canadian Labour Congress (CLC). It is not, however, the only trade union central.

Quebec has three trade union centrals. The Confédération des syndicats nationaux (CSN, Confederation of National Trade Unions), formed in 1960 as the successor to the Canadian Catholic Federation of Labour, is the largest organization and the main rival to the CLC. The Centrale des syndicats démocratiques (CSD, Quebec Federation of Labour), a much smaller organization, was formed in 1972 as a consequence of a split in the CSN. And the Centrale des syndicates du Québec (CSQ, Quebec Teachers Union) originated as a teachers' organization, but from the 1970s on extended its coverage to other workers in the school system. As well, the Quebec Federation of Labour, while affiliated with the CLC, has, since 1994, had sovereign status and carries out many of the functions in Quebec that are the responsibility of the CLC in the rest of Canada (Boivin and Deom 1995: 462–68).

Quite apart from the Quebec situation, rivals to the CLC have been established from time to time as a consequence of conflict within the CLC over direction and policies. In 1969 the Council of Canadian Unions (CCU) was created for the express purpose of creating a purely Canadian trade union movement (see chapter 4). The CCU established a handful of locals, but its appeal for the Canadianization of unions was eroded by the growth in national unions (especially in the public sector). In 1962, 72 percent of trade union members in Canada were in international unions. By 1978 the number had declined to 50 percent. In 2006 it was down to 28.5 percent (HRDC 2006). As well, throughout the 1970s and 1980s international unions ceded greater autonomy to their Canadian branches, and some major unions (the autoworkers in 1985, for example) made an outright break of formal ties with international unions.

A more serious situation developed in 1981, when the CLC suspended fourteen international building trades affiliates for non-payment of dues to the CLC. A number of issues were involved in the conflict, including the political activities of the CLC, the involvement of the Quebec Federation of Labour in organizing construction workers, and the method of delegate selection to CLC conventions. The construction trades union argued that the formula for selecting delegates — one delegate per local up to one thousand members and an additional delegate for each additional thousand members — favoured public-sector unions at the expense of the construction trades. In 1982, ten of the construction trades unions formed the Canadian Federation of Labour (CFL) (Craig and Solomon 1993: 85–87). The CFL opposed most of the CLC's positions and policies (supporting, for example, the Free Trade Agreement and calling for greater co-operation with employers), but it never did expand beyond its initial base and did not gain much influence. Faced with declining membership in the 1990s, the CFL disbanded in 1997 and most of its affiliates rejoined the CLC.

Table 2.1 Union Membership by Congress Affiliation, 2006

	Congress Affiliation	
Membership	**Number**	**Percent**
Canadian Labour Congress	3,197,600*	72.0
Confederation of Canadian Unions**	9,390**	0.2
American Federation of Labor/ Congress of Industrial Organizations	74,650	1.7
CSN	284,280	6.4
CSD	59,160	1.3
CEQ	123,510	2.8
Unaffiliated National Unions	531,720	12.0
Independent Local Organizations	158,085	3.6
Other	2,605	<1.0
Total	4,441,000	100.0

* Includes 818,770 members of international unions also affiliated with the American Federation of Labor/Congress of Industrial Organizations.
** Formerly the Council of Canadian Unions.

Source: Human Resources Development Canada, 2006.

THE ROLE OF THE CANADIAN LABOUR CONGRESS

The CLC (and other trade union centrals) perform four main functions for affiliated unions. First, the CLC attempts to influence federal government policies that will have an impact on workers. It does this both by monitoring and making representations on federal legislation and policies, and by promoting legislation and policies beneficial to its members and working people in general. The CLC also organizes campaigns either in support of or in opposition to federal government initiatives.

For the past thirty years the CLC has faced an onslaught of policies detrimental to the interests of working people. As a result it has organized campaigns to oppose, amongst other things: wage controls; restrictions on collective bargaining and the imposition of back-to-work legislation, primarily in the public sector, ordering striking workers to end strikes and return to work; free-trade agreements; cuts to social welfare programs; negative changes to the unemployment insurance program; budgetary measures (tax and expenditures changes) that provide disproportionate benefits to corporations and the wealthy; and the use of monetary policy to maintain high unemployment. Related to this role, the CLC also produces useful research on labour-related matters (see, for example, Jackson 2005).

In many of these campaigns the CLC participated in coalitions with other organizations such as the National Action Committee on the Status of Women and the National Anti-Poverty Organization. As well, the CLC was one of the prime movers in the formation, in 1980, of the Canadian Centre for Policy Alternatives (CCPA) in Ottawa — a progressive research centre established to counter the growing influence of right-wing think tanks funded by corporations.

A second CLC role is the regulation of relations between member organizations. This function involves mediating and resolving conflicts that arise either when two or more unions are seeking to organize the same group of workers or when one union raids, or attempts to take over, the membership of another union. These sorts of conflicts can create serious problems for the CLC if they become protracted and divisive, diverting the energies of the leadership away from its other tasks and undermining both internal solidarity and the public face of organized labour. A major conflict erupted in 2000 when members of eight locals of the Service Employees International Union (SEIU) in Ontario bolted to the Canadian Auto Workers (CAW). The SEIU filed a complaint with the CLC accusing the CAW of raiding. In April 2000 the CLC found in favour of the SEIU and imposed sanctions on the CAW that could culminate in expulsion. CAW president Buzz Hargrove responded by threatening to take the CAW out of the CLC and establish a new trade union central. A justification process (established in 1987 as a result of similar accusations against the CAW by the United Food and Commercial Workers involving fishermen in Newfoundland) exists within the CLC for resolving such disputes, but it was not invoked in this case (Weinberg 2000).[4]

Third, the CLC also seeks to regulate and police the conduct of member unions. Its code of conduct is intended to discourage corruption, ensure that democratic practices are adhered to, and safeguard the rights of union members. Unions that contravene this code of conduct are subject to disciplinary action. As well, there is a code of obligations for delegates to the CLC and its organizations.

A fourth CLC role is to provide support for member unions in organization campaigns, collective bargaining, and strikes or lockouts (when employers deny workers access to their jobs until they accept terms and conditions demanded by the employer). Such support is particularly important for small unions that sometimes lack the resources and expertise required to deal effectively with employers. But larger unions also benefit from the moral support and tangible demonstrations of solidarity (solidarity pickets, the promotion of boycotts, publicity campaigns, and government lobbying) when they are involved in confrontations with employers and/or governments.

The CLC was also involved in the formation of the New Democratic Party in 1961 and since then has sought to promote union affiliation with the NDP and co-ordinate union participation in electoral politics. These efforts have been hampered because, while the NDP may be more labour friendly than other political parties, it is not a labour party in the sense that its agenda and electoral platforms are established by labour (Archer 1990). As a consequence, CLC efforts in this regard have had little impact at the federal level. Somewhat more success has been achieved in Saskatchewan, British Columbia, Manitoba, and Ontario, where labour's political participation has contributed to the election of NDP governments. In Quebec, organized labour has supported the Parti Québécois in provincial elections.

> Brandon District Labour Council Statement of Aims, 2007:
> "Peace! Freedom! Democracy! Social Justice! Equality! A fair deal for all! Safe air and water! Safe communities! A green world! These are the things we believe in. These are the things we struggle for. The struggle continues."

Provincial federations of labour and local labour councils are the affiliates of the Canadian Labour Congress and perform functions similar to the CLC in provincial and local jurisdictions. Currently, ten provincial federations of labour exist, as well as equivalent organizations in the Yukon and Northwest Territories and Nunavut. The country also has 137 local labour councils (HRDC 2006).

Unions affiliated to the CLC are entitled to affiliate with and participate in the activities of provincial federations and local labour councils. A majority of the larger unions affiliate with and actively participate in provincial federations. Rates of affiliation and participation tend to be much lower at the local level. This is especially true of participation, as many of the locals contributing dues neglect to elect delegates to represent them at labour council meetings.

This lack of involvement at the local level is unfortunate, because most union activity — organization, collective bargaining, strikes, political action, coalition-building — occurs at a local level, and the bulk of the support that local unions receive during periods of crisis comes from union members in their own geographical areas. Moreover, all campaigns launched by the CLC and provincial federations of labour must ultimately be put into action at a local level by labour councils and the members of local unions. For example, the CLC announced the initiation of a **living-wage** campaign based on a similar, and successful, campaign in the United States. The purpose of the campaign was to persuade local levels of government to require that all contractors and suppliers doing business with them pay a living wage (which is invariably higher than minimum wages). The task of advancing this campaign in Canada fell to labour councils. But with low levels of participation, the labour councils have a constrained ability to carry out such campaigns effectively because the handful of active members become overextended and "burn out."

At recent CLC conventions, some local labour councils have presented resolutions calling for compulsory affiliation to labour councils of all CLC member unions. These resolutions have been rejected on the grounds that affiliation should be voluntary. As an alternative, the CLC has promised to vigorously promote affiliation with and participation in labour councils.[5]

One explanation for the lack of participation in labour councils is that as unions have increased in size and complexity the role of the local union and its members has diminished in importance. With the concentration of greater power and resources in the parent body, local members tend to become more remote from and defer to the leadership, as well as to the union employees hired to provide the expertise required in negotiating and administering collective

> Before they are accepted as delegates, delegates to labour councils must make a declaration:
>
> "I solemnly promise and declare that I will support and obey the by-laws of this Labour Council, and the Constitution of the Canadian Labour Congress. That I will, if within my power to do so, assist my fellow members, or their families, when they are in distress, that I will not purposely, or knowingly, wrong a member of the Council, that I will not divulge, except to a delegate, any of the affairs of this Council, that I will not recommend any person to become a delegate to this Council whom I believe unworthy to be a delegate. I do hereby solemnly promise and declare that I will undertake a faithful performance of this obligation."
>
> *Source: Brandon and District Labour Council 1979: 9.*

agreements and the internal affairs of the union. The flip side of this is that they become disengaged from activities in both their locals and the local labour movement. While this argument does contain an important element of truth, the result pointed to is not inevitable. In the end, the shaping of union participation depends on the practices and policies of the parent union regarding integration of members into the movement.

UNION DEMOCRACY

When workers form or join unions, they do so in the expectation that through their participation they will gain the power necessary to give them some control over decisions that have an impact on their lives. Indeed, one of the promises that the union movement holds out to workers is: join the union and you will have a voice in the union, in the workplace, and your community.

The starting point to gaining and exercising power is in the local union and in how the local union nurtures and promotes participation and engagement by its members. All unions have constitutions and bylaws that define member rights and establish procedures for participation. Members have the right to vote on union matters such as the approval or rejection of collective agreements and strike action. They have the right to seek office in the union and represent their local union as a delegate to union conventions and other bodies that their union is affiliated with, such as labour councils. These procedures are prerequisites for, but not the substance of, union democracy.

Union democracy requires that local unions and their memberships act in an all-inclusive way: women's voices and the voices and interests of people of colour — including Aboriginal people — must be fully heard and their interests represented. This difficult goal almost always requires struggle on the part of those who would otherwise be excluded. But unless the union is inclusive, it is not democratic; and once achieved, inclusiveness must be nurtured and entrenched.

If a union is to achieve true democracy, the members — all of the members — of a local must be able to control their union's agendas. They must be able to determine which issues go forward in collective bargaining and how their representatives conduct bargaining. They must be able to submit resolutions to union conventions — resolutions that will be placed on the agenda and properly debated. They must be able to establish the issues that local and parent unions address in their dealings with governments. Union members may sometimes get it wrong — that is, they may make the wrong decisions. But who doesn't make wrong decisions? The necessity is that those decisions are their own, and when they are wrong the members will have to accept the consequences, learn from their experience, and ensure that the mistakes are not repeated.

Women Fight For and Get Respect in the Labour Movement:
"Prior to the mid-1970s, women simply weren't taken seriously as trade unionists by men in the labour movement in Manitoba, and issues of particular concern to women were not considered to be labour issues. Women put up with a good deal of abuse and humiliation, and their attempts to involve themselves in the union movement were treated with scorn...

Darlene Dziewit [president of the Manitoba Federation of Labour (MFL)] recalls that in the early 1970s a CLC convention was a place for verbal harassment. 'It wasn't possible to go to a mike on a convention floor; the obscene comments weren't worth it,' recalls Susan Hart-Kulbaba [MFL president in the late 1980s and early 1990s]. When women spoke about child care at a 1975 convention attended by Dziewit, men responded with laughter. Although by this time there was a Women's Committee of the MFL, it operated more like a social auxiliary... concerned with the social side of the trade union movement, and the organizing of events such as the Miss Union Label Pageant. The existence of the Committee was tokenism on the part of the male MFL Executive.

Darlene Dziewit came on the UFCW staff in 1977, and was their first female staff representative in Manitoba. She worked to push other women forward, including Susan Hart (now Hart-Kulbaba), who recalls: 'When I first got involved, it was horrible. There were the two of us, and every time we moved, they were accusing us of caucusing. If you argued, you were called shrill. It was paternalistic and condescending.'

Dziewit, Hart and Astrid Zimmer all recall a confrontation over the Choice issue as being an important symbolic turning point for women in Manitoba's labour movement. In 1983 the Equal Rights and Opportunities Committee (EROC) of the MFL joined the Coalition for Reproductive Choice. The next day the all-male Executive of the MFL had a meeting and passed a resolution ordering the EROC to disaffiliate from the Coalition, despite the fact that the CLC had a pro-choice policy. Women went in one at a time to see Dick Martin, MFL President, and yelled at him all the next day. Dziewit was the last to go in. She told him: 'You have two problems. You have no business in telling us what to do, and you have no women on that Executive Board.'

Dziewit and Hart met with Martin on the second issue and said: 'Look we want women on the Executive Board. We're banding together. There'll be a blood bath. Either you work with us or we'll fight.'

There really wasn't any coalition of women behind these threats. Dziewit and Hart met in Dziewit's basement and talked about the issue and decided that you have as much power as the other side thinks you have. 'They thought we had power.' Martin became convinced, and at the next MFL Convention six women were added to the Executive, and a pro-Choice resolution was passed. The Choice issue, says Astrid Zimmer, made a new kind of women's politics felt in the MFL.

The way the MFL women worked and related to each other is important. For example, at one MFL conference in the mid-1980s women brought in a speaker to talk about battering. About sixty women were in attendance, and somebody said that given the statistics on battering, chances are that about a dozen women who were there had experienced what was being talked about. Three women got up crying. Other women talked to them in the hallway. The three women got together, and two ended up going to Klinic for counseling. Women trade unionists support each other, on labour matters and on personal matters.

The point is that labour women were talking about issues not usually addressed in the labour movement — or elsewhere for that matter. They were struggling over issues not traditionally seen to be union issues. And they forced men to take those issues seriously."

Source: Black and Silver 1991: 61–64.

In many cases, though, union members have relinquished control of their local unions to their union representatives or their union leaders, many of whom lack detailed knowledge and understanding of the local situation. This abandonment leads to the apathy evident in many locals, as reflected in low turnouts at meetings, in the reluctance of members to seek office or run for shop steward positions, and in the lack of support for local labour councils. Those situations are most likely to emerge in locals in which membership involvement has either not been actively promoted or perhaps even discouraged as a result of a "we know best" attitude on the part of union bureaucrats and leaders.

In the short run, a union may find it advantageous to have a passive or quiescent membership. Collective bargaining and the handling of grievances become less problematic and impose less of a strain on union resources when members get the sense that they really can't do much to influence their union — when members resign themselves to having decisions imposed from on high. In the long run, however, local unions and the union movement as a whole will suffer. Dissatisfied union members will turn against their union and against unions in general. They will become more susceptible to criticisms of unions levelled by employers and governments. They will be less likely to support the leadership's calls for strike action and more likely, if a strike vote goes against their wishes, to cross picket lines. Moreover, when union members have bad experiences in one place of work, they will be less likely to support a union in the next.

Building and sustaining vigorous and engaged memberships in local unions is a difficult task. The difficulties are particularly great once workplaces are already unionized and new workers become members more or less by default — not because they have been part of a union organization drive, but rather because the union is just there. But in the long run, for a parent union the creation of a vigorous and involved membership constitutes a wise investment of effort and resources. Local unions with active memberships are less dependent on the parent union because they can draw on their own resources — their active members — to provide leadership. This ability frees up the resources of the parent union to do more of the other things required to support a growing and robust trade union movement — organizing the unorganized, negotiating improvements in wages and benefits and the terms and conditions of employment, and challenging government policies and actions that hurt workers. (For discussions of these issues see Moody 1997: 275–77, 1998: 303–30; Parker and Gruelle 1993; and Goddard 1994: 235–42.)

The differences in union practices can have sharp, and contrasting, practical consequences. Say, for instance, in one union — Union A — a local's agenda for collective bargaining is established by union representatives in consultation with the president and perhaps other members of the local union executive. In many cases, the agenda reflects a common core of issues that the international union is pushing in comparable bargaining situations. The leaders in the parent union have no formal consultations with the members, although members of the local executive may consult with them informally, at coffee breaks and lunch breaks, perhaps. The members are, in short, all but excluded from the bargaining process. The union representative from parent or regional headquarters is the union's chief bargainer. The local president and perhaps another member of the executive are also on the team. Union members may be advised when bargaining sessions occur, but they are not provided with details.

Then an impasse arises in bargaining because the employer refuses to concede improvements in wages and conditions requested by the union. The union has a couple of options: it can decide to accept the employer's position and recommend it to the membership on the grounds that this is the best they can do; or it can ask the members to take a strike vote. But because local members have not been directly involved in the sequence of events leading to the impasse, they must accept at face value the recommendations of the union representative and the bargaining team. In essence, they lack the detailed knowledge required to make an informed decision. Whatever the outcome, the experience is likely to generate discontent and dissension within the local, alienate some of the members, and weaken support for the union.

In another union — Union B — members at the local level are involved in matters from the beginning. The local holds formal meetings to discuss the bargaining agenda and establish priorities. A parent union representative attends these meetings to provide information and statistics and otherwise facilitate the deliberations. The agenda that goes forward is the members' agenda. The bargaining may be structured in the same way as it was for Union A, but local representatives will tend to have greater scope for participation in the give and take of the process. As well, the local representatives will be responsible for keeping their members informed of the progress in bargaining. If an impasse develops, and members must choose between accepting the employer's offer and taking strike action, they are in position to make an informed decision — to evaluate the pros and cons of choosing one course of action or the other. Whatever the outcome, local members will be able to accept it as *their* decision and abide by it. This does not mean that no friction resulting from the vote occurs within the local. The difference is that discontent and dissension are more likely to be reflected in internal debate within the local about what its members should be trying to achieve as a union, rather than being directed at the union itself.

Employers and governments frequently attack unions for being undemocratic, citing unionization drives, strike votes, and trade union political action. The arguments today are the same as they have always been: decisions to unionize and strike are either dictated by outside agitators and "big union" bosses or otherwise rigged and manipulated. The critics only make this claim, however, when workers vote to join a union, to take strike action, or to endorse political action; never when they vote to move in the opposite direction. Employers and governments detest union democracy because it conflicts with authoritarian rule in the workplace and the economy. Anti-union laws legislated by governments in Ontario and Manitoba in the mid-1990s — for example, the replacement of a card-based system of certification with a vote-based system in both provinces and the repeal of anti-scab legislation in Ontario — were clearly designed to undercut workers' democratic rights and restore power to employers and the state.

Union leaderships and staffs are, in most unions, committed to the principles of union democracy. They recognize that without an active membership the capacity of unions to sustain themselves and grow is tenuous. They also recognize that no silver bullets exist to create and entrench union democracy once and for all. As unionist and writer Sam Gindin (1995: 276) puts it:

> Democracy is not supplied by a constitution. Nor can it be reduced to a mechanism for keeping leaders in line (as relevant as that need is). Union democracy is primarily about workers making changes: changing themselves, changing their immediate world, and laying the basis for eventually changing the larger world. Union democracy is built by workers in their struggles to build the union, which acts as their line of defence and base for progress. Democracy is

therefore not separate from struggles, nor is it static; it must constantly be redefined, recreated, and reinvented.

Union democracy, then, is something that must be built; and ultimately only the members themselves can do the building.

THE CHALLENGE OF RACIALIZED LABOUR FORCES, RACIALIZED WORKPLACES, AND RACIALIZED COMMUNITIES

A challenge of profound complexity confronting trade unions and trade union centrals in this century is the pervasive racialization of labour forces and workplaces in Canadian cities — that is, the growing proportion of individuals in the workforce from non-Aboriginal visible minorities. This phenomenon is a result of two main changes in the flows of population: a dramatic change in the composition of the immigrant population; and an increase in the proportion of Aboriginal peoples moving to cities from reserves and rural communities.

In his analysis of minorities in the workforce, Andrew Jackson (2005: 101–22) observes that visible minorities accounted for 13.4 percent of the population in 2001, compared to only 4.7 percent in 1981. This proportion is expected to reach 20 percent by 2016. The composition of this segment of the population was 26 percent Chinese, 23 percent South Asian, 17 percent blacks, and 34 percent other. Now and for the foreseeable future, the growth in Canada's labour force will be fed primarily by immigrants, and the bulk of these immigrants will belong to visible minorities.

Along with immigrants, Canada also recruits offshore workers to come here on a work permit to meet specific labour force needs. In December 1, 2005 some 151,720 individuals were working in Canada on work permits, including 99,141 people who had entered the country in 2000. The flow of permit workers consists not only of credentialed and skilled workers, who come primarily from the United States, Japan, and European countries, but also of less skilled workers who come primarily from Mexico and other Central American countries, the Caribbean, and Africa and are

Unionization Rates for Workers of Colour and Aboriginal Workers, 2001:

Union Coverage	
Visible Minority	21.3%
Men	21.2%
Women	21.4%
Visible Minority Workers	
As % All Workers	9.3%
As % Unionized Workers	6.9%
Union Coverage	
All Aboriginal Workers	30.4%
Men	29.1%
Women	31.8%
As % all Workers	2.7%
As % Unionized Workers	2.7%

Source: Jackson and Schetagne 2003: 36–37.

Table 2.2 Average Annual Earnings of Visible Minorities and All Canadians, 2000

	All		Male		Female	
	Number	% Average	Number	% Average	Number	% Average
All Earners	$31,757	100%	$38,347	100%	$24,390	100%
Visible Minorities – All	27,149	85.5%	31,623	82.5%	22,301	91.4%
Visible Minorities – Canadian Born	22,781	71.7%	25,701	67.0%	19,737	80.9%
Chinese	28,846	90.8%	33,350	87.0%	24,069	98.7%
South Asian	28,072	88.4%	33,222	86.6%	21,610	88.6%
Black	25,156	79.2%	28,441	74.2%	21,984	90.1%
Immigrants 1990–94	25,560	80.5%	30,292	79.0%	20,553	84.3%
Immigrants 1995–99	23,889	75.2%	29,014	75.7%	18,113	74.3%

Source: Jackson 2005: 105

recruited to work as domestics, do seasonal work in agriculture, and fill vacancies in meat-packing and other plants with high rates of turnover (Citizenship and Immigration Canada 2007).

Labour markets in cities are augmented not just by immigrants and foreign workers, but by Aboriginal migrants who move to cities seeking to improve their lives. The impact of this flow is particularly significant in Prairie cities in Manitoba and Saskatchewan. Michael Mendelson estimates that the Aboriginal workforce in those provinces will climb to 17 percent of the total workforce by 2020: "To no small degree, the Aboriginal children who are today in [Prairie] homes, child care centres and schools represent the economic future of the two provinces. The increasing importance of the Aboriginal workforce to Manitoba and Saskatchewan cannot be exaggerated. There is likely no single more critical factor for these provinces" (Mendelson 2004: 35, 38).

Despite our growing economic dependence on immigrants, people in visible minorities, and Aboriginal peoples, workers in these groups are disadvantaged in the labour market relative to other workers. In brief, they are: more likely to experience unemployment; be concentrated in jobs in

Table 2.3 Aboriginal People in the Workforce, 2001, Selected Indicators

	Total Population	Aboriginal Population	Aboriginal as % of Total
Average Income of People			
15 and Over	$29,769	$19,132	64%
Incidence of Low-Income			
Families	12.9%	31.2%	242%
Single People	38.0%	55.9%	147%
Employment Rate			
All	61.5%	49.7%	81%
Men	67.2%	52.5%	78%
Women	56.1%	47.1%	85%
Unemployment Rate			
All	7.4%	19.1%	258%
Men	7.6%	21.4%	282%
Women	7.2%	16.7%	232%
Percent of Employed Working Full-Time/Full-Year			
All	53.9%	40.5%	75%
Men	59.6%	42.0%	70%
Women	47.4%	38.9%	82%
Average Employment Income Full-Time/Full-Year			
All	$43,298	$33,416	77%
Men	49,224	37,370	76%
Women	34,892	28,851	83%
Average Employment Income Not Full-Time/Full-Year			
All	$19,207	$13,795	72%
Men	23,370	16,119	69%
Women	15,625	11,437	73%

Source: Jackson 2005: 116.

service, clerical, and unskilled or semi-skilled manual occupations; have lower annual earnings; and be poor (See Tables 2.2 and 2.3).

While a number of factors contribute to these disparities, discrimination and racism play, as always, a critical role in determining the opportunities and rewards that are accessible to workers of visible minorities,

Union Statements on Race

Canadian Labour Congress, "Unions Make a Difference in the Community," Committee Report, June 15, 2005:

"The CLC will embark on a campaign to defend the rights of migrant workers. This campaign shall include lobbying for legislation at all levels of government and internationally to ensure that migrant workers have the same rights as Canadian workers when they work in Canada.

"This campaign will also include:

- the education of our members, the public and politicians about fair treatment for migrant workers;
- resist the racist, anti-worker free-trade policies that allow businesses and governments to deny migrant workers: fair wages, right to access to employment insurance, full health and safety protection, labour law protection, the right to unionize..."

National Automobile, Aerospace, Transportation and General Workers Union of Canada, (CAW-Canada) Constitution:

"Article 2 Objectives
Section 1
To unite all workers who are under the jurisdiction of CAW-Canada into one organization without regard to race, sex, creed, colour, marital status, sexual orientation, disability, political or religious affiliation or place of national origin. Every member must receive equal treatment under this constitution."

Canadian Union of Public Employees Constitution: Appendix "D" Equality Statement

"Union solidarity is based on the principle that union members are equal and deserve mutual respect at all levels. Any behaviour that creates conflict prevents us from working together to strengthen our union....

"CUPE's policies and practices must reflect our commitment to equality. Members, staff and elected officers must be mindful that all sisters and brothers deserve dignity, equality and respect."

including Aboriginal peoples.

The challenge confronting the labour movement and its various components is to provide the leadership and action required to obliterate the conditions in our society that nurture and sustain racism, or, to put it another way, obliterate the obstacles that impede the achievement of racial equality. The starting point for unions and trade union centrals must be to

United Food and Commercial Workers Successful in Organizing Migrant Mexican Farmworkers at Mayfair Foods, Manitoba:

For many years, the UFCW has been in the forefront of a campaign to achieve labour rights and human rights for migrant workers in Canada. To this end, the UFCW provides an array of support services, including information, training, and advocacy for off-shore workers who are brought to Canada under the Seasonal Agriculture Workers Program; lobbies federal and provincial governments to get them to amend health and safety, employment standards, and other labour legislation to extend coverage to migrant workers; and seeks to unionize migrant workers in provinces where they have the right to join unions.

In June 2007 the UFCW achieved a major breakthrough in Manitoba when the Manitoba Labour Board granted certification to UFCW Local 832 to represent sixty-five offshore migrant workers at Mayfair Farms near Portage La Prairie. However, the ruling of the Labour Board has been challenged by Mayfair Farms with the support of various employer groups who are concerned that the Mayfair Farms success will result in further certifications at other workplaces dependent on offshore workers.

In an insightful analysis of the implications of Mayfair Farms certification, Dave Hall observed that the "Mayfair workers are under a lot of pressure to drop the union," because of signals from both Mexico authorities and local employers that they will not be able to return next year if they belong to a union.

Hall says that "unions, the NDP and other progressive organizations need to speak clearly in support of the UFCW and the right of migrant workers to organize. Silence leaves migrant workers at risk of being intimidated for fear of losing the opportunity to work in Canada."

Source: Hall 2007: 2.

recognize that racism exists and is pervasive, and to resolve to work with the victims of racism to empower them and overcome the conditions that oppress them. "An anti-racist perspective begins by accepting that the perceptions of people of colour are real," and the struggle for racial equality must include "members of racial minorities as full and equal participants" (Henry et al. 2000: 379). The struggle to overcome racism must, as Galabuzi (2006: 235–36) suggests, be reflected in all union activities, including organizing, collective bargaining, and the work of local labour councils in seeking to create communities that serve the collective interests of working people.

Most unions are committed to combating and overcoming racism in their own organization, in the workplaces they have unionized, and in society as a whole. The extent to which the labour movement is successful in overcoming the forces that give rise to racism is likely to have a profound influence on the vitality and strength of the movement in the coming years.

NOTES

1. Goddard (1997) categorizes union activities into five roles: economic; workplace democratization; integrative; social democratic; and conflict. Our categorization combines (with a little give and take) Goddard's workplace democratization and integrative roles into an industrial citizenship role and his social-democratic and conflict roles into a political-voice role.
2. In 1925 the Toronto Electric Commission challenged the constitutionality of the *Industrial Disputes Investigation Act*, arguing that the federal government could not apply the law to local utilities and municipal employees. The case was finally referred to the Judicial Committee of the Privy Council in Britain (the final court of appeal at that time) for resolution. The Judicial Committee ruled that the power of the federal government to legislate in industrial relations matters was restricted to workers in the federal jurisdiction (Craig and Solomon 1993: 137–38). Today the federal jurisdiction covers workers in: air, rail, shipping, and trucking firms engaged in interprovincial or international activities; banks, uranium mines, broadcasting, and grain elevators; and the federal civil service and agencies and Crown corporations of the federal government. All other workers are covered by provincial laws (Carter 1995: 27–29).
3. In many jurisdictions a process was in place for civil service associations to make presentations to governments on employment-related issues. Governments would then impose their decisions, which might or might not reflect the concerns presented by the associations. Similar arrangements existed in other public-sector institutions such as universities. Robert Florida, a member of the Brandon University Faculty Association, which was certified in 1978, characterized the process as "binding supplication."
4. In a CBC interview, July 11, 2000, Nancy Riche, a CLC spokesperson, reported that twenty applications had been filed under the justification process since 1987 by employees seeking to change unions. Of these applications, nine were granted; the other eleven situations were resolved through mediation and negotiation.
5. The Brandon and District Labour Council, for example, is a strong proponent of compulsory affiliation. On its own the Labour Council has conducted intensive efforts to encourage increases in affiliation and participation. These efforts usually result in a few more affiliations (which often lapse after a year or two) but not much increase in participation. Moreover, so far the promises made by CLC convention delegates and the CLC leadership to promote more involvement by affiliates in labour councils have had little impact.

CHAPTER 3

ACTING FOR MEMBERS, ACTING FOR SOCIETY

A number of questions immediately arise in any discussion of trade unions. What exactly have unions and the labour movement achieved in their roughly 150 years of existence? What have they done for their members? What have they done for labour in general? And what have they done for society?

These questions can be answered by considering contexts: the success of unions in building their memberships; the representation of member interests in their dealings with employers (through collective bargaining, strikes, and related activities); the establishment and entrenchment of rights for members in workplaces and in the economy as a whole; and the creation of a strong voice for members in politics.

BUILDING THE MOVEMENT

Union organizing has always been difficult, but it was especially so before workers secured trade union rights. Before 1944, discontented workers who tried to form a union were subject to dismissal, **blacklisting** (placed on a list of union activists/malcontents circulated among employers), and other forms of reprisals from employers. In many situations employers compelled workers to sign, as a condition of employment, **yellow-dog contracts** stating that they did not belong to and would not join a union. PC 1003 (and the legislation that incorporated PC 1003 provisions in the immediate postwar era) declared that such practices, which were intended to interfere with and frustrate the formation of a union, were unfair labour practices and contrary to the law.

Today union representatives handle most union organizing drives. The drives start either when a disgruntled worker approaches a representative and asks how to go about forming a union, or when a representative initiates contact with workers at a particular workplace and finds interest in forming a union. Some unions have experimented with more innovative techniques for assessing worker interest in forming unions. For example, United Food and Commercial Workers Local 832 in Manitoba has run newspaper ads inviting workers who want to join a union to contact it. This tactic led to successful organizing drives at a number of private-sector security firms.

If the expressed interest is strong, the union will undertake a drive. It asks the individuals who first showed an interest in unionizing to sign union membership cards and often enlists them to help the representative sign up other workers. Representatives will organize both one-on-one and group meetings with the most likely prospects. They may hold group meetings on a regular basis to report on progress, build morale, and encourage newly signed-up members to become involved in the campaign. This approach is designed to prevent the employer from finding out that the workers are organizing, which is especially important in jurisdictions that give employers the right to talk to their workers about the consequences of unionization. Such "talks" usually take the form of threats — either overt or veiled — that establishing a union will bring layoffs or relocation of the plant, or promises that workers will get improvements in wages and benefits if they do not unionize.

In recent years, following the rapid growth in the numbers of women and people of colour in the workforce, more and more union organizers are taking great pains to ensure that these workers are sought out and encouraged to become union members. The extent to which unions can improve workers' sense of dignity and respect in the workplace has become an important issues in organizing drives.

Certification by a labour board legally establishes a union as a bargaining agent for a group of employees. But before a union can file an application for certification in a workplace, the law requires a sign-up threshold, which ranges from 35 percent to 45 percent depending on the province (except for Saskatchewan and Prince Edward Island, where a percentage is not defined). In some jurisdictions the labour board is empowered to grant union status based on membership cards. In the federal jurisdiction and in Quebec, Saskatchewan, and Prince Edward Island, certification can be granted if more than 50 percent of workers in the bargaining unit have signed cards. In Manitoba the figure is more than 65 percent; and in New Brunswick the labour board can certify at more than 50 percent, and must certify at more than 60 percent. Newfoundland, Nova Scotia, Ontario, Alberta, and British Columbia require mandatory votes. A disadvantage for workers and unions of mandatory voting is that, in the period between the announcement of a vote and the actual vote itself, employers get a chance to threaten and intimidate employees in an effort to dissuade them from voting for a union.

The laws relating to certification matter — as Felice Martinello (2000) demonstrated in a study of the impact in Ontario of the replacement, in 1995, of a card-based system of certification (automatic certification with 55 percent of members signed up) with a system requiring votes in all situations. Applications for certification dropped significantly as a result of the change. Legislation was also changed to make it easier to **decertify** (vote to get rid of) a union. The result was a significant increase in decertifications.

In the past, it seems, each successive wave of unionization was followed by either stagnation or decline (see Table 3.1). The initial wave peaked in 1920, but declined in the 1930s as a result of the Great Depression and intensified employer resistance to unionization. A second wave, involving a growth in industrial unions, peaked in 1955. While union membership continued to grow in absolute terms through to the mid-1960s, union density declined. The decline reflected a slowdown in union growth relative to the growth in overall employment and an increase in employment in non-unionized industries relative to unionized industries — specifically the growth in service industries relative to goods-producing industries. The extension of union rights to public-sector workers in the second half of the 1960s provided a fresh impetus to union membership. From 1965 to 1975, the number of union members increased by 1.3 million, and union density rose by six percentage points. Union membership continued to grow after 1975 but at a much slower rate, and union density levelled off at about 36 percent in the 1980s. In the 1990s union growth slowed even more, and union density declined. In recent years union density has been at its lowest level since the 1970s. The average for the period 2000–06 was 30.9 percent, which is 10 percent less than the average for 1990–99.[1]

Possibly, the union movement in Canada has now run up against the limits of the expansion made possible by the extension of trade union rights to public-sector workers. Given that virtually all public-sector workers in Canada now have trade union rights, if unions are to regain their momentum and generate a fourth wave of union growth they will have to do it by organizing the unorganized. This means focusing on industries in private-sector services in which unionization rates are very low, and non-unionized firms in sectors such as manufacturing and construction, where unions are already entrenched but some slippage in membership has occurred in recent decades.

Compared to other industrialized countries, Canada is roughly somewhere in the middle in **union density**: the number of unionized workers relative to the total number of employed workers. The Scandinavian countries — where rates range from 60 percent to 90 percent — and Italy, Belgium, and Austria all have higher rates than Canada does; while Australia, Germany, Japan, the United States, and France have lower rates.[2] Moreover,

Table 3.1 Union Membership and Density, Selected Years, 1920–2006

		Union Membership as a Percentage of	
Year	Union Membership (000s)	Civilian Labour Force	Non-agricultural Paid Workers
1920	374	9.4	16.0
1925	271	7.6	14.4
1930	322	7.9	13.9
1935	281	6.4	14.5
1940	362	7.9	16.3
1945	711	15.7	24.2
1951*	1,029	19.7	28.4
1955	1,268	23.6	33.7
1960	1,459	23.5	32.3
1965	1,589	23.2	29.7
1970	2,173	27.2	33.6
1975	2,884	29.9	35.6
1980	3,397	29.2	35.7
1985	3,666	28.3	36.4
1990	4,031	28.5	34.5
1995	4,003	27.0	34.3
1999	4,010	26.0	32.6
2000	4,058	25.8	31.9
2001	4,111	25.7	31.3
2002	4,174	25.7	31.1
2003	4,178	25.0	30.4
2004	4,261	25.2	30.4
2005	4,381	25.5	30.7
2006	4,441	25.6	30.8
Averages			
1980–89	3,668	28.7	35.7
1990–99	4,034	27.4	34.4
2000–06	4,229	25.5	30.9

* No survey of union membership was done in 1950.

Sources: For the years 1920–75, Benjamin, Gunderson and Riddell (1998: 489); for 1980–98, HRDC (1998b: 15); and for 1999–2006 HRDC (2006).

Table 3.2 Union Density Rates* by Selected Characteristics, 2006

	Union Density (Percent)	Percent of All Employees
Total	29.7	100.0
Men	29.4	50.6
Women	30.1	49.4
By Age		
15–24	13.3	17.2
25–44	29.5	47.5
45–54	39.3	23.5
55 and over	35.5	11.9
By Education		
Less than grade 9	27.6	2.4
Some high school	21.9	10.8
High-school grad	27.1	20.6
Some post-secondary	21.6	8.8
Post-secondary certificate/diploma	33.4	34.8
University degree	33.7	22.5
By Work Status		
Full-time	31.2	81.7
Part-time	23.2	18.3
By Job Status		
Permanent	30.2	87.4
Non-permanent	26.3	12.6
By Job Tenure		
1–12 months	14.6	22.8
Over 1 to 5 years	23.0	31.6
Over 5 to 9 years	32.1	15.9
Over 9 to 14 years	36.7	9.3
Over 14 years	52.0	20.5
By Workplace Size		
Under 20 employees	13.4	32.4
20–99 employees	29.7	32.9
100–500 employees	41.4	21.3
Over 500 employees	50.9	13.3
By Sector		
Public**	71.4	23.4
Private	17.0	76.6
By Industry		
Goods-producing	28.8	23.3
Agriculture	4.8	0.9
Natural resources	21.7	1.9
Manufacturing	28.4	14.6

Construction	30.2	5.0
Utilities	68.5	0.9
Service-producing	30.0	76.7
Professional, scientific, and technical	4.3	5.2
Accommodation and food	6.3	6.5
Finance, insurance, and real estate	8.3	6.2
Other services	9.3	3.5
Business, building, and other support	12.5	3.7
Trade	12.6	16.8
Information, culture, and recreation	24.9	4.5
Transportation and warehousing	42.9	4.8
Health care and social assistance	54.2	11.2
Public administration	67.3	6.0
Education	68.3	8.3
By Occupation		
Management	7.6	7.3
Occupations unique to primary industry	15.4	2.0
Sales and service	20.0	24.9
Natural and applied sciences	23.4	7.1
Business, finance, and administrative	24.1	19.5
Culture and recreation	26.1	2.4
Trades, transport, and equipment operators	36.5	14.4
Occupations unique to production	36.8	7.0
Social and public service	60.7	8.3
Health	61.7	6.2
By Province		
Alberta	22.4	10.9
New Brunswick	26.4	2.2
Ontario	26.7	39.8
Nova Scotia	27.5	2.8
Prince Edward Island	28.9	0.4
British Columbia	30.2	12.8
Manitoba	34.8	3.6
Saskatchewan	35.0	2.8
Newfoundland	36.3	1.3
Quebec	37.0	23.3
Newfoundland	38.0	1.4

* Union members as percent of paid employees.

** Public sector includes employees in government departments or agencies, Crown corporations or publicly funded schools, hospitals or other institutions. The private sector includes all other paid employees.

Source: Statistics Canada 2006: 66–67.

most other countries have had, like Canada, stagnant or declining density rates in the 1980s and 1990s (see chapter 1 for additional data relating to trends in union density rates in different countries, and also Akyeampong 1997; Mainville and Olineck 1999). Significantly, the higher rates of union density in the Scandinavian countries correlate directly with the greater access to public-sector benefits and supports enjoyed by workers in those countries.

Certainly, the labour movement in Canada should be concerned about two important trends: the long-term decline in private-sector union membership; and a growing hostility to unions from both employers and governments. As well, the relationship between unionization rates in Canada and the United States should be of particular concern. In 1951 unionization rates (percentage of non-agricultural paid workers in unions) in Canada and the United States were almost identical: 30.2 percent and 31.7 percent, respectively (Murray 1995: 164). Since 1951 the rate in the United States has declined continuously. In 2006 the rate for Canada was more than twice that of the United States: 30.8 and 12.5 percent, respectively (Human Resources Development Canada 2006; U.S. Department of Labor 2007).[3]

Numerous studies have attempted to isolate the key factors underlying these divergent trends. Among the factors identified are: more favourable laws in Canada (in particular the use of card-based certification in many jurisdictions and the absence of right-to-work laws); the existence of a social-democratic alternative, the NDP, in Canada; a more inclusive union movement in Canada and more effective unionization strategies by Canadian unions; and a larger public sector in Canada. As well, a number of authors have cited both the presence of a strong anti-union bias in the enforcement and administration of labour laws and concerted and sustained opposition to trade unions from employers in the United States[4] (see Murray 1995: 164–65; Goldfield 1987; Kumar 1993; Riddell 1993; Robinson 1993).

Some of the factors that have protected unions in Canada from the long-term decline experienced in the United States have weakened significantly in the past decade and a half. Labour laws in Canada are becoming less favourable to unions as provincial governments seek to make their jurisdictions more attractive to private-sector investment. The social-democratic alternative offered by the NDP has been diluted as the NDP itself and its provincial governments have moved to the right in an attempt to remain politically viable (see chapter 5). At the federal level a persistent erosion of public support has sharply reduced NDP influence. Growth in the public sector has given way to stagnation and decline in many jurisdictions as governments adopt neo-liberal policies aimed at cutting both taxes and government expenditures and altering market regulations for the benefit of business. Added to the mix is a constant barrage of anti-labour stories and analyses originating with employer-financed research bodies and in much of the mainstream (that is, corporate) media.

The decline of union density relates to the character and dimensions of the problems confronting trade unions in their organizational activities (see Table 3.2). The rates of unionization are lowest for young workers (fifteen- to twenty-four years old) and workers in the age group of twenty-five to forty-four. Evidently, workers with post-secondary credentials (certificates, diplomas, or university degrees), full-time workers, workers with permanent jobs, and workers with over five years in a particular job are much more likely to be union members than are those with no post-secondary credentials, part-time jobs, non-permanent jobs, and less than five years' tenure in their jobs.

Of these factors, the most critical would seem to be the characteristics of the jobs held by workers. One of the more pervasive trends in the labour market in recent decades has been the casual nature of significant numbers of jobs, as reflected in increases in part-time and temporary jobs, both of which are concentrated among young people and women (Broad 1999). In 2006, 18.3 percent of paid workers were in part-time jobs, and 12.6 percent were in temporary or non-permanent jobs (calculated from data in Table 3.2). Of the part-time workers, 37.5 percent were age fifteen to twenty-four, and 68.2 percent were women (Statistics Canada 2006c). Unionization rates for these two categories of workers were 23.2 percent and 26.3 percent, respectively. Workers in these sorts of jobs are more difficult to unionize because of high turnover and, often, a short-term attachment to the jobs. As well, employers in the service and retail trade sectors, who employ a significant proportion of casual workers, are more likely to oppose unions.

Some onlookers have argued that personal characteristics determine whether individuals want to join unions or not. At one time, for example, researchers believed that, compared to men, women were less likely to join unions because their attachment to the workforce was more tenuous and, in the case of married women, their earnings were of secondary importance to their families. As well, women in professional occupations, such as nursing and teaching, were supposedly preoccupied with the public-service aspects of their jobs rather than with more mundane matters such as wages and working conditions. These beliefs were supported by the low proportion of women in unions: in 1966, 320,000 women, a mere 16 percent of women workers, were union members. The inference proved to be incorrect, however, as became apparent with the expansion of union rights in the parapublic and public sectors and the intensification of unionization efforts in occupations and industries dominated by women workers. After 1966 the number of women union members increased significantly, reaching 2,054,325 in 2006. As well the unionization rates of men and women are

Standing the Fraser Institute on Its Head!

The Fraser Institute, which is funded by corporate dollars, is a relentless opponent of any and all rights that could potentially improve conditions for working people in Canada and other countries, including trade union rights. Most of what the Institute publishes is mere propaganda — and not even very good propaganda at that. A recent paper by Keith Godin and Milagros Palacios, "Comparing Labour Relations Laws in Canada and the United States," exemplifies the Institute approach to labour issues.

Godin and Palacios trot out something called the Index of Labour Relations Law (ILRL), which ranks jurisdictions on the basis of three criteria: procedures for certification and decertification; union security (which focuses on the issue of whether or not workers are obligated to become union members and/or join unions); and regulation of unionized firms (the extent to which the laws prevent unions from exercising rights and powers to win improvements in wages and working conditions). The value of the index ranges from 0 to 10, with 0 the worst possible outcome and 10 the best possible outcome, from a Fraser Institute point of view. The jurisdictions that would qualify for a 10 are those in which: it is almost impossible to certify and easy to decertify; workers are not obligated to belong to unions or, if they are in a bargaining unit that has been certified, to pay union dues; and unions are denied access to the tools they require to become entrenched and achieve sustainable benefits for their members.

Godin and Palacios conclude that the results of the application of the ILRL to jurisdictions in North America "suggest four distinct groups of jurisdictions." At the top of the heap are the twenty-two right-to-work states (predominantly the old slave states in the South and agrarian states in the Midwest), which fell a bit short of perfection but did score a combined 9.2. Group two, which consists of the other twenty-eight states, weren't too shabby either, scoring 7.5 on the ILRL. The states in this group were docked points mainly because they allow unions to collect dues from individuals who benefit from collective agreements negotiated by unions; or to put it another way, because they don't promote free riders.* Alberta stands alone as a group, with a score of 6.0. The other nine provinces and the federal jurisdiction comprise the final group, with all of them scoring less than four. The federal government is at the bottom of the Fraser Institute league table, with a score of 1.0.

Of course, anyone who believes that workers should have basic rights and who subscribes to the idea that trade unions and the labour movement are a bulwark of democracy, human rights, and progressive politics would immediately flip the Institute index over and rank the four groups in reverse order, with the federal jurisdiction in Canada at the top rather than the bottom of the league table.

*Godin and Palacios don't comment on this, but given their dislike of workers and unions it seems likely that one of the things that appeals to them about the situation in the United States is the impunity with which private-sector employers fire workers whom they suspect of union activity, and the great lengths they are prepared to go to thwart a union drive by hiring union busters, forcing employees to attend one-on-one meetings with their own supervisors, and forcing employees to attend industry-organized closed-door anti-union meetings.

Source: Godin and Palacios 2006

now virtually identical (see Table 3.2).

Given this evidence, neither the personal characteristics of workers nor the characteristics of their jobs would appear to be significant deterrents to joining unions. On the contrary, the evidence suggests that if workers are dissatisfied with their jobs, believe that unions can improve their situation, and have a positive view of unions, they will, given the opportunity, join up (Murray 1995: 168–70).

Surveys of how workers feel about unions consistently generate two main results: most workers already in unions are relatively content with their status and prefer to remain union members; and 30 percent to 35 percent of non-members are favourably disposed to joining unions (Murray 1995: 169; Riddell 1993: 118–22). The results of more recent CLC surveys confirmed this tendency: "Two-thirds of current union members are satisfied with their own national union and three-quarters [are] satisfied with their local unions." Moreover, the results of a 2003 survey showed that 43 percent of non-union workers "would be 'very or somewhat likely' to join a union if there were no grounds for fear of employer reprisal." This survey also revealed "Underlying support for unions is even higher among young workers aged 18 to 29 (52%), visible minorities (54%), and women (50% vs. 37% for men)" (Jackson 2005: 182).

Of much greater importance are the characteristics of workplaces and the industries in which workers are located. Indeed, it would seem that any future impetus to growth in union membership will have to come from the private sector (see Table 3.3). The public sector now accounts for 56.2 percent of union members but only 9.5 percent of non-unionized paid workers, while the private sector accounts for 43.8 percent of union members and 90.5 percent of non-unionized paid workers. In short, nine of every ten workers who are not unionized are in the private sector.

The private sector does have the potential for some gains in manufacturing and construction, which between them have 2,705,000 paid workers, or 19.6 percent of the total. Of this number, 1,924,000 do not belong to unions. As well, large numbers of non-unionized employees work in private-sector services (in recent years the fastest-growing sector of the economy, a trend likely to continue in the immediate future). In this sector, six of the industries (professional, scientific, and technical; accommodation and food; other services; finance, insurance, and real estate; business, building, and other support; and trade) have unionization rates of 12.6 percent or less (see Table 3.2). The number of non-union members in the six service industries is 5,221,000. These areas — manufacturing, construction, and the six service industries — account for 81 percent of non-union members in the private sector.

Obstacles to Unionization:
Hotels employ a high percentage of workers on a part-time or casual (as-needed) basis. Because of the irregularity of their working hours, these workers tend not to be integrated into the core workforce, and in a unionization drive they are more difficult to identify and contact than full-time workers. Because they lack any form of protection they are more exposed and susceptible to intimidation by their employers. Turnover is also high in these jobs, which means that even in unionized hotels union activists and leaders must guard against employer initiatives aimed at convincing new employees that they would be better off without a union. Cycles of certification followed by decertification are common in hotels.

Similar problems exist in many retail establishments. Fabricland, a franchise operation that sells materials for clothing and drapes, warns employees in a company handbook: "Discussion of wages between employees [or] the release of information confidential to the company to any person not employed by the company [such as] personal employee information including names, phone numbers and addresses will result in disciplinary action which may include dismissal without notice."

A key obstacle to unionization in many of these fields is the relatively small size of the workplaces; a positive correlation exists between workplace size and union density rates. Small workplaces with under twenty employees have a density rate of 13.4 percent, whereas large workplaces with over five hundred employees have a rate of 50.9 percent. The problem for unions is that almost one-third of paid employees are in workplaces with less than twenty employees, and close to two-thirds are in workplaces with less than one hundred employees. Moreover, 73.3 percent of all non-unionized workers are in workplaces with less than one hundred employees. The costs to unions in terms of money and staff time involved in organizing small workplaces is much higher per potential member than it is in large workplaces. Small employers are also more likely to detect unionization drives in the early stages and take action to thwart them.

Alberta and Ontario — two of the fastest-growing and most industrialized provinces in the country — have the lowest unionization rates. These two provinces account for 50.7 percent of all paid employees, but just 44 percent of union members.

Unions themselves must bear some of the blame for the slow growth in union membership and the recent decline in union density, because they

Organizing Dilemma:
Declining union membership has created a dilemma both for trade unions in the private sector, where membership losses are concentrated, and for the labour movement as a whole. Unions require expanding resources to meet the demands of existing members for improved services, and also to initiate and sustain the organizing drives that will add new members. The problem is that declining membership also results in declining resources, which makes it very difficult to maintain services for existing members and to launch and carry through to fruition new organizing drives. This problem has intensified in recent years because of the concentration of anti-union employers in the least organized sectors of the economy (among them the banks, Wal-Mart and its competitors, and major hotel and restaurant chains), and the growing tendency of provincial governments to favour businesses over workers and their organizations.

There is no easy way out of this dilemma for private-sector unions. They must expand membership to retain their membership base, but given their lack of resources they sometimes lack the capacity to organize the unorganized. The danger, therefore, is that increasingly they will look to the cannibalization of existing memberships through hostile raids. This in turn creates serious problems for the labour movement as a whole, because not only does internal strife undermine the credibility of the movement, but the loss of private-sector members also undermines the movement's capacity to challenge both employers and governments.

Table 3.3 Potential for Union Growth by Sector, 2006

	Public Sector	Private Sector	Total
Paid employees	3,229,000	10,575,000	13,804,000
As percent of total	23.4	76.6	100.0
Union members	2,305,506	1,797,750	4,103,256
As percent of total	56.2	43.8	100.0
Non-union employees	923,494	8,777,250	9,700,744
As percent of total	9.5	90.5	100.0

Source: Calculated from data in Statistics Canada 2006c: 66–67.

have committed only limited resources to organizing. In 1995, the last year for which comprehensive data on trade unions' revenues and expenditures were collected under the *Corporations and Labour Union Returns Act,* all unions combined spent $18.3 million on union organizing, which represented a mere 1.7 percent of total expenditures and 1.9 percent of dues

Organizing a Union Local:
Heather Smith, a union representative for the Canadian Union of Public Employees in Red Deer, Alberta, gets a telephone call from a young woman. The caller asks about what workers need to do to establish a union. Heather explains how the certification procedures work and then asks her why she wants this information. The caller, Joan Robinson, says she works for a private day-care owner with seven employees. They haven't had a wage increase in three years, and when employees raise concerns about the operations of the facility they are either warned that they can be dismissed or told to look for a job elsewhere. Heather proposes that they meet over coffee and talk about the possibilities in more detail.

They have the meeting. Heather, convinced that Joan is sincere about trying to establish a union, tells her that the starting point is for her to sign a union membership card and pay a one dollar initiation fee. She does this and Heather then asks her for the names and phone numbers of others in the group who share her interest. Joan gives Heather the names and phone numbers of two other employees. Heather asks her to talk to them and see if they will agree to a meeting. Joan doesn't want to do that, though, because she doesn't want her employer to find out. Heather contacts them directly, explains that she has been told they might be interested in forming a union, and asks for a meeting with them. They agree. The meeting takes place and they too sign membership cards.

Heather now has the 40 percent sign-up required to apply for certification, but she knows from experience that it would be desirable to have better than half of the employees signed up before a representation vote. She meets with the women who have signed cards and tells them they need at least one more member, preferably two, before applying for certification.

They talk about the other four employees. They rule out one of the others because she often talks about setting up her own day-care centre and more often than not sides with the employer when they talk about wages or other matters. They rule out a second employee because her husband has his own business, which he operates from his home, and at social functions they have heard him criticizing unions — especially public-sector unions. They agree that all of them should meet with the other two and try to convince them to join. The meeting is held and the two agree to join. Heather has now signed up five of the seven employees. She files an application for certification with the Labour Board, which sets a date for a vote. When the employer finds out, she advises the employees that if the employees vote for a union, she could be forced to close the day-care centre. When the vote is held, four of the seven employees — four of the five who signed union cards — vote in favour of the union. The Labour Board certifies the local union.

collected from members. International unions, which organize primarily in the private sector, spent 6.2 percent of dues on organizing. National and government unions spent 1.2 percent (Mainville and Olineck 1999: 29). These figures, though, may understate the total amount spent on organizing because part of the affiliation fees paid to trade unions may also be used for that purpose.

Still, as a whole, the union movement in Canada has been effective in sustaining its membership base since the 1950s, at least relative to the union movement in the United States, and it has managed to avoid the serious slippage in union memberships experienced in many other countries in recent decades. This solidarity has been achieved, moreover, despite two deep and protracted recessions, in the early 1980s and early 1990s, persistently high rates of unemployment, and a constant turnover of plants and firms (plant closures and firm failures, on the one hand, and the start-up of new firms and the opening of new plants, on the other hand), all of which have contributed to a high rate of attrition in union members.

REPRESENTING MEMBERS: COLLECTIVE BARGAINING

A primary function of unions is to negotiate collective agreements with employers on behalf of their members. Certification establishes a union as a bargaining agent for a group of workers and compels employers to bargain with them with a view to achieving a collective agreement that specifies the terms and conditions of all members of the **bargaining unit** — all employees covered by certification and therefore represented by the union. The bargaining unit may be very small — for example, a couple of employees in a funeral home — or very large — as, for example, in the case of General Motors, which has thousands of workers in its Canadian plants.

Irrespective of the size of the bargaining unit, the process of collective bargaining is essentially the same. It starts in the union with the establishment of a bargaining committee, which usually includes representatives from the local.[5] That committee then formulates a bargaining position, which specifies the demands that the union will place before the employer. In many unions the membership of the local contributes to and approves the union proposals. In others the bargaining committee, with the help of a union representative, makes the decision about what to include in the union position. The process is more complicated than it seems because it involves establishing a consensus among often disparate segments of the workforce — skilled versus unskilled workers, women versus men, and older workers versus younger workers, for instance. Indeed, the union's process of **internal bargaining** to establish unity on the issues that go to the bargaining table can sometimes be more difficult than bargaining with employers. As well, in developing a package of demands, the standard practice is to include proposals that the local can give up during bargaining. This strategy leaves room to make gains on the issues that are particularly important to members. The added items are not, as a rule, "blue-sky" proposals (that is, proposals that the union knows the employer can never accept), but rather proposals that address issues of concern to some union members. They signal, in effect, that these are matters that employers will eventually have to deal with; they could be on the union's bargaining agenda in subsequent rounds of collective bargaining.

The union must also establish a strategy that will guide its efforts at the bargaining table. The objective is not simply to reach an agreement, but rather to get an agreement that will be acceptable to its members. Therefore the union must define a lower limit (a sticking or resistance point) on the scope for give-backs or **concessions** on particular issues. This task is simplified if the position is based on a principle. For example, a union may have a principle of negotiating equal absolute increases in wages for all members of the bargaining unit because this maintains internal equity within the bargaining unit. In this situation there can be no compromise on the principle; the only issue that the union will bargain on is the amount of the equal absolute increase. The union must also know what it is going to do if the employer insists on concessions that would move the union below its sticking point.

For much of the postwar era the practice in bargaining was for the union to present its proposals to the employer, and then the employer would respond with counterproposals. For example, on the wages issue, the union might propose an across-the-board increase (an increase for everyone in the bargaining unit) of 10 percent, reflecting increased productivity, increases in the cost of living, and the union's assessment of the capacity of the employer to pay, as measured by the profitability of the firm. The employer might counter with an offer of, say, 4 percent. This exchange establishes a bargaining range for wages, with both sides attempting to move the other side closer to its position.

Wages are always a particularly contentious issue. For workers, wages determine their income. For employers, wages are the major component of labour costs. In general, the higher the proportion of total costs accounted for by labour costs (the more labour-intensive production is) the more reluctant employers are to concede the union's demand. Benefits are a similarly contentious issue, for the same reasons. Another issue that becomes particularly contentious involves union proposals interpreted by employers as encroachments on **management rights**, that is, management's right to deal unilaterally with all matters not covered by the collective agreements — such as control of production and labour processes. Union-security articles — such as the establishment of a union shop that requires all employees to become members of the local within a specified period of time — are yet another area of contention.

In recent decades, and especially since the 1980s, employers have become much more aggressive in collective bargaining, and they often bring their own demands to the table. Frequently these demands call for union give-backs or concessions on wages and fringe benefits previously gained in collective bargaining, on the grounds that the employer must cut costs to stay competitive. Or the demands call for the union to give up wording in the collective agreement that prevents the employer from **contracting out** to another firm work done by members of the bargaining unit or that imposes restrictions on the ability of the employer to control how workers are utilized on the job. These articles may, for example, restrict the ability of employers to transfer workers between jobs or promote whom they want by establishing seniority either as the sole criterion, or one of the key criteria, to be applied in these sorts of decisions.

Once they are together at the bargaining table, the two sides will first of all negotiate a bargaining protocol, that is, a set of procedural rules that establish the locale for bargaining (often away from the workplace in a hotel or hall). They will set out the dates for bargaining sessions and prescribe how they will construct a tentative agreement. It could be on an issue-by-issue basis or as a total package, for example. When these preliminaries are out of the way, they will concentrate on the "nuts and bolts" — the substantive issues each side has brought to the table.

For the union, it is also imperative that the bargaining strategy established beforehand defines roles for the members of the bargaining team. Usually the local identifies a particular individual to act as the chief bargainer. Preferably this is someone who has experience in bargaining, has the ability to effectively argue the union's position, and is respected by other members of the team and the members of the local. Other members of the team may also be designated to speak on particular issues. A big part of what is involved takes place away from the table, when the bargainers prepare for bargaining sessions by scripting their words and actions and rehearsing their roles. Insofar as possible, the team leaves nothing to chance; they carefully orchestrate everything, although even the most careful preparations will not guarantee complete protection from the influence of Murphy's Law, which states that if anything can go wrong, it will.

Notwithstanding the skill of the negotiators and the justness of their position, collective bargaining is ultimately a power relationship. The power of both parties lies in their members' abilities to persuade members of the other party that the costs of accepting the proposed terms of settlement are less than the costs of an impasse that results in either a strike or lockout. As bargaining progresses, the parties will make concessions that reduce the cost to the other side of accepting the proposed settlement. At the same time, each party will be seeking to alter the other's perception of the costs of holding out for further concessions.

The union, for example, will seek to persuade the employer that any deal that provides less for its members than what the union is proposing will almost certainly result in a protracted strike or, alternatively, harm morale and productivity within the firm. Eventually one or both of the parties will reach a point at which it determines that the costs of agreeing are less than the costs of disagreeing to the other party's terms, and together they will conclude a deal (Chamberlain 1965: 231–37).

The employer's power derives from ownership of the assets used in production and the ability to withstand a stoppage of production. That power is also influenced by the ability to close the workplace altogether and either transfer production to another plant or relocate production facilities to another locale; and that ability in some industries in Canada has been strengthened in recent decades by technological change and free-trade agreements that have eliminated barriers to capital movement.

For the union, power rests with the local membership and the willingness of members to incur the costs of strike action, most notably the loss of income while on strike and the potential loss of their jobs if the establishment is closed or the strike broken. But such power is tempered by the social, economic, and political context of the bargaining. During times when the economy is booming and unemployment is low, for example, unions have a bargaining advantage, both because employers are reluctant to forego potential profits and lose market share and because striking workers have less fear of being replaced while on strike. When the economy is stagnant or slumping, the bargaining advantage shifts to employers.

A collective bargaining dispute between Maple Leaf Foods and the United Food and Commercial Workers in 1997 provides an example of how this power relationship works. Maple Leaf, a food conglomerate with a major interest in the meat-packing industry, was negotiating simultaneously with workers at plants in Edmonton, Burlington, the Battlefords (in Saskatchewan), and Winnipeg. The employer demanded major cuts to wages upwards of 40 to 60 percent as well as cuts to fringe benefits. Workers in all plants resisted these demands. In Edmonton UFCW Local 312A members voted overwhelmingly to take strike action to defend their wages and benefits. Maple Leaf warned them that strike action would result in permanent closure of the plant. The workers struck, and the company closed the Edmonton plant. Workers in other Maple Leaf plants quickly fell into line and grudgingly accepted the concessions demanded by their employer. Moreover, Maple Leaf then negotiated a collective agreement with UFCW Local 832 (which had obtained the right to represent employees in the new plant as part of a deal between the Manitoba government and Maple Leaf for a plant in Brandon). The agreement at the Brandon plant entrenched the new wage scales and conditions of employment.

The most difficult collective agreement to negotiate is often the first one, both because all the terms and conditions of employment must be established and because employers who oppose unions will often seek to sabotage the bargaining process through delaying tactics and by refusing to compromise on key issues. Such tactics are designed to force strike action, a situation employers sometimes exploit to try to break a union. After recognizing these problems, eight jurisdictions in Canada established legislation designed to provide an alternative method of resolving first-contract disputes (the exceptions are Alberta, Nova Scotia, and New Brunswick), either through arbitration or imposition of a first contract by a labour board.

Once a collective agreement is in place, subsequent rounds of negotiations usually focus on articles that are subject to dispute, and on wages and benefits. Collective bargaining does not necessarily become any easier, but generally there are fewer issues to deal with.

When a tentative agreement is reached, the outcome goes to a vote of the union membership for **ratification** or approval of the proposed collective agreement. If the membership approves the agreement, the deal is done; if the agreement is rejected, the parties go back to the bargaining table to try to get the agreement modified to address the concerns that led to rejection.

If an agreement cannot be reached then, collective bargaining is at an impasse. All jurisdictions in Canada have articles in their labour relations acts providing for **conciliation** and/or **mediation**, which involves appointment of a conciliator (usually a government employee) or mediator (a private person) to assist the parties in reaching a voluntary agreement. The basic difference between conciliation and mediation is that a mediator is normally more aggressive in trying to get the parties to reach an agreement. In most jurisdictions, appointment of a conciliator or mediator is at the request of one or both parties or the discretion of the minister responsible for labour relations.

The ultimate step in the resolution of disputes in the private sector is either a strike or a lockout of union members by an employer. A strike must, as stipulated in legislation in all jurisdictions, be voted on by bargaining unit members in a secret ballot and is decided by a majority of those who vote. The situation regarding public and parapublic-sector workers varies significantly. Disputes between civil servants and governments in Alberta, Ontario, Nova Scotia, and Prince Edward

Most collective agreements are established without resort to strike or lockout. In 1990, for example: 56 percent of agreements involving 500 or more workers were achieved through direct bargaining between the parties; 31 percent were negotiated with the help of conciliation or mediation; 5 percent were resolved through arbitration; and 8 percent through stoppages (strikes or lockouts).

Source: Craig and Solomon 1993: 209.

Negotiating a Collective Agreement:
Local 1604 is preparing to negotiate renewal of a collective agreement for 112 members employed by Brown Steel Fabricating Works Ltd. When the last collective agreement was negotiated three years previously, Brown was in a precarious situation because of slumping sales of granaries and steel buildings. The union agreed to forego wage increases and accept compulsory overtime to give the company a chance to turn things around. Now the company's situation has improved significantly. Production, revenues, and profits are way up and the company has acquired another plant.

At a meeting of the members called for the purpose of planning for the current round of bargaining, 86 of the 112 members show up. They are agitated and vociferous. Real wages have been eaten up by inflation at the rate of 3 percent per year. The workers are under constant pressure to speed up production, and overtime is out of control. Health and safety conditions have deteriorated, as reflected in a rising incidence of both accidents and the number of employees on stress leave. There have been no improvements to plant and equipment. As the top priorities in bargaining the members recommend to the union leadership a catch-up for the loss in real wages and further increases over the life of the collective agreement, as well as an end to compulsory overtime. They also propose that Peter Slomiany, a young, up-and-coming union activist, join the union representative, the local president, and the chief shop steward on the bargaining team. These recommendations are accepted.

When negotiations start, the union proposes a 9 percent increase in wages in the first year of the contract and 3.5 percent in each of the next two years and an end to compulsory overtime. It becomes immediately apparent that the company is not much interested in either conceding major improvements in wages or relinquishing control over the assignment of overtime. The company offers 2 percent per year over a three-year contract and insists that the overtime is not negotiable: "We must be able to control overtime hours to ensure that we are able to meet production commitments."

Negotiations drag on with no discernible progress. Two weeks before the expiry of the collective agreement the union conducts a strike vote. There is overwhelming support — 94 percent — for strike action. The day after the vote, the membership walks off the job to protest the lack of progress in negotiations and demonstrate to the company that they mean business. At the bargaining session the next day company representatives are fuming about the stoppage of work and condemn the union representatives for their inability to control the members. The union representatives counter with an allegation that the company is responsible for the **wildcat** — illegal — strike and warn that significant movement must be made in the next few days or the plant will be totally shut down when the agreement expires.

The pace picks up over the next few days. The company raises its wage offer to 3 percent per year but remains adamant on the overtime issue. Union representatives suggest that they might be able to sell the wage offer, but there is no possibility of a settlement unless something is done about overtime. The company finally modifies its position on overtime, proposing that it retain control for the assignment of up to four hours of overtime a week; overtime above four hours would be voluntary.

With twenty-four hours to go before the expiry of the agreement, conditions in the plant become tense. The workers are on the job, but they are not much interested in sustaining the pace of production. They are talking strike, getting themselves ready to walk the picket line the following morning.

The next morning the picket line is up and workers are digging in for a long strike. One week into the strike, the company notifies the union that it wants to resume bargaining. Complaints have been received from customers who want their orders filled, and other customers are switching their business to the company's competitors. The company indicates that it is now willing to make overtime voluntary and grant wage increases of 3 percent per year. The union representatives reply that they are pleased the company has moved on overtime, but that there will have to be an additional inducement on wages for them to be able to sell the package to the members. The union proposes a signing bonus of $500. The company agrees.

A membership meeting is scheduled for the following day to review the tentative agreement and conduct a ratification vote. The members are restive; now that they are out on strike they argue that they should stay out until the company ups its wage offer. The union representative suggests that this is the best they are going to be able to do and that the leadership is recommending the agreement be approved. This view is echoed by other members of the bargaining team, including Slomiany. The ratification vote is held and the agreement ratified by a margin of 58 percent to 42 percent.

Island must be settled through compulsory arbitration. In all jurisdictions where civil servants have the right to strike, except Saskatchewan, there are requirements that workers providing essential services remain on the job. In some jurisdictions — Alberta and Ontario, for example — hospital workers are prohibited from taking strike action. In most jurisdictions, employees in fire and police departments do not have the right to strike (see Craig and Solomon 1993: 257–92). But while these kinds of restrictions reduce the likelihood of strike action, they do not guarantee that there will be no strike action. On the contrary, in some situations conditions become so desperate that union members will strike illegally despite the threat of fines and jail sentences. This happened in Alberta in 1988 when nurses defied legislation and waged a nineteen-day strike (Panitch and Swartz 1993: 105–09) and again in 2000 when hospital workers walked off the job.

Most unions maintain a **strike fund**, an amount of money created by the union and paid by the members over time, which is intended to partially offset the lost wages and benefits incurred by workers when they are on strike or locked out. **Strike pay** helps workers meet costs of subsistence, but is generally much less than normal pay and usually tied to participation on the picket line. For short strikes such payments may be sufficient to tide workers over. With longer strikes, workers may be forced to deplete their savings, cash in insurance policies, or give up houses and durable goods purchased on a time-payment basis. In some cases, if the plant is closed, they may lose their jobs permanently. Understandably, then, workers are loath to take strike action unless they are certain that the potential gains (better wages and benefits and enhanced conditions on the job) will compensate them for the costs they incur.

Relatively unskilled workers are at a particular disadvantage in strike/lockout situations because they can easily be replaced by employers, especially when unemployment is high. As well, they are the ones least likely to have resources they can draw on to sustain themselves and their families during a lengthy strike. They are especially vulnerable given that only two jurisdictions, Quebec and British Columbia, have legislation prohibiting the hiring of replacement workers, or **scabs**.

These dangers notwithstanding, strikes and the threat of strikes are essential to the success of both individual unions and the trade union movement as a whole. Without the threat and the real possibility of strike action, workers have little power to advance their interests and make gains in collective bargaining. Unions' greatest strength in collective bargaining is an informed and mobilized membership. As a preliminary to bargaining, therefore, it is vital that the bargaining agenda that goes forward is one that is achievable (that is, a set of demands consistent with members' views about what is fair and possible and that does not raise expectations unduly). It must also be linked to a long-term view of acceptable goals. Unions have a number of ways of gathering the necessary information for formulating demands and goals, but the usual and most effective method is to do it at membership meetings, where members can debate and agree on issues. It is also vital that members of the local who are elected to the bargaining team and union representatives be knowledgeable about and sensitive to conditions in the local: the weaknesses in existing collective agreements; the composition of the membership and how it is changing; how the terms and conditions of employment of members compare to what other workers are getting in the local labour market, in the industry, and in similar situations in other cities and other provinces; and the nature of the relationship

The importance of community-oriented campaigns became clear in Alberta in May 2000, when hospital workers staged an illegal strike (they have not had the right to strike in Alberta since 1983). The unions involved went into the strike with unified support from their members and the support of a general public convinced that the deterioration of wages and working conditions in hospitals was linked to a decline in the quality of health care. Alberta's government caved in within two days and conceded the union demands — although the government subsequently gained a measure of revenge by prosecuting the unions for breaking the law.

between union and employer.

In the first couple of decades after the entrenchment of union rights, most major employers accepted unions and operated on the assumption that they would be obliged to concede wage increases and benefit improvements in each round of bargaining. Firms were also aware that failure to make such concessions could provoke a strike that would lead to lost sales and profits. In an expanding economy, employers could accommodate continued improvements in collective bargaining. As a consequence, bargaining became somewhat ritualistic and routine. Unions were able to deliver the goods, and members accepted direction from their leaders. When the union recommended ratification, the members voted to ratify. The union called for a strike vote, the members voted for a strike.

This cozy arrangement started to unravel in the late 1960s and 1970s as changing economic conditions — most notably the advent of **stagflation** (simultaneous increases in prices and unemployment)[6] and pressures on profits — generated increasing conflict at the point of production. As the economic crisis intensified, employer resistance to unions increased, and unions not only found it more difficult to make new gains but also more difficult to simply maintain past gains. More and more often, employers demanded concessions: wage and benefit cuts, changes to work rules, and more scope for management to impose unilateral changes in working conditions. They cited low profits and increased competition and threatened workers with plant closure or relocation and layoffs if they didn't yield. Fearing for their jobs, union members became more reluctant to support strike action as a means of making gains or warding off concessions. In the absence of member support for strike action, the bargaining power of unions was eroded (for a more detailed discussion of the process of collective bargaining see Chaykowski 1995; Yates 1998).

To rectify this situation, unions could no longer just have member participation in the formulation of bargaining demands. Unions now had to **mobilize** members prior to collective bargaining to ensure that they were solidly behind the union position and prepared to take job action to back up their demands. As part of the preparations for collective bargaining most unions now include the formulation of a strategy based on member support for dealing with deadlocks in bargaining. These strategies include getting the members mobilized in support of strike action. They also include mounting a campaign to gain community support, which is especially important in disputes involving services provided through the public sector and financed out of taxes, such as health care or education, and disputes in the private sector involving activities that produce major dislocations in the economy and society, such as transportation and communications services.

REPRESENTING MEMBERS: GRIEVANCE PROCEDURES

After a collective agreement is established, the union has to ensure that the agreement is applied in the way it was intended and that members are treated fairly in the administration of the agreement. All collective agreements contain a **grievance-arbitration article**, which provides a mechanism for resolving disputes that arise out of the application (policy grievances usually initiated by the union) and/or administration of the collective agreement (individual grievances originating with members). These articles prescribe a number of steps for resolving the grievance voluntarily and stipulate time lines that must be met for the grievance to proceed to subsequent steps.

Shop stewards play a particularly important role in the grievance process as it relates to the processing of grievances filed by individuals. They determine the validity of the grievance, questioning whether the employer has contravened the collective agreement. They help the member draft the grievance, making sure it is done properly, citing the articles in the collective agreement that have been violated, and specifying the **redress** sought — that is, the action that management must take to resolve the grievance. They attend and participate in the meetings between the aggrieved member and management at the various steps to try to get the grievance resolved.

Grievance procedures are a particularly significant advantage of union membership. They place limitations on the extent to which management can act arbitrarily, and thus, to some extent, they bring the rule of law to the workplace. In the absence of a union, and the grievance procedures set out in a collective agreement, workers' rights are much more fragile; management is able to act much more arbitrarily.

Most unions provide shop stewards with intensive training in the grievance procedures to ensure that they are able to perform this important function effectively. As well, union representatives will work closely with shop stewards at all stages of the process, gradually taking on a more active role as the grievance progresses to higher levels.

To ensure compliance with the rule of law that the union brings to the workplace, the union must take all member grievances seriously. Unions have a legal requirement to provide fair representation for all members of the bargaining unit (whether members of the union or not). Quite apart from this legal obligation, for many members a grievance provides a personal test of the union's willingness and capacity to represent member interests. Failure to process a grievance in a timely and effective fashion could sow seeds of dissatisfaction amongst the members and weaken loyalty to the union. This is especially true of grievances involving unjust disciplinary action and dismissal, which is often described as the workplace equivalent of capital punishment, because it could damage permanently the work and life prospects of the individual in question.

If the grievance is not resolved through internal negotiations, the final step is arbitration, which involves either a single arbitrator or a three-person arbitration board consisting of representatives named by each of the parties and a "neutral" chairperson.[7] In most cases, the arbitrators are either lawyers or individuals with a knowledge of labour relations issues.

While these procedures normally result in the resolution of disputes, they are open to a number of criticisms, most notably that:

- individuals may be deterred from filing a grievance because either they fear that such action will jeopardize their future prospects with the employer or they lack confidence in the resolve of the union to see the matter through to completion;
- the arbitration process is too lengthy (sometimes taking years to complete) and too costly (because the process involves lawyers);
- the employer will find ways of getting back at the grievor;
- individuals who file grievances may be forced to continue to put up with the employer actions that prompted the grievance in the first place;
- arbitrators place undue emphasis on management rights at the expense of the interests of individuals; and
- employers intent on breaking the collective agreement and/or the union will simply ignore the provisions of the agreement with impunity, knowing full well that the union does not have the resources required to prosecute them successfully.

All of these criticisms are valid, the obvious importance of grievance procedures notwithstanding, and some unions have experimented with innovations designed to overcome the defects in grievance procedures. Some unions, for example, try to reduce the costs by training their own employees to represent the union in arbitrations. As well, some collective agreements and labour relations acts include expedited arbitration articles designed to move important grievances (usually grievances that arise from disciplinary actions by the employer) more quickly through the process. In some situations unions have tried grievance mediation designed to expedite the resolution of grievances voluntarily. These sorts of innovations have

Grievance-Arbitration:

Section 24 Adjustment of Grievances

24.02 Any grievance arising out of or in any way involving the interpretation, application or operation of the terms and conditions contained in this Agreement shall be settled and resolved by the procedures and in the manner hereinafter set forth.

***

24.04 Any employee, the Union or the Company may present a grievance. Any grievance which is not presented within fifteen (15) working days following the event giving rise to the grievance shall be forfeited and waived by the aggrieved party....

24.05 All grievances shall be submitted in writing.

24.06 The procedure for adjustment of grievances and disputes by an employee shall be as follows:

(1) By a discussion between the employee and the Union representative, with the employee's immediate superior.

(a) When an employee takes a grievance to the Union Representative, Step 1 of the grievance procedure shall be considered complied with, providing the Union Representative files the grievance in writing with the Company's Labour Relations Official or designate. The Labour Relations Official... shall reply to the grievance in writing within seven (7) working days to the union. After seven (7) working days, the Union Representative may proceed to Step 2.

(b) If an employee takes a grievance to his or her immediate supervisor and satisfactory settlement has not been reached within seven (7) working days, then:

(2) The Union Representative... may take the matter up with the Company Official designated by the Company to handle Labour Relations matters. If the matter is not taken up within ten (10) calendar days of the date the Union received the written reply to the grievance in Step 1, it will be deemed to have been abandoned and further recourse to the grievance procedure shall be forfeited.

24.07 If a satisfactory settlement cannot be reached then upon request of either party, within fourteen (14) days of receiving the final, written decision from either party, but not thereafter, the matter may then be referred to an Arbitrator, selected in accordance with Section 25.

Section 25 Arbitration

25.01 If the Union and the Company cannot reach a settlement to the grievance, then upon request of either party, the grievance shall be submitted to an Arbitrator. If agreement cannot be reached within seven (7) days in respect to the selection of an Arbitrator by the parties involved, the matter shall be referred to the Manitoba Labour Board, who shall appoint said Arbitrator.

25.02 The person selected as Arbitrator shall in no way be involved directly in the controversy under consideration or be a person who has a personal or financial interest in either party to the dispute.

25.03 The Arbitrator shall receive and consider such material evidence and contentions as the parties may offer and shall make such independent investigation as he or she deems essential to a full understanding and determination of the issues involved. In reaching a decision, the Arbitrator shall be governed by the provisions of this Agreement and shall render a decision as soon as reasonably possible.

25.04 The Arbitrator shall not be vested with the power to change modify or alter any of the terms of this Agreement....

25.05 In the event of termination discharge or suspension of an employee, the Arbitrator shall have the right to sustain the Company's action or reinstate the employee with full, part or no back pay, with or without loss of seniority, or to settle the matter in any way he or she deems equitable.

25.06 The findings and decision of the Arbitrator, on all arbitrable questions, shall be binding and enforceable on all parties involved....

25.07 The expenses and fee of the Arbitrator shall be borne equally by the parties to the arbitration proceedings.

Source: Union Agreement Between UFCW Local No. 832 and A.E. McKenzie Co. Inc. — Production Unit — August 1, 1998–July 31, 2001.

Arbitration:
In February 2000, Glen Green, a welder at ABC corporation in Brandon and a member of Local 861 of the United Steelworkers, was fired from his job. He grieved. The grievance progressed through all the steps in the collective agreement without resolution. An arbitration board consisting of a lawyer appointed to represent the company, a union representative from CAW appointed to represent the steelworkers union, and a chairperson — also a lawyer — agreed to by the employer and union representatives was established to hear the grievance and make a ruling. The venue for the arbitration was the Crocus Room of the Canadian Inn.

Both the union and the company were represented in the hearings by lawyers. The hearings lasted a day and a half. The grievance form, a copy of the collective agreement and the company policy manual, and the worksheets were submitted as evidence. The company called four witnesses, the union six, including Glen Green, the grievor.

The essential elements of the evidence presented were not in dispute. On February 6, Green, who was welding a component for a front-end loader, opened a side door to get some fresh air. A supervisor, Jim Grant, spotted the open door, and closed it. When Grant left the floor, Green again opened the door. Grant came back to the floor, saw the open door and slammed it shut. He went over to Green and asked, "Are you the one that keeps opening that damn door?" Green replied, "Yes, I can't work in these fumes; they're making me sick." Grant retorted, "Well, Glen, when you start paying the heating bills around here you can open the door; otherwise leave it shut." In response Green shut down the welder and told Grant, "I can't hack this; I'm out of here." He left for the change room. Grant followed him to the change room and advised him that he needed permission to leave the plant. Green ignored him and changed out of his work clothes. Grant continued to tell him he needed permission to leave; Green continued to ignore him. Finally, Grant said, "Alright. Fuck off then." Green left.

The following day, February 7, Green came back to work. His card wasn't in the time clock. He went to the personnel office and asked, "Where's my time card?" He was told that as far as the company was concerned, Green had quit his job. He then filed a grievance claiming that he was unfairly dismissed.

In discipline/dismissal cases, the onus is on the company to justify its action. The company lawyer argued that it was the company's position that Green had quit. If the board determined that he hadn't quit, then, the lawyer argued, the company's position was that he was dismissed for just cause — his failure to comply with an article in the collective agreement that required employees to get permission before leaving the workplace.

The union lawyer argued that Green's return to work the day following the altercation on the floor was clearly not the action of a person who had quit his job. He had not quit. The lawyer further argued that when the supervisor had told Green to "fuck off," he had given him permission to leave the plant.

After the hearing was over, the board members met for three hours to review the evidence and talk about a possible award. The union representative on the board argued that the board should find in favour of the union; that Green was unjustly dismissed. Moreover, he should be compensated for a partial loss of wages over the last six months (Green was working in another welding shop for $2 an hour less than what he had been getting at ABC) and have his seniority and benefit entitlements restored. The company lawyer conceded that Green had not quit his job, but argued that the company was justified in its actions. He further suggested that, in the event that the board decided Green had been unfairly dismissed, the appropriate award would be to substitute a six-month suspension without pay for dismissal.

The final award found in favour of the union and ordered Green reinstated with full compensation for the time he had lost from his job. Green returned to work the following week, collected his cheque, and promptly resigned.

improved things where they have been tried, but only marginally.

Other critics of the grievance-arbitration process argue that this sort of tinkering is inadequate. Instead they propose the restoration of the right to strike during the life of a collective agreement. Having the right to strike over grievances would restore the initiative to unions and their members and produce a quick resolution in most circumstances because employers are ill-equipped to deal with unanticipated strikes. It would give members the incentive to police their agreements more vigilantly. It would lay the foundation for continuous as opposed to episodic member mobilization, which would in turn strengthen the position of unions in collective bargaining (see Haiven 1995 for an especially strong statement of this view).

REPRESENTING MEMBERS: STRIKES

Strikes are an especially important aspect of trade union activities. They are the ultimate action available to unions as a means of trying to win gains for members in collective bargaining. They are, however, high-risk actions with potentially devastating results for the union and its members if they fail. Therefore a union resorts to strike action only after a careful evaluation of the likelihood that going on strike will produce benefits for both the union and its members.

From the perspective of the union, the role of the strike is to raise the costs to the employer of refusing to agree to the union's position. In all jurisdictions, unions are required to conduct strike votes by secret ballot, and in all jurisdictions, except Quebec, where the vote is restricted to union members, all members of bargaining units, whether members or non-members, have a right to participate. Before initiating a vote, the union must be reasonably certain that a positive strike vote will improve the outcome of collective bargaining. The union must also be confident that a vote will be supported by members and that they will be prepared to follow through, that is, take strike action, if necessary. A union that obtains a solid mandate for strike action — 70 percent or better — will have its position strengthened in the bargaining process. A lukewarm result — 60 percent or less — will signal to both union and employer that in this particular round of bargaining members are reluctant to take strike action.

The costs of a strike can be high to both employer and union. For the employer a stop in production means, as a rule, lost sales and revenues and reduced profits. Moreover, a long strike can force customers to switch to competitors to obtain their required goods or services. When the strike ends some of these customers may return, but others may stick with their new suppliers, which means a loss in market share. As a strike deadline approaches, the likelihood increases of incurring undue costs, putting pressure on the employer to think about improving its offer to the union. Some employers may be able to avoid or reduce these costs in the short-term by drawing down accumulated inventory, switching production to workplaces not affected by the strike, or using non-union employees or replacement workers to maintain production.

For unions the main costs of a strike are the wages and benefits lost by members and the strike funds paid out, especially on strike pay. Another danger is a possible misreading of the situation — perhaps underestimating the employer's resolve or overestimating the employer's capacity to pay better wages and benefits — which could lead to the loss of the strike and to the workers either returning to work no better off than before or even losing their jobs. A negative outcome could damage the credibility of the union and impair its efforts to organize other groups of workers and maintain existing locals.

In evaluating the potential benefits and costs of a strike both parties must also take the long view. The current round of negotiations is immediately important, but the prospect of future negotiations also comes into play. The base on wages established in current negotiations, for example, could potentially be compounded in future negotiations. If, for example, the union succeeds in raising wages from $14.00 to $14.50 through strike action, the $14.50 establishes the base for the next round of negotiations.

Unions recognize that if their members don't strike from time to time, the threat of a strike may lose its force in collective bargaining. There are

Strike at the Victoria Inn in Brandon, Manitoba:
On October 8, 2000, 200 employees of the Victoria Inn, members of United Food and Commercial Workers Local 832, went on strike to back up their contract demands. Many of the strikers were young people, including women heading single-parent families. The owner of the Victoria Inn also owned the Royal Oak Inn in Brandon and hotels in Flin Flon and Thunder Bay. The union was seeking wage parity with the hotel in Thunder Bay. While a bartender in Brandon was getting $6.00 an hour to start, the starting wage for a bartender job in Thunder Bay was $9.16. As well, the union wanted an increase in the proportion of full-time jobs in the bargaining unit.

The hotel continued operations using bargaining unit members who crossed the picket line and replacement workers recruited with ads in the local media. As well, the hotel hired a local security firm to monitor the activities of workers on the picket line. Strikers speculated that the cost to the hotel for security services could be as high as $35,000 a week.

With the brutal weather in December there was further attrition in the ranks of the strikers as more employees decided to return to work. By the end of December the number of workers doing picket-line duty was down to twenty-four. The hotel claimed that fifty-one bargaining unit members had returned to work.

Picket-line pay is tied to the number of hours on the picket line. Workers picketing full-time received about $200 a week (more, some say, than they would get in pay from the Victoria Inn). Strike pay was doubled for one week just prior to Christmas.

Other unions provided modest support for the Victoria Inn strikers: Brandon University Faculty Association, $1,000; United Transportation Union, Local 548, $250; UFCW members at Springhill Farms in Neepawa, $350; the Brandon and District Labour Council, $40 gift certificates at Safeway. The Brandon and District Labour Council also organized solidarity pickets to bolster the picket line.

The hotel lost considerable business after the strike started, especially around Christmas when other unionized establishments cancelled functions scheduled for the Victoria Inn. However, it soon became apparent that the hotel was intent on freezing or starving out the strikers and breaking the union.

Some three months into the strike the Victoria Inn tabled a new proposal of $1.20 over six years and some improvements in benefit plans. Al Patterson, UFCW representative, said the offer not only was for less than the last offer on the table in October, but also imposed conditions for a back-to-work protocol unacceptable to the people on the picket line.

When the strike first started in October, the union and its members were optimistic that there would be a quick settlement. By late December that optimism was gone and they were wondering if they would ever get a settlement. One of the union activists said, "Either way it looks like we're going to starve. But better to starve with dignity on the picket line than to work any longer for poverty wages at this hotel."

In January Becky Barrett, Minister of Labour, appointed mediator Wally Fox-Decent to try to settle the dispute. Fox-Decent was able to broker an agreement, but the proposed agreement was subsequently rejected by a vote of forty to twenty-eight. A report in the January 30 *Brandon Sun* suggested that the forty members who had defied the union and returned to work voted against the agreement, while the workers still walking the picket line voted for it.

The strike finally ended in early March, after 150 days, when the UFCW and the Victoria Inn announced an agreement to end the strike. As part of the terms of settlement the twenty active picketers were offered the option of either returning to work or taking a severance package (ranging from $500 to $5,000). Sixteen of the twenty took the severance package. As well, the union agreed that it would not oppose an expected application for decertification.

Source: Interview with Al Patterson, union representative in Brandon, UFCW Local 832.

also times when working conditions have deteriorated so far that the air can only be cleared through a strike that gives workers the chance to indicate the extent of their discontent.

Strikes are complicated matters involving careful preparations. When a workplace is closed through strike action, the union has to establish a picket line around the employer's facility as a means not only of informing the public that a strike is in progress but also of monitoring the employer's activities, and especially to ensure that the employer does not attempt to resume production. To maintain the picket line and ensure that participants comply with picket-line protocol, the union appoints picket captains. When union members cross the picket line to continue work and/or replacement workers are recruited to maintain production, the problems on the picket line are compounded. No workers like to see others going into a workplace to do their jobs when they are on strike. In these circumstances picket captains have the responsibility of preventing altercations between strikers and people crossing the picket line. Though the union wants to hold firm, at the same time it wants to avoid any behaviour or incidences on the picket line that could lead to police intervention and charges. It also wants to avoid any picket-line confrontations that could undermine public support for the union and striking workers.

During a strike, unions and employers both seek to gain public support through media advertising, news stories, and interviews. Both parties also seek to build the support of other organizations in the community, especially in situations where the employer is maintaining production. Employers will ask their customers for continued patronage and solicit support from other businesses in the community. Unions will call on local labour councils, women's organizations, and other groups for support on the picket line and in the media. (See Hyman 1977 for a useful account of the nature and importance of strikes.)

The capacity of the respective parties to cope with the costs that accompany a stoppage of work ultimately determines the outcomes of overt conflicts. Eventually one party or the other will decide that the costs of continued disagreement exceed the costs of accepting the other party's terms, and the conflict will end. In some cases, the realization will come too late; either the company will go under or the union will be broken.

THE RESULTS OF COLLECTIVE BARGAINING

How Have Unions Fared in Collective Bargaining in Recent Years?

Most of the standard indicators show a reduction in union effectiveness in recent years. For one thing, during the twenty-year period ending in 1999, negotiated increases in base wage rates of large bargaining units (500 or more employees) failed to keep pace with inflation. Since 1999, however, the situation has improved marginally (see Table 3.4).

The incidence of strikes, the number of workers involved, the person-days not worked, and the time lost due to strikes all declined. These declines in strike activity reflected the suspension of bargaining rights and the de facto curtailment of the right to strike in many jurisdictions for public-sector workers, as well as the high rates of unemployment that effectively regulated the bargaining demands and propensity to strike of private-sector workers.

Still, despite these declines, unionized workers, both men and women, did maintain an advantage over non-unionized workers in wages and fringe benefits (see Tables 3.5 and 3.6).

Clearly, unionized workers have higher hourly wages than do non-unionized workers. Many factors (time on the job, firm size, and age, for instance) contribute to these wage differentials. Estimates that control for the impact of these other factors suggest that the union wage premium (the component of the wage differential attributable to unionization alone) accounts for about 25 percent of the overall differential (Jackson and Robinson 2000: 99–100). The evidence also suggests that the union wage premium tends to increase when the economy is in a slump and unemployment is increasing and to shrink when the economy is growing and the unemployment coming down.

The wage impact of unions may well spill over into the non-unionized sector. Because of negotiated increases in the unionized sector, non-union employers may be forced to adjust wages to remain competitive in labour

Table 3.4 Wage Settlements and Strike Action,* Selected Periods, 1980–2005

	1980 –84	**1985 –89**	**1990 –94**	**1995 –99**	**2000 –04**	**2005**
Average Percent Wage Increase in base wage rates						
Public sector	8.6	4.1	2.3	1.2	2.6	2.2
Private sector	8.5	4.1	2.9	1.9	2.3	2.4
Both sectors	8.5	4.1	2.5	1.4	2.6	2.3
Average Change in Consumer Price Index	8.7%	4.3%	2.8%	1.6%	2.4%	2.2%
Strikes and Lockouts						
Number	823	684	440	347	324	293
Workers involved (000)	355	377	172	217	175	429
Person-days not worked (000)	6,401	4,538	2,566	2,669	2,370	4,107
Percentage of estimated working time lost	0.26	0.17	0.09	0.09	0.09	0.11

* For bargaining units of 500-plus members.

Source: Akyeampong 1999: 65; Statistics Canada 2006: 71.

markets and to avoid unionization of their firms (Goddard 1994: 370–71). Given these spillovers, the standard figures will tend to understate the union wage premium achieved through collective bargaining.

As well, the incidence of union members in low-paid jobs (jobs that pay two-thirds of the economy-wide median wage) is much lower than it is for non-union members. Only 9 percent of unionized women were in low-wage jobs, as compared to 47 percent of non-unionized women. The comparable figures for men are 6 per cent and 32 percent respectively (Jackson and Robinson 2000).

Part of the explanation for the smaller incidence of union men and women in low-wage jobs is that unions have historically sought to reduce inequalities in the distribution of wages by raising the wages of the lowest-paid workers relative to the highest paid. In 1995 the ratio of earnings between top and bottom deciles (the top and bottom 10 percent of workers in the earnings distribution) was 2.50 for unionized women and 3.30 for non-unionized women, and 2.45 for unionized men and 3.64 for

Table 3.5 Average Hourly Wages of Men and Women by Union Status and Selected Characteristics, 2006

	Women			Men		
	Union $	Non-Union $	Non-Union as % of Union	Union $	Non-Union $	Non-Union as % of Union
All	21.86	16.15	73.9	23.58	20.43	86.6
Age						
15–24	13.57	10.34	76.2	13.85	11.52	83.2
25–44	22.16	17.70	79.9	23.44	21.94	93.6
45–69	23.01	18.02	78.3	25.78	24.20	93.9
Education						
Less than high school	14.76	10.62	72.0	18.69	13.94	74.6
High school graduate	17.79	14.10	79.2	21.09	17.59	83.4
Certificate/ diploma	21.12	16.66	78.9	23.95	21.12	88.2
University degree	27.42	22.66	82.6	29.54	28.55	96.6
Work Status						
Full-time	22.45	17.58	78.3	24.00	21.67	90.3
Part-time	19.71	12.20	61.9	17.57	11.60	66.0
Occupation						
Managerial, Admin.	31.25	27.27	87.3	33.38	33.32	99.8
Professional	27.14	26.49	97.6	30.71	30.93	100.7
Clerical	18.94	15.16	80.0	19.70	15.84	80.4
Sales & Services	14.66	11.03	75.2	17.93	13.93	77.7
Blue Collar	16.65	12.69	76.2	22.40	17.52	78.2
Firm Size						
Under 20 employees	17.92	13.99	78.1	20.95	16.45	78.5
20 to 99	18.59	15.52	83.5	21.53	19.26	89.4
100 to 500	20.94	16.88	80.6	22.15	21.80	98.4
500 plus	22.69	17.62	77.6	24.47	23.08	94.3

Source: Statistics Canada "Labour Force Survey" 2006.

non-unionized men (Jackson and Robinson 2000: 103).

But wages are only part of the story. In collective agreements unions also seek to establish benefits. Union members are much more likely to be covered by private pension plans, dental plans, and medical plans than are workers who are not in unions (see Table 3.6).

Under collective agreements unions also provide their members with a broad range of other benefits that are not usually available to non-unionized workers — except those workers whose skills are essential to the employer and/or workers of privilege within enterprises. These benefits may include job security, superior vacation plans, more statutory days off, voluntary overtime and compensation rates for overtime in excess of what is mandated under employment standards legislation, equitable procedures for determining promotion, layoff, and recall, access to training opportunities, and more rigorous standards pertaining to health and safety.

There is also evidence that unions are sensitive to changes in the composition of their memberships and attempt to ensure both equity for all members and that the special needs of particular groups of workers — for example, women or recent immigrants — are addressed in collective agreements (see White 1990 for a careful case study of how one union, the Canadian Union of Postal Workers, responded to the particular needs of women; and White 1993 for a general discussion of how women have fared in Canada's union movement).

At their very roots, collective agreements extend the rule of law to the workplace. They afford to workers certain rights, and place limits on the arbitrary power of employers. They specifically include grievance-arbitration articles that give members rights in the workplace — rights to due process and fair treatment — not available to other workers except through the courts. The value of rights entrenched in collective agreements cannot be converted readily to dollar terms. The value to individuals of having some control over workplace conditions and of having protection against arbitrary (and, in disciplinary matters in particular, often harsh) treatment by

Table 3.6 Benefits Coverage by Union Status, 1999

Benefit	**Union**	**Non-Union**
(Percent receiving benefit)		
Employer Pension Plan	79.9%	26.6%
Medical Plan	83.7%	45.4%
Dental Plan	76.3%	42.6%
Life/disability insurance	78.2%	40.8%

Source: Akyeampong 2002: 42–43.

The Union Advantage:
An increasing proportion of collective agreements contain articles dealing with anti-discrimination (60.5 percent), sexual harassment (51.7 percent), flextime, or a variable work schedule (34.9 percent), supplemental benefits for maternity leave (52.0 percent), and seniority during adoption leave (48.1 percent); and many other articles geared to providing individuals with greater scope for reconciling the competing claims of work and family life. What is more, the proportion of collective agreements containing such articles rose dramatically during the period 1985–98. In 1985, for example, only 20.6 percent of agreements had articles on sexual harassment; and only 17.5 percent on flextime. In 1985–98 the proportion of agreements with an article on equal pay increased from 5.4 percent to 27.6 percent; those with an article on unpaid personal reasons leave went from 34.1 to 52.9 percent.

Source: Jackson and Robinson 2000: 106–09.

employers is incalculable. There can be no doubt, however, that union members recognize the importance of gaining access to these rights and place a high value on them.

From the perspective of society as a whole, unions have often been criticized for generating unfavourable results that undermine the health of the economy and conditions for workers in the non-unionized sector. Employers and their organizations, right-of-centre governments, and employer-funded research bodies such as the Fraser Institute blame unions for generating unemployment and inflation, reducing productivity, and making gains at the expense of non-unionized workers. Employers make those accusations in attempts to discredit unions, to make it more difficult to organize and achieve gains in collective bargaining, and to marginalize unions' influence in society. Governments, more often than not, attack unions in a kind of scapegoating intended to deflect public attention from both their own ineptitude and the more fundamental causes of economic and social problems.

These critics muster little evidence in support of their positions, and what they do put forward is often counterintuitive and spurious (for an assessment of some of these positions, see the arguments in Freeman and Medoff 1984). This is especially true of accusations that single out unions as the main cause of either unemployment or inflation — complex phenomena that defy easy explanation. In the inflationary era of the 1970s and 1980s, for example, critics cited unions as a major contributor to escalating prices. But in-depth studies revealed a variety of forces at work, including the actions of monopoly firms and increases in commodity prices, most notably increases in the prices of oil engineered by the Organization of Petroleum Exporting Countries. Wages followed other prices as unions responded to rising inflation by doing what they are supposed to do: seeking to protect the real wages of their members. Similarly, the high rates of unemployment in the 1980s and 1990s had little to do with unions. They were a result, rather, of deliberate government policies instituted to keep unemployment at a high level as a means of disciplining labour and controlling wages — especially negotiated wages, but also wages administered by employers (for a discussion of these issues see Black 1998; Goddard 1994; Gordon 1996; Stanford 1998, 1999).

The basic activities (the nuts and bolts) of unions — organizing, collective bargaining, the processing of grievances, and the conduct of strikes — are, then, complex; and they are shaped by a dynamic economy and frequent changes in political, legal, social, and ideological conditions. For the most part, the things that unions do are determined by their members through democratic practices entrenched in constitutions, traditions, and organizational structures. The members themselves ultimately decide what should be negotiated in collective bargaining and sanction the outcome of the bargaining process: the collective agreement. The members decide which grievances should get priority and which grievances should be pushed to arbitration. The members decide when to take strike action and when to end a strike.

For union members, the outcomes of union activities in Canada have, moreover, brought significant benefits. Union members enjoy a wage advantage over their non-unionized counterparts. They are protected by the rule of law in the workplace. In their collective agreements they have entrenched rights and entitlements that are not part of the terms and conditions of employment of most non-unionized workers. The very success in making these gains is undoubtedly one of the main reasons why unions have historically been opposed, and why they will continue to be opposed, by employers and governments.

NOTES

1. Three sets of union membership statistics exist for Canada. Human Resources Development Canada (formerly Labour Canada) conducts an annual survey of unions, publishing the results in a *Directory of Labour Organizations*. Prior to 1995 unions were required as well to submit annual membership and financial statistics under the *Corporations and Labour Union Returns Act*. These statistics were reported in an annual publication with the same title. Finally, since 1997 Statistics Canada has included questions about union membership in its *Labour Force Survey*. The first two surveys are based on union administrative statistics, while the Statistics Canada survey is of individuals. There are some differences in the union membership and density figures published in the various reports, but the fluctuations and trends reflected in the data tend to be consistent.
2. There are some anomalies in such comparisons. For example, in France, which has one of the most militant and combative workforces in the world, 95 percent of workers are covered by collective agreements, but a mere 9 percent of workers are union members (Akyeampong 1997: 54).

3. Significant variations in union density rates exist across individual states, ranging from rates above 20 percent in Hawaii (24.7), New York (24.4), Alaska (22.2), and New Jersey (20.1) to rates below 5 percent in North and South Carolina (3.3), Virginia (4.0), Georgia (4.4), and Texas (4.9). (U.S. Department of Labor 2007).
4. U.S. capitalists and governments have always been much more bloody-minded in their opposition to unions than are their Canadian counterparts. For a discussion of the U.S. experience, see Boyer and Morais (1955); for Canada, see Jamieson (1968).
5. Pattern bargaining (where bargaining takes place initially with one firm in the industry and the union then seeks to impose the same settlement on other firms, as is the case, for example, in the automobile industry) and multi-employer bargaining (where bargaining takes place between a union and an employer organization representing major firms, as in some segments of the construction industry) are features of collective bargaining in concentrated, highly unionized industries.
6. Stagflation involves simultaneously slow (or no) economic growth and increasing rates of inflation. In an economy with a growing workforce a lack of growth generates rising unemployment, resulting in simultaneous increases in the unemployment rate and the rate of inflation.
7. The chairperson may be chosen by mutual agreement between the union and employer representatives on the board or, failing agreement, appointed, in most jurisdictions, by the minister of labour or the labour board.

CHAPTER 4

CREATIVE ORGANIZING AND DETERMINED MILITANCY

A Brief History of Trade Unions in Canada

Hard work for long hours at low pay in difficult, often appalling conditions — that was the lot of most workers, especially women and children and the most recently arrived immigrants, during the first half of the nineteenth century in what would become Canada. The vast majority of the population — 85 percent in 1850 — lived and worked on the land. Those who did not toiled at a variety of tasks: as day labourers on construction sites and on the docks; building canals; rafting logs downriver to mills; as domestic labourers; in small workshops. Factories were rare, and even by 1850 workshops employed an average of just over three workers. Among the few instances of collective labour were the large numbers of workers, predominantly Irish, who dug the St. Lawrence canals in the 1830s and 1840s. Conditions there were especially harsh, and strikes and riots were frequent. But no "working class" existed as yet. Workers were fragmented and stratified along regional, occupational, and income lines, as well as on the basis of ethnicity and gender. Difficult though the conditions were, very few doing such "semi-skilled" work would enjoy the benefits of unionization until well into the twentieth century.

CRAFT UNIONS

Unions did emerge in the first half of the nineteenth century, though, formed by those at the top of the labour force, the crafts workers — carpenters, stone masons, printers, tailors. At the heart of craft unionism was the apprenticeship system. A boy was bound by contract to a master craftsperson for anywhere from three to ten years, during which time he learned the craft under the guidance of the master, eventually becoming a skilled tradesperson — a journeyman and, in some cases, a master.

Apprentices, journeymen, and masters were united in a common dedication to their craft. It was a dedication reinforced with rituals and celebrations: lavish banquets with speeches about the honour of the craft; colourful parades with banners on festive occasions. The crafts workers were the elite of the nineteenth-century labour movement — the "aristocracy of labour." They were proud of their skills, and they worked at maintaining the tradition of their craft.

In the course of time, some masters began to think of themselves and to act as capitalists — more committed to accumulating profits than to maintaining the craft. At the same time some apprentices and journeymen began to see that they had interests differing from their masters. Class differences began to emerge. Apprentices and journeymen established craft societies to represent their collective interests to their employers, the masters.

Some of these craft societies evolved into unions: a handful of them early in the nineteenth century (carpenters, mechanics, tailors, and printers, for example); more by the 1830s–1840s (coopers, blacksmiths, painters, bakers, shipwrights). These craft unions were rarely confrontational; the line between master and journeymen was still too blurred for that. Attachment to a craft identity was still stronger than the emergent working-class identity. The desire to be a "respectable" part of their communities — respectability was a central element of craft unionism — was still too strong.

Craft workers sought to preserve the values and traditions — the culture — of the craft. The craft tradition was one of collectivism, mutuality and solidarity, and the dignity of labour and of the craft. These were *alternatives* to the more dominant, individualistic, bourgeois values of capitalism.

Especially after the 1850s and the spread of the railway system, craft workers frequently travelled in search of work. Because they moved back and forth across the Canada-U.S. border, they sought affiliations with the similarly emerging craft unionism in the United States. These bodies gradually came to be called **international unions** — or unions with members in both Canada and the United States. By 1873 Canada had at least 123 local and international unions, many of them relatively bureaucratized, with constitutions for conducting union affairs and rule books with pay schedules and standardized work rules.

In the second half of the nineteenth century, mechanized factories slowly began to emerge, resulting in the beginnings of a demand for semi-skilled factory labour and, in industries such as clothing and shoemaking, female factory labour. At the same time, small handicraft workshops that continued to exist alongside the emergent factory system employed women and children in growing numbers. Most women factory workers were not only poorly paid but also young, because they tended to leave their employment upon marriage. Many married women worked for wages, but most often in the **"putting out" system** (they did consignment work at home, usually on a piecework basis, at even lower wages than women in the factories).

KNIGHTS OF LABOUR

The first serious attempt to organize these new industrial workers, including women, was made by the Holy and Noble Order of the Knights of Labour. Formed in Philadelphia in 1869, the Knights of Labour established their first "local assembly" in Canada in 1881, in Hamilton. By 1886 the organization had exploded to one million members in Canada. Workers could join "trades" assemblies of particular crafts or "mixed" assemblies of various occupations — which meant that semi-skilled as well as skilled workers, and women as well as men, were for the first time able to join a union. The Knights were the first example, albeit in a modified form, of industrial unionism. By the end of the 1880s the Knights were playing important roles, alongside the crafts unions, in most of the trades and labour councils established in cities and towns.

Like the crafts unions, the Knights of Labour promoted a working-class culture as an alternative to the acquisitive and individualistic norms of capitalism. Workers' festivals, picnics, dinners, and dances all served to create a culture of collectivity, of mutual aid and solidarity. The Knights' emphasis on education — the regular promotion of lectures and various other educational events, the establishment of newspapers and reading rooms — encouraged the flowering of a working-class intellectual tradition. By the 1880s significant numbers of working-class intellectuals added further to the ability of the emergent working class to build a distinctive, solidaristic culture.

The Knights declined precipitously in the late 1880s to early 1890s. The decline was the result of several factors: the timidity of their leadership in promoting strike action in pursuit of members' interests; their growing split with the crafts unions; and, most importantly, their inability to respond adequately to the dramatic changes being wrought by the end-of-the-century transition to monopoly capitalism. But they were an important nineteenth-century example of what a union might be: inclusive of all workers, irrespective of occupation or gender, and committed to building a culture of mutuality and solidarity rather than the greed and individualism of the emerging monopoly capitalism.

MONOPOLY CAPITALISM

By the turn of the century the relatively slow and gradual growth of the factory system had given way to the full-fledged arrival of **monopoly capitalism**. Giant corporations emerged in new industries such as automobiles, steel, rubber, electrical parts, oil, chemicals, and pulp and paper. These corporations — Ford and General Motors, Standard Oil, U.S. Steel, General Electric, Du Pont, Goodyear Tire and Rubber Company, for example — organized production in great factories. Mergers were frequent;

corporations grew ever larger. U.S. investment in Canada expanded rapidly, creating the branch-plant structure that would characterize twentieth-century Canadian industry.

Factories were increasingly organized on the basis of **scientific management**, introduced and promoted by the U.S. engineer Frederick Taylor. His "Taylorism" broke up factory production into its various tasks. The system assigned each small task to one worker, and to speed up the pace of work managers used a stopwatch to establish the fastest possible time in which workers could complete each task. At its heart, scientific management separated the conceptualization of how work was to be done from the actual execution of the work tasks. Relatively unskilled workers, as opposed to crafts workers, could do work organized in this way. This **deskilling** strategy eroded the control over their work traditionally exercised by crafts workers, placing more power in the hands of managers. Henry Ford's introduction of the assembly line was the prototype of this new way of organizing industrial work, and with his five dollar a day plan — he paid his workers this high wage not only to increase productivity by securing a stable workforce and reducing training and turnover costs, but also to ensure buyers for his cars — the foundation was laid for the age of mass production and mass consumption.

Workers resisted this reorganization of work and their loss of control over the labour process. The number of strikes exploded between 1901 and 1914. Capital responded aggressively, even brutally, with industrial spies, strikebreakers, and stool pigeons, detective agencies like Thiel and Pinkertons, and firing and **blacklisting** — circulating among employers a list of those not to be hired — of strike leaders and union organizers. On more than twenty occasions between 1895 and 1914 the state used the militia to crush strikes. The working class became what labour historian Bryan Palmer (1992: 163) calls a "community under siege."

The state's response to this turn-of-the-century militancy was not only to send in the militia, but also to engineer a more subtle and sophisticated approach to industrial relations under the direction of the young William Lyon Mackenzie King, who would later become Canada's longest-serving prime minister. King oversaw the establishment of a federal Department of Labour in 1900, and the passing of the *Industrial Disputes Investigation Act* (IDIA) in 1907. The IDIA was King's attempt to have the state intervene in industrial disputes involving utilities, railways, and coal mines as an "impartial umpire," ostensibly representing the interests of the community. The provisions of the IDIA included compulsory conciliation, a "cooling off" period, and the establishment of tripartite boards of conciliation.

The IDIA did not include the right to form a union. It was primarily a means of averting strikes, and for this limited purpose it worked. From 1907 to 1911 the IDIA was used in 101 disputes, and in nine of ten cases strikes

Women and the Work Force: The Early Years:

"The story of Canada's women workers in the years from 1870 to 1939 is, in many ways, a grim tale." —Frager and Patrias, *Disconnected Labour*, p. 147

Women's work has often been "homework" — work done in the home and paid for on a piecework basis — with the women very often working as subcontractors for the garment industry, and typically combining paid work with domestic and child-care responsibilities. Wages have always been extremely low: "Isolated from each other and competing for scraps of work, they desperately underbid each other" (Frager and Patrias 1005: 27). In many parts of the world, including Canada, these conditions continue to be in effect today.

When women began to enter the paid labour force — in some cases because the "family wage" of their husbands was simply not enough to support their families — they were confined to a limited number of low-paid occupations. Better-paid and more skilled positions were for men, especially Anglo-Saxon men.

Employers exploited women even more than they did men. A late nineteenth-century clothing manufacturer said: "I don't treat the men bad, but I even up by taking advantage of the women. I have a girl who can do as much work, and as good work as a man; she gets $5 a week. The man who is standing next to her gets $11" (p. 35).

Teaching was a job open to women in the early twentieth century. It was poorly paid, and teachers were tightly controlled. A 1923 contract for a female teacher in Ontario provided a number of requirements: "She was not to use face powder and mascara or dye for her hair. She was also forbidden to ride in a carriage or automobile with any man except her brothers or father. Nor was she to leave town without permission, loiter downtown in ice cream parlours, smoke cigarettes, or drink beer, wine or whiskey" (p. 58).

Women were often treated badly by unions and male union members: "Many male workers and male unionists were, at best, ambivalent towards women workers, and some were overtly hostile. These men thought that women did not belong in the workplace, and feared that low-wage women workers might undercut their own wages or take their jobs" (p. 121).

Women did make gains in later decades, but they have yet to achieve equality. Every gain that women workers have made has been the result of hard-fought struggles against intransigent employers, often-rigid union members, and a powerful patriarchal ideology that seeks to justify women's being slotted into jobs low down in the hierarchy and the pay scale.

Source: Frager and Patrias 2005.

Family Wage:
The notion of a "family wage" includes the view that men ought to work for wages and be paid enough to support a family, which would include a wife whose work was confined to the home and was not for wages. This notion of a "male breadwinner" who had the primary responsibility for providing for a family was a powerful ideological force that undercut the possibility of economic independence for married women, who were to be confined to the (unpaid) roles of wife and mother. Associated with the ideological notion — the patriarchal notion — of a family wage was the belief that married women joining the labour force and working for wages would represent a threat to men's jobs. A woman ought to be in the home; her true vocation was motherhood. The net effect of this belief in a family wage was to confine women to particular, largely supportive, roles in society.

were averted. Workers grudgingly accepted this state intervention, even though the settlements could rarely be considered complete victories, in large part because they recognized that in an all-out war with capital, labour would be the loser. Significantly, in this new, twentieth-century form of state intervention in Canada's industrial relations, the state was intervening only when labour militancy threatened to upset industrial peace — it was militancy that triggered state intervention, as it still does. The purpose of the state intervention was simply to restore relative industrial harmony, to regulate the relations between capital and labour so that profit-making could proceed without undue interruption from militant workers.

Although increasingly militant, workers in the early twentieth century were still by no means a unified "working class." The new demand for workers less skilled than crafts workers was met in large part by a dramatic, turn-of-the-century increase in immigration from Europe, including Eastern and Southern Europe. Between 1896 and the outbreak of the Great War in 1914, a massive wave of mostly non-English-speaking immigrants flooded into Canada, filling the newly opened Prairies with farmers and the emergent factories of monopoly capitalism with semi-skilled labour. Their arrival added to the growing need for **industrial unionism** — the establishment of unions representing *all* workers in a workplace, irrespective of craft or task. It also added to the fragmentation of the working class. It would not be until the 1940s that industrial workers from Eastern and Southern Europe would become fully a part of the labour movement.

It was harder still to unionize women. A large proportion of women continued to work in relatively isolated workplaces: in domestic service in the homes of the well-to-do; in the small sweated workshops of contractors, or at home as part of the putting out system that was so common in the clothing and textile industries; in small retail shops, where young women commonly worked twelve hours a day and sixteen hours on Saturday. Wages were low. A commentator in 1913 noted, "The average female factory worker in Montreal earned $4.50 to $5.50 per week, at a time when the lowest estimate of the minimum living wage was $7.00 per week" (Frager 1983: 45). In the factories, abuse, including the imposition of fines for laughing or talking on the job and even physical beatings by employers, was not uncommon. But because women typically left the workforce when they married, too often they "were deprived of the opportunity to build experience in collective action, to discuss and pass on knowledge of work relationships, to develop a history of action and to provide leaders with years of work and union experience" (White 1993: 13). This was not invariably the case. In the clothing industry, for example, women were enthusiastic participants in strikes, and by the 1930s were struggling to become active in their unions (Steedman 1997: 251). In most cases — the Knights of Labour were to some extent an exception — unions themselves and their mostly male members were opposed to having women in the workforce, arguing that women would drive down wages. The commonly held view was that male workers ought to be paid a **family wage** sufficient to support a family, and that women ought to be in the home.

If unions were less than welcoming to women in the workforce, they were downright hostile to workers of colour. Chinese workers, for example, were brought to British Columbia from China in the 1880s as contract workers to lay the track in the last leg of the cross-country CPR. They were brutally exploited:

> Accidents were frequent, with far more Chinese than Whites as victims. Many workers died from exhaustion and rock explosions and were buried in collapsed tunnels. Their living conditions were appalling. Food and shelter were in insufficient supply, and malnutrition was widespread. There was almost no medical attention, contributing to a high fatality rate from diseases such as scurvy and smallpox. It is estimated that there were six hundred deaths in British Columbia of Chinese labourers working on the construction of the railway. (Henry et al. 2000: 73)

Once the rail line was completed, the government passed legislation to prevent further Chinese immigration: the *Chinese Immigration Act* in 1885; and the imposition of a head tax of $50 in 1888, which grew to a prohibitive $500 in 1903. The Canadian labour movement was among those organizations in support of these and later anti-Chinese policies. For example, one group of researchers pointed out, "The white labour movement of British Columbia proudly shared credit for the Canadian government's discriminatory $50 head tax on Chinese entering Canada, the first in an escalating series of anti-Chinese measures adopted by the provincial and dominion governments" (Iacovetta, Quinlan, and Radforth 1996). Chinese

> The Effects of Racism on Union Solidarity:
> "As cyclical economic recessions reduce job opportunities, many domestic workers perceive immigrants to be taking away their jobs. Since many immigrants come from a different racial and ethnic background than the dominant group, competition for high-paying jobs often surfaces as inter-ethnic antagonism. These ethnic divisions among employees reduce unity among the work force by diverting attention from the fundamental contradictions of capitalist accumulation to inter-ethnic and inter-racial competition. In this way, artificial cultural divisions among the work force facilitate social control [by employers. As a result]... one of the effects of racism is to weaken the solidarity of the working class and of union organization, thus strengthening the position of employers."
>
> *Source: Li 1988: 51*

workers were excluded from some white unions; in other cases wage differentials were embedded in collective agreements allowing for lower wages to be paid to "oriental" than to "occidental," or white, workers (Henry et al. 2000: 73). This is an early example of what has been called the **split labour market**, in which employers benefit from the lower wages that can be paid to workers of colour, and workers as a whole are divided along colour lines and thus weakened (Li 1988: 43; for a discussion of the devastating effects of this phenomenon on the U.S. working class, see Roediger 1991). Further to this, Chinese workers were barred from various occupations and institutions, with the result that many of them ended up working in the service sector, in restaurants, laundries, and domestic work, for example, because nothing else was open to them. These conditions provide an early example of how the labour force became stratified along ethnic and racial lines, to the detriment of all working people.

Still, some great and noble attempts at establishing industrial unionism were made late in the nineteenth and early in the twentieth centuries. These attempts were often associated with some variant of socialism — with socialist ideas and leaders. This was the case, for instance, with the Wobblies — the Industrial Workers of the World — and would be the case right through to the late 1940s. In important respects, this association with socialism reveals the importance of ideas in the struggle to develop new forms of unionism.

But, early in the twentieth century it was the crafts unions that persisted and even grew in strength. In 1886 U.S. crafts unions had formed the American Federation of Labor (AFL), headed by Samuel Gompers, and earlier that same year Canadian crafts unions together with other elements of organized labour met as a Canadian central, the Trades and Labour Congress (TLC). The TLC struggled towards the end of the century. While 109 delegates had attended the first session in 1886, only 39 were in attendance in 1895, and 44 in 1898. However, at the turn of the century the crafts unions of the AFL launched a dramatic organizing drive aimed at the emergent corporate giants of monopoly capitalism and their Canadian branch plants. Between 1899 and 1903 thousands of workers in many industries signed up in U.S.-based unions in what was the biggest organizing campaign since the Knights of Labour in the 1880s. Building on their success, the U.S.-based crafts unions seized control of the Trades and Labour Congress at its 1902 convention by expelling the few remaining Knights of Labour assemblies and other **dual unions** — unions representing workers in industries in which U.S.-based unions operated. The bulk of the Canadian trade union movement was, to a considerable extent, now under the control of U.S.-based unions. The struggle to break away from what some would see as American domination, like the struggle to form industrial unionism, would be an important theme in the history of trade unionism in Canada in the twentieth century.

Samuel Gompers and Business Unionism:
Samuel Gompers, an English-born cigarmaker, became the first president of the American Federation of Labor (AFL) in 1886 and remained in that role for almost forty years. His philosophy came to dominate craft unionism. He believed that unions should concentrate first and foremost on collective bargaining, because what workers wanted was simply "more, more, more." This pure and simple unionism would result in significant gains for skilled crafts workers. Gompers opposed industrial unionism, as represented by the Knights of Labour and the Industrial Workers of the World, because less-skilled workers would weaken crafts workers' bargaining strength, and because he believed that radical politics was detrimental to workers' interests. Gompers favoured a "pragmatic" politics by which labour would seek to advance its interests within the existing two-party system in the United States. Labour's strategy should be to "reward its friends and punish its enemies," regardless of their political affiliation. The result was Gomperism, a cautious and conservative form of unionism, often called "business unionism" or "bread and butter unionism."

By the First World War "international" craft-based unionism was dominant in Canada, as in the United States. It was guided by **Gomperism**, named after the approach of AFL president Gompers. This was pragmatic, bureaucratic, non-political, and especially non-socialist "bread and butter" unionism, or **business unionism**, aimed almost solely at getting more for its members within the existing system. Effective though this approach often was, craft unions had a glaring flaw. They represented only the skilled crafts workers and excluded the rapidly growing numbers of semi-skilled industrial workers being created by the burgeoning factories of monopoly capitalism. The struggle for industrial unionism had a long way to go.

WORKERS' REVOLT AND THE 1919 WINNIPEG GENERAL STRIKE

The First World War and especially the 1917 Bolshevik Revolution in Russia inspired an accentuation of the labour militancy of the early twentieth century. In 1917 the record shows 218 strikes involving more than 50,000 workers, double the numbers for 1916 and more than any year since the turn of the century. In 1919 another attempt at radical industrial unionism was made with the establishment of the One Big Union (OBU), based largely in Western Canada and a breakaway from the increasingly cautious, crafts-based Trades and Labour Congress based largely in the East. Many of the OBU leaders — including Winnipeg General Strike leaders R.B. Russell and Dick Johns — were members of the Socialist Party of Canada, established in 1904. The groundwork for the radical OBU was laid at the Western Labour Conference in Calgary in March 1919. The OBU not only decided to secede from the much more conservative TLC but also identified openly with the revolutionary situation in Russia and Germany.

The OBU's approach to labour politics added to the widespread radical tone of the times, which became the context for the Winnipeg General Strike, one of the most important moments in Canadian labour history. The 1919 strike was, indeed, the centrepiece of a pan-Canadian labour revolt that saw in 1919 alone, 150,000 workers taking part in 427 strikes — twice the number for 1917. Union membership was exploding too, from 140,000 in 1915 to 205,000 in 1917, 250,000 in 1918, and 378,000 in 1919 (Heron 1998: 269). But Winnipeg was the heart of the uprising.

Industrial militancy had been growing in Winnipeg, as in the rest of the country, in the first two decades of the century. Winnipeg was then one of Canada's fastest-growing cities, a rail and industrial centre whose North End was teeming with European working-class immigrants. Economic inequalities, deep class divisions, steep wartime inflation, and frequently dreadful working and living conditions were the context in which industrial unions sought recognition and the right to negotiate the conditions of their work and wages with employers. It was a battle. Winnipeg industrialists were rigidly anti-union. Bitter strikes had been fought in 1906 by streetcar workers and the metal workers at Vulcan Iron Works. In the summer of 1918, when the City of Winnipeg workers went out, they were joined by between 1,400 and 1,700 other Winnipeg workers. The situation was explosive: "Confrontation was in the air. Martial law and arrests were threatened from the outset. Working class solidarity with the civic workers was palpable and explosive.... The machinists called for a general strike" (Mitchell and Naylor 1998: 180).

Workers in the metals trades in Winnipeg were establishing a Metals Trade Council, headed by Russell, to co-ordinate their attempts to bargain collectively with employers in those industries. The employers were intransigent. E.G. Barrett, owner of Vulcan Iron Works, typified their stance: "This is a free country and... as far as we are concerned the day will never come when we will have to take orders from any union" (Smith 1985: 42). Barrett and the other metal-shop owners simply refused to meet with any union representatives. Russell and the Metals Trades Council — another attempt, in effect, at industrial unionism — appealed to the Winnipeg Trades and Labour Council for support. The Council called for a general strike, and in the following week member unions conducted a referendum. The result was overwhelming: 11,112 in favour and 524 against the call for a general strike. On May 15, 1919, some 25,000 Winnipeg workers, including many non-unionists led by 500 female telephone workers, walked off the job to start the largest general strike in Canada's history.

The strike lasted six weeks. An initial two-hundred-member Central Strike Committee proved too cumbersome and was replaced by a fifteen-member committee that met daily to co-ordinate strike efforts, maintain order, and ensure the provision of essential services in the city. Essential goods, such as milk, were allowed to get to citizens "by authority of the Strike Committee" — making it appear as if the strikers were in control of the city. Indeed, this was at least partly true.

The business and professional class responded by forming the Citizens Committee of 1,000, an extension of the Citizens Committee of 100 formed the year before during the civic workers' strike. When the Winnipeg police force was dismissed en masse on June 9 because its members refused to sign a no-strike pledge, the Citizens Committee organized their replacement by untrained but sympathetic "special constables," whose one-sided aggression precipitated what little violence occurred. The Canadian government rushed through changes to the *Immigration Act* to enable it to deport foreign-born strike leaders, and on the night of June 16–17, police swooped down on the homes of the strike leaders to arrest them and haul them off to Stony Mountain Penitentiary. A mass rally on Saturday, June 21 — "Bloody Saturday" — led to four Royal North-West Mounted Police charges down Main Street. On the last charge the police fired shots into the crowd, killing two strikers. Shortly after, on June 25, the Winnipeg General Strike came to an end. About 3,500 strikers lost their jobs; many were blacklisted.

In the main, the leaders of the strike, most of them British immigrants steeped in the non-revolutionary politics of their homeland, appear to have been simply trying to achieve collective bargaining rights. They wanted union recognition and the right to collectively bargain their working conditions and wages. To them, the General Strike was a trade union issue. But to many others, the larger context of the strike — almost twenty years of labour militancy as industrial unions, often led by socialists and promoting socialist values, struggled with aggressive employers and governments in what amounted frequently to industrial warfare — seemed to be revolutionary. The revolutionary tone of the times was accentuated by the dramatic 1917 Bolshevik Revolution in Russia, which threatened for a time to spread to Western Europe and from thence to who knows where, and which had a significant impact on workers across North America. Local labour councils across Canada passed motions supporting the new revolutionary government; Winnipeg strike leader Johns said he would be proud to be called a Bolshevik; over 1,700 Winnipeggers crowded into the downtown Walker Theatre in December 1918 to hear prominent left leaders express solidarity with the Russian Revolution.

Moreover, as labour historian Greg Kealey (1984: 12) observed after surveying the speeches, writings, and activities of local leaders of the many pan-Canadian strikes in 1919: "The message was the same across the country. The capitalist system could not be reformed; it must be transformed. Production for profit must cease; production for use must begin." After all, a general strike is not an industrial technique, but a political tool. It is virtually a revolutionary weapon. A general strike replaces the elected and legitimate authorities with rule by workers — as the strikers' use of placards reading "by authority of the Strike Committee" would suggest. Thus, although most of the leaders of the General Strike were not revolutionaries, and the intent of the General Strike was not revolutionary, the business and professional class and their state supporters believed that it was a revolutionary situation, and in a sense they were right — the situation was potentially revolutionary. Thus from their perspective, it had to be crushed, and it was. An important aspect of this was the remarkable process by which the federal government and the leaders of the Citizens Committee of 1,000, in what can only be described as a conspiracy, afterwards railroaded the strike leaders into jail (see Chaboyer and Black 2006).

THE 1920S: LABOUR'S LOW POINT

In the immediate aftermath of the 1919 Winnipeg General Strike, labour elected representatives in 1919, 1920, and 1921 at each of the municipal, provincial, and federal levels of government. This success, though, was short-lived. In 1921 the Communist Party of Canada (CPC) was formed, and the workers and trade unionists on the left were split. The more revolutionary and Soviet-linked CPC was on one side, and the more moderate, social-democratic Independent Labour Party and later Co-operative Commonwealth Federation (the CCF, forerunner of the New Democratic Party, or NDP) were on the other. By 1921–22 the workers' revolt in Canada was largely over, save for some vicious battles in which the state intervened with armed troops in the coal fields of Cape Breton from 1922 to 1925. Much about the union movement for the next thirty years would be coloured by the increasingly destructive split between the country's communist and non-communist left.

> "Hidebound, the TLC perversely clung to its craft mentality. It launched no organizing campaigns, hired few organizers and spent little money.... By the end of the decade [the 1920s] it had lost much of its membership and was on the verge of bankruptcy. It was impotent, rudderless, in total disarray, and its very survival seemed in the balance."
>
> *Source: Abella 1973: 2.*

The long, twenty-year struggle to establish industrial unionism had been defeated once again. The efforts of the Knights of Labour, the Wobblies, the One Big Union — all had suffered the same fate. By 1921, despite a remarkable twenty-year period of creative industrial militancy — despite a massive labour revolt all across Canada — most industrial workers in Canada were still without the democratic rights and protections that a union can provide. By the end of 1922, union membership had dropped by 100,000 since its 1919 peak, and matters were only getting worse. As labour historian Irving Abella (1973: 1) puts it: "For the Canadian labour movement, no period was more dismal than the 1920s. Organization was at a standstill, membership declined dramatically, and union leadership was divided and paralyzed."

The crafts union movement had distanced itself from the great labour revolt and, like the Gompers-led American Federation of Labor, pursued a relatively narrow and apolitical path of caution and complacency. Indeed, the TLC, like its U.S. counterpart, was unwilling and unable to respond to the challenge created by the rise of the mass-production industries and the growth in the numbers of factory workers. Its leaders opposed industrial unionism and continued to believe that only highly skilled crafts workers should be organized.

At the same time, other union centrals were emerging alongside the TLC, and unlike the mostly international unions of the TLC they were Canadian-based. The Canadian and Catholic Confederation of Labour — dominated by the Roman Catholic Church and concerned about the TLC's lack of interest in the particular problems of French-Canadian workers — emerged in Quebec in 1921. The All-Canadian Congress of Labour (ACCL), comprising unions expelled from the TLC for their advocacy of industrial unionism and led by the Canadian Brotherhood of Railway Employees and the remnants of the OBU, was established in 1927.

THE WORKERS' UNITY LEAGUE

Early in 1930 the CPC announced the creation of yet another union central, the Workers' Unity League (WUL), which became "a storm centre of new unionizing efforts in the darkest years of the early 1930s" (Heron 1989: 70). By 1933 the WUL had eleven affiliated industrial unions. Its creative militancy and core of highly skilled union organizers kept alive the dream of industrial unionism during a time when the TLC was adrift and largely

> Organizing in the Relief Camps:
> "Anyone caught attempting to organize or distributing Relief Camp Workers' Union [RCWU] leaflets would be expelled from camp immediately and blacklisted throughout the DND [Department of National Defence] camp system. Such people would also be on blacklists in the cities which meant they would be unable to obtain relief. Many were imprisoned, usually for vagrancy. Nevertheless, the organizing continued and took the form of secret 'bush committees' in the camps, which would distribute leaflets, coordinate and generalize individual grievances, and provide leadership in strikes and other actions of this nature. When they were discovered and blacklisted they would try to enter other camps under assumed names. A skillful organizer might last some months before the authorities finally caught up with him. Before long the majority of protest actions and the most effective strikes were led by supporters of the RCWU."
>
> *Source: Brown 1987: 63.*

ineffectual. Moreover, the socialist-inspired WUL, like the OBU before it, recruited Chinese workers and included them on union executives and strike committees to overcome employers' racially-based divide and rule tactics (Das Gupta 1998: 318-319).

Most of the strikes in the first half of the 1930s were led by WUL affiliates, and many of those strikes as well as organizing drives were met with brutal state repression. In the Estevan miners' strike of 1931, a parade of four hundred miners in cars and trucks was met with RCMP and local police gunfire. The shots killed three miners, and the police arrested another fifty. The next day sixty RCMP constables raided the union's headquarters and conducted a house-to-house search for union members. In a furniture workers' strike in 1933 in Stratford, Ontario, the authorities sent in troops with brand new machine-gun carriers to put down the strike. In a Bloedel's lumber strike in Vancouver in 1934, police made mass arrests and evicted strikers from their homes.

The state always has at least two options available for dealing with labour militancy: the relatively subtle use of industrial relations legislation and mechanisms to restore industrial peace, as for example with the IDIA; and the use of force to repress militant workers. In the 1930s, force was frequently the preferred option.

The same repression halted the On-to-Ottawa Trek in Regina in 1935. In the early 1930s, the Great Depression left many tens of thousands of young, single men unemployed. Fearful that these men might be radicalized if they gathered in large urban centres, in October 1932 the federal government of R.B. Bennett passed an order-in-council setting up rural relief camps. Single unemployed men were then denied relief in towns and cities, effectively forcing them into the camps, where conditions were harsh and the pay was paltry. Strikes and other disturbances soon became a frequent occurrence. Out of these conditions arose the Relief Camp Workers'

Union (RCWU), affiliated to the WUL. Conditions in the camps were tough for union organizing.

In June 1935, after spending months protesting in Vancouver, more than a thousand RCWU members, led by Slim Evans, an experienced WUL organizer who had previously worked with the Wobblies and OBU, began the On-to-Ottawa Trek to present their grievances to Prime Minister Bennett and rally support for their cause. The federal government, fearful of the Trek's political potential, decided to stop it before it reached Winnipeg, with that city's radical tradition and large left-wing movement, and where hundreds more people were waiting to join up. Despite the Trekkers' efforts to reach a peaceful resolution, the RCMP attacked them at a mass meeting on July 1 in Regina's Market Square. By the end of the "Regina Riot," one city policeman was dead, scores of people were injured, and several Trekkers and citizens were hospitalized with gunshot wounds. The On-to-Ottawa Trek was over.

The WUL came to an end as well, as the result of instructions from Moscow. The Communist Party of Canada, the driving force behind the WUL, was closely tied to the Soviet Union. Indeed, the Party's great weakness was the extent to which it was controlled from Moscow. The connection frequently led to sudden and otherwise inexplicable policy shifts in the Party's relationship to the Canadian labour movement. For example, in the early 1920s the CPC abandoned the OBU on Moscow's instructions in order to work within the Trades and Labour Congress; then it reversed that decision in 1927 by supporting the establishment of the ACCL.

Yet another shift in strategy led to the WUL being ordered by Moscow to fold up in 1935. Its unions were instructed to rejoin the TLC, and the most vibrant union central in the country was disbanded. However, the now-seasoned WUL organizers would be at the heart of the campaign by which the Committee for Industrial Organization, the CIO, made its way into Canada from south of the border.

THE CIO

At the 1935 convention of the American Federation of Labour the leader of the United Mineworkers, John L. Lewis, took what would turn out to be a historic step. Reacting against the caution of the AFL and its determination to divide industrial workers by organizing them on the basis of craft, Lewis announced the formation of the Committee for Industrial Organization, which would work within the AFL to organize factory workers into industrial unions. The letters CIO became a battle cry. Overnight, the CIO made spectacular gains in hitherto non-union U.S. industries such as steel, automobiles, electrical, rubber, and other mass-production industries. The greatest organizing drive of the twentieth century took flight. The tactic at the heart of the drive was simple, powerful, and unprecedented: the

The Sit-Down Strike:
Autoworkers in the midst of a sitdown strike chanted this defiant and descriptive song:

When they tie the can
to a union man,
Sit down! Sit down!
When they give him the sack,
they'll take him back,
Sit down! Sit down!
When the speed-up comes,
just twiddle your thumbs,
Sit down! Sit down!
When the boss won't talk,
don't take a walk,
Sit down! Sit down!

"sit-down" strike. Factory workers simply downed tools and occupied a plant.

Although the U.S.-based CIO confined almost all of its efforts to the huge organizing task in the mass-production industries of the United States, the magic of the CIO name was picked up and used in Canada by scores of highly skilled Canadian organizers. But despite the use of the name, it was Canadian organizers and Canadian money that fuelled the CIO drive in Canada. A large proportion of these organizers were Communist Party workers who had honed their considerable skills with the WUL. The craft unions opposed this organizing drive. In the United States the American Federation of Labor expelled the CIO in 1937 (it then became the Congress of Industrial Organizations, and thus still the CIO). In Canada the Trades and Labour Congress followed suit in 1939 and expelled the CIO unions and their more than 20,000 members, just as it had expelled the remnants of the Knights of Labour in 1902. These actions were an expression of an intense opposition to industrial unionism. The CIO unions in Canada responded by amalgamating with the ACCL to form the new Canadian Congress of Labour (CCL) in 1940.

But the CIO drive for industrial unionism developed more slowly in Canada than in the United States. The main reason was the strong opposition to industrial unionism, from both the TLC and the companies and the Canadian state. For example, when the CIO-inspired Steel Workers Organizing Committee (SWOC) attempted in 1937 to organize a foundry in Sarnia, where Eastern Europeans made up a significant minority of the workers, enraged citizens of Sarnia, "united in their hatred of the foreigners, descended on the foundry with an assortment of anti-union devices — crowbars, baseball bats, bricks and steel pipes. A bloody battle ensued, and within an hour the union was broken, as were the arms, legs and heads of many of the 'sit-downers'" (Abella 1973: 7). The Sarnia police refused to intervene, and the sit-down strikers were convicted in court of trespassing. No charges were laid against the strikebreakers. It was clear whose side the state was on.

In the United States, by contrast, a key element of Franklin Roosevelt's New Deal was the 1935 *National Labor Relations Act* (usually called the **Wagner Act,** after the senator who initiated the legislation), which protected those trying to organize a union from the anti-labour practices of the past and compelled employers to bargain collectively with unions chosen by a majority of workers in a bargaining unit. In Canada in the 1930s the government passed no such legislation; compulsory recognition of unions when they had the support of a majority of workers was still almost a decade away.

The first significant breakthrough for the CIO in Canada occurred at the General Motors plant in Oshawa. In January 1937, General Motors announced its largest profit ever, $200 million, and then imposed the fifth wage cut in five years on its Oshawa workers. In April the workers struck. Ontario premier Mitchell Hepburn, vowing that the CIO would not succeed in Oshawa, described the strike as "a fight to the finish." According to Hepburn, a CIO victory in Oshawa would lead to an organizing drive directed at the Northern Ontario mines, which would demoralize shareholders and drive down stock prices. The strike was successful, although to win the union organizing team had to disavow its involvement with the CIO. The agreement signed was between the General Motors Company of Canada and the employees of the company at Oshawa: neither the CIO nor the United Auto Workers were mentioned. Hepburn used this element to claim victory, but in the end the victor was industrial unionism. As Abella (1973: 22) puts it, the workers' victory against the combined power of big business and the state "gave the CIO the impetus it so badly needed to begin organization in the mass production industries of the country."

The Padlock Laws:
The Padlock Act (Act Respecting Communistic Propaganda), a 1937 Quebec statute enacted by Quebec Premier Maurice Duplessis, authorized Quebec's attorney general to close for one year any building being used to propagate "communism or bolshevism." Neither of these terms was defined in the act, with the result that the powers under the act could be widely applied. Under the provisions of the act the attorney general could confiscate and destroy printed matter that "propagated communism or bolshevism," and could imprison for up to one year, without appeal, anyone distributing, printing or publishing such material. The act was ruled unconstitutional by the Supreme Court in 1957.

But in the absence of legislation comparable to the Wagner Act, gains continued to be slow in coming, even after Oshawa. By October 1937, CIO organizing had ground to a halt. Hepburn won a landslide re-election in Ontario on an anti-CIO platform in fall 1937, while in early 1938 Quebec premier Maurice Duplessis used the infamous **Padlock Laws** to raid the homes of SWOC organizers and confiscate their union records. Membership in CIO unions declined in 1938, and it would only be under wartime conditions that Canadian industrial labour could finally make its big breakthrough.

THE SECOND WORLD WAR

The Second World War was a turning point for labour in Canada. The war acted as a catalyst for union activity much as the First World War had done during the great labour revolt of twenty years earlier. Union membership doubled, from 359,000 in 1939 to 744,000 in 1944. Unemployment plummeted: 900,000 people were registered as unemployed in 1939; by 1941 a labour shortage had set in. During the war the cost of living rose, and so too did workers' expectations and demands, especially the demand for the right to unionize and to negotiate working conditions and wages.

The result was an outburst of labour militancy in the early 1940s comparable to that of 1917–19. Work stoppages doubled between 1941 and 1942, and doubled again the following year. By 1943 one in every three union members in Canada was on strike. Of particular symbolic importance was the long and bitter gold miners' strike at Kirkland Lake in the winter of 1941–42. The mining companies refused to negotiate, even after a board of conciliation unanimously recommended recognition of the union. The federal government refused to intervene in support of the conciliation board's report; the provincial government provided armed protection for strikebreakers. The miners were eventually defeated, but their loss crystallized in workers' minds the need for compulsory recognition legislation and further fuelled labour militancy, which peaked in 1943.

Many of the leaders of this renewed burst of labour militancy had developed their organizing skills during the tough times of the 1930s and were associated with some form of radical politics. Growing numbers were members of the Co-operative Commonwealth Federation. The CCF, formed in Calgary in 1932, would become the social-democratic and non-communist branch of the divided Canadian socialist movement. The party's electoral fortunes took flight in the early 1940s, at the very time when industrial militancy was exploding. Throughout 1942 the CCF attracted more and more members, especially among trade unionists in Ontario. In 1943 the party placed a strong second in the Ontario provincial elections — where nineteen of its thirty-four members were trade unionists — and a month after the election a national Gallup poll showed the CCF ahead of both the Liberals and Conservatives in Canada-wide popularity.

The simultaneous rise in labour militancy and CCF electoral strength finally forced the federal government to act. As always, labour militancy induced state intervention. The Inquiry into Labour Relations and Wage Conditions in Canada, conducted by the National War Labour Board at Prime Minister Mackenzie King's request, called for a labour code similar to the U.S. *Wagner Act*, something that would prevent the increasingly bitter strikes over the basic right to unionize. King feared that unless he acted, he risked losing labour's support, thus threatening the chances of a Liberal re-election. The result, almost seven years after the victory at Oshawa's

General Motors plant, was PC 1003, enacted in 1944 in an attempt to control labour militancy and win back labour's political support from the surging CCF. Like other such turning points — including the *Industrial Disputes Investigation Act* of 1907 — PC 1003 was the result of labour militancy.

Labour militancy continued in the immediate postwar period, with strike activity especially aggressive in 1946–47 as the new industrial unions determined to prove their merits to their members by winning industry-wide agreements. The militancy contributed to the establishment of the Rand Formula and the 1948 passage of the *Industrial Relations and Disputes Investigation Act* (IRDIA), which together made permanent the gains embodied in PC 1003. Trade unions in Canada benefited enormously from the terms of the IRDIA, but the government intervention would also carry significant long-term costs.

THE POSTWAR COMPROMISE

The state intervenes in industrial relations when labour militancy — whether in the form of strikes, or political gains by labour's representatives, or both — threatens to upset the balance between capital and labour. In these circumstances the state makes certain concessions to labour, but also exacts a price in arranging a new class compromise to promote industrial and political peace. PC 1003 and the IRDIA formed the basis of the postwar industrial relations compromise.

In PC 1003 and the IRDIA trade unions won the basic right of recognition and the right to negotiate the terms of employment. The regulations legally bound employers to recognize and deal with any union that could demonstrate the support of a majority of the workers in a workplace. The long struggle for industrial unionism had been won; the benefits for legions of semi-skilled factory workers were immense.

But many of labour's gains were also weaknesses. The creation of grievance procedures, for example, represented a dramatic gain for workers because that system placed strict limits on managements' ability to treat workers in an arbitrary manner. The rule of law replaced, to a considerable extent, the arbitrary power of management. But the existence of a legal framework meant that many workplace problems were now to be resolved by professionals — lawyers and arbitrators. The problems were no longer to be solved by the direct and collective actions of workers.

In addition the system limited strikes, which became illegal during the period covered by a collective agreement. Workplace problems therefore could not be resolved by workers' direct and collective action, and if workers did make any such attempts, union officials would be expected, under the terms of the legislation, to push the employees back into the established mechanisms. Union representatives took on a policing role, in effect acting on behalf of the state to prevent **wildcat strikes** — strikes that violate the collective agreement and are not authorized by the union — thus, at times, setting them against their own union members.

Under this new regime, union officials spent a large proportion of their time negotiating and servicing collective agreements and spent much less time mobilizing workers — the main preoccupation of the 1930s and 1940s. Administration replaced mobilization and political education. The focus of member education shifted to their learning to use the rules prescribed in legislation and collective agreements. In effect, the union movement became bureaucratized and service-oriented, and the tasks of mobilizing and politically educating existing membership, and organizing in new industries, became more difficult.

These characteristics would pose particular problems later in the century, as the global capitalist system underwent dramatic changes that created a host of new challenges for the trade union movement — challenges to which labour would have difficulty responding.

WOMEN AND THE POSTWAR COMPROMISE

One of these challenges involved the role of women in unions. As Anne Forrest (1995: 139) argues, the postwar labour relations machinery was "fundamentally about the rights of working-class men." PC 1003 and the IRDIA were premised on the old notion of men as breadwinners and women as economic dependants, and so women's rights to good jobs and wages would be tightly restricted. Thus the rights contained in PC 1003 and IRDIA were exercised mostly by men, with the result that, in the following half-century, women in the private sector remained largely unorganized — and continue to be so today. The legislation's focus on single-establishment certification and its virtual preclusion of sympathy strikes discriminated against unionizing attempts in smaller, non-industrial, service and retail establishments that were part of multi-unit operations and were more likely to employ women. The postwar legislative framework represented "a construct of workers' rights shaped by the needs of blue-collar workers and men employed in the mass-production and resources industries" (Forrest 1995: 146). Not surprisingly, women in the service and retail sectors had much greater difficulty winning union recognition and satisfactory collective agreements; witness the long and unsuccessful struggles at Eaton's and at the Canadian banks, fought largely by, and lost by, women (see, for example, Sufrin 1982; Baker 1993; McDermott 1993). Even where unions were successfully established, in the industrial and resources sectors, women continued to be segregated in low-paid positions, union executives remained largely a male preserve, and women members' interests were generally ignored when bargaining demands were being constructed.

The situation was worse still for women of colour. Consider the case of those — many from the Caribbean and the Philippines — who came to

Canada under the Domestic Workers Program of 1955, to fill positions whose rates of pay and working conditions were sufficiently unattractive that they were hard to fill otherwise. As has so often been the case in Canadian history, people of colour were brought into the country to do the work that nobody else would do. In their countries of origin many of these women had been skilled workers — nurses, secretaries, teachers, for example. But as domestic workers in Canadian homes they were easily exploited and hard to unionize, even if unions had made the attempt to do so. In a labour force stratified along gender and ethnic/racial lines, women were particularly subject to exploitation, while women of colour — often confined to marginalized jobs such as domestic work — were even lower down on the scale.

THE COSTS OF THE POSTWAR COMPROMISE

The result of these various limitations to the postwar industrial relations system was that unions lost much of the capacity for mobilizing and educating rank-and-file members. Members became increasingly separated from their union representatives. Unions ceased to focus on the need to educate their membership. Attempts to create and maintain a distinctive working-class culture were largely abandoned. The postwar boom and the relatively attractive collective agreements that it made possible altered the whole character of the trade union movement. What emerged was much less radical, more settled and stable and bureaucratized. As Craig Heron (1996: 89) puts it, "Much union administration, collective bargaining and grievance work could be carried out in an orderly fashion from behind a desk or across a table." The changes led to a union movement whose structure and culture would not be fully adequate for dealing with the dramatic changes of the last quarter of the twentieth and the beginnings of the twenty-first centuries.

A hard-fought attempt by the Retail, Wholesale and Department Store Union to organize the T. Eaton Company's 15,000, mostly female, employees in Toronto revealed the limits of the new postwar industrial relations regime. The campaign started in 1948, financed by the Steelworkers and headed by Eileen Tallman, a first-rate, experienced CIO organizer. Some three years and $250,000 later, and despite a remarkable and frequently creative campaign, the union was defeated, in no small measure as a result of the atmosphere of fear created by the employer's virulent and expensive propaganda campaign. The postwar pattern was set: unions might now, finally, succeed in the mass-production industries where they had struggled unsuccessfully for fifty years; but the rapidly growing numbers of poorly paid and mostly female workers in the service and retail industries, and the growing numbers of workers of colour who would fill the **precarious jobs** — part-time, low-wage jobs without benefits — that would grow rapidly in the latter part of the twentieth century, would face the same frustrations as the industrial unions had encountered in the first half of the century.

COMMUNIST PURGE

Meanwhile, as the anti-left mentality of the **Cold War** — the post–Second World War period of high tension between the Soviet Union and its allies and the United States and its allies, during which the fear of and antagonism towards the U.S.S.R. grew dramatically in the West — fully set in, the Communist Party was being driven out of the Canadian trade union movement. Between 1948 and 1950 the Canadian Congress of Labour expelled the Mine, Mill and Smelter Workers' Union, United Electrical Workers, International Leather and Fur Workers, and International Woodworkers of America, in each case because of the strong Communist influence in the union. In 1949 the Trades and Labour Congress suspended the Communist-led Canadian Seamen's Union (CSU), leading to its replacement by the corrupt, gangster-ridden, U.S.-based International Seafarers' Union, headed by Hal Banks. Described as "the stuff of the Capones and Hoffas — a bully, cruel, greedy, dishonest, power hungry, contemptuous of the law" (Palmer 1992: 296) — Banks led a vicious campaign, supported by the employers and the Canadian government, to drive the CSU out of the Canadian shipping industry. "A decade later the price of this 'victory' over 'Communist domination' was revealed: 2,000 seamen had been blacklisted, not by employers but by the union; wage costs in the industry declined; employers and union officials defied the law to the detriment of workers in the trade" (Palmer 1992: 297). By the early 1950s the Communist influence in the Canadian trade union movement was largely erased — this despite the enormous contribution made by the party's organizers in the Workers' Unity League and then in the CIO drive in Canada, and even though Communist unions were generally democratic and fought effectively for the interests of their rank-and-file members.

So at the same time as the state-engineered compromise between class forces was being put firmly in place in the postwar period, and the union movement was being, to some extent, tamed and bureaucratized, many of the most militant and most effective trade unionists and trade unions were being driven from the house of labour, further diluting the movement's radicalism and capacity for militant action.

A CERTAIN COMPLACENCY

Times were good for most trade unionists in the 1950s. It was a time of unparalleled prosperity, and relative labour tranquillity. Business unionism prevailed. A certain complacency had set in. Union leaders serviced contracts; members were largely passive. Organizing was limited: the mass-production industries were largely unionized; and the postwar industrial relations framework made organizing in the rapidly growing service and retail sectors extremely difficult. New members were most easily gained through **raiding** — the attempt by one union to induce members of another union to defect and become members of the first, the raiding, union. Raiding had become a serious problem between TLC and CCL unions by the early 1950s. It was to bring this damaging practice under control, to overcome the long-standing split between the TLC and the CCL, and to secure the postwar gains that accrued to labour in a time of prosperity that the two major Canadian labour centrals agreed to their 1956 merger — made possible by the 1955 merger of the AFL and the CIO in the United States. The first Canadian Labour Congress convention was held in April 1956. While in the United States the cleavage between the AFL and the CIO was reflected in the name of the merged organization, the AFL-CIO, in Canada the organizers attempted to bridge the divide with an entirely new name. Further, the CLC and the social-democratic political party, the CCF, merged in 1961 to form the New Democratic Party.

In some ways, trade unionists had been lulled into what would later be seen as a false sense of security. The postwar economic boom carried on throughout the 1950s and 1960s, making possible increasingly high levels of consumption. Unionized working-class families were suddenly able — in a way they hadn't been in previous decades — to take out mortgages on homes in the suburbs and buy cars and a range of home appliances and even TV sets. The corporate media's constant message was that what existed in North America was the best of all possible worlds. The increasingly bureaucratized unions made relatively little effort by way of mobilization and education to counter these forces. Unions became increasingly distanced from their memberships; most of their members were passive recipients of the wage and benefit gains that unions were able to win. Still, at that very moment, the seeds of future problems were germinating.

THE END OF THE LONG BOOM, AND RENEWED LABOUR MILITANCY

Though seemingly tamed, the Canadian labour movement was still capable of outbursts of militancy. In the decade from the mid-1960s to the mid-1970s — at the end of the long post–Second World War boom — strikes rose consistently, from 274 in 1960 to a record 617 in 1966. From 1960 to 1965 the strikes were relatively small: the number of workers involved averaged 241; the amount of working time lost averaged 1,381,607 days and 0.10 percent of working time. In 1966, however, an average of 661 workers engaged in strikes, and the time lost jumped to 5,179,993 days and 0.34 percent of working time, the highest levels since 1946.

In his analysis of disputes in the 1960s, Stuart Jamieson (1968: 395–486) revealed that an increasing proportion of strikes were illegal wildcat strikes: "In 1965 they numbered 149 or 21 percent of the total 501 strikes, and in 1966, 210 or about one-third of the total 617" (Jamieson 1968: 401). Many of the strikes occurred when union members refused to ratify collective agreements, and a growing number involved "physical violence or intimidation, property damage, personal injury or death, arrests and convictions" (Jamieson 1968: 403). In 1957–59, nine such strikes had occurred; in 1960–66, seventy-five took place. Consistent with other studies, Jamieson noted that the increase in strikes reflected growing militancy and restlessness among union members aimed not only at employers, but also in many cases at union leadership.

Jamieson suggested that part of the explanation for this phenomenon was a significant increase in the proportion of young people in the workforce and in unions. In contrast to workers in the 1950s, who were preoccupied with job security and pensions, these younger workers were mainly concerned with rates of pay, shorter hours, and longer vacation times. They were dissatisfied with "the monotony, bureaucratic regimentation and submission to authority that is imposed by the discipline" of the authoritarian workplace (Jamieson 1968:482). While employers were prepared to bargain on rates of pay and vacation periods, they resisted all proposals that would give workers greater control over their working lives.

The renewed militancy continued for a decade. Of all the industrial disputes after 1900, one-quarter occurred in the period 1971–75, with the peak year being 1976 (Heron 1989: 105).

QUEBEC

A good deal of this militancy emanated from Quebec. In the post–First World War period, trade unionism in that province had been heavily influenced by the Catholic Church. The Canadian and Catholic Confederation of Labour (CCCL) was the product of the Catholic Church's attempt to nurture francophone culture and to keep the Quebec labour movement from falling into radical, secular, foreign hands. **Confessional unions** — founded and led by Catholic priests who promoted the ideal of co-operation between management and labour — were committed to recognizing the common interests of workers and employers and to using conciliation and arbitration rather than strikes to settle disputes. As a result of their conciliatory, conservative approach, between 1915 and 1936 only 9 of 507 officially reported strikes in Quebec involved confessional unions. The confessional unions' caution was complemented by the provincial government's anti-union and anti-left repression, including, most notoriously, the Padlock Act. Nevertheless, despite — or perhaps because of — this repressive atmosphere, labour militancy grew in Quebec in the 1940s, with a record-breaking number of strikes in 1942–43.

In 1945 a new leadership took over the CCCL. The Confederation recruited aggressive young organizers from Laval University, and the unions' link with the Church was weakened. Manufacturing employment, and union membership, grew dramatically. A new working class and a new union movement were being created in Quebec, with their emergence symbolized by a dramatic 1949 strike at the asbestos mines in Quebec's Eastern Townships. For seven months there, 5,000 militant workers in the CCCL battled the U.S.-based employer and the provincial government. The company brought in strikebreakers and evicted union members from their homes. Workers responded by setting up picket lines and barricades and effectively seizing control of the town of Asbestos. The riot act was read, strikers were beaten by police, and hundreds of them were arrested. The union was finally defeated.

But in defeat came victory. The Quebec unions' image of Catholic control and cautious conservatism was shattered, and the rallying of Quebec nationalists and intellectuals to the cause of the embattled asbestos workers made the strike a turning point in Quebec's social history. In effect, the event was an opening salvo in what would become known, after 1960, as Quebec's **Quiet Revolution**. In 1960 the Liberals under Jean Lesage formed the government in Quebec and set in motion the dramatic changes of that revolution, which included rapid urbanization, modernization, and secularization, an important part of which was a further radicalization of the province's labour movement. The former Catholic trade union central became the Confederation of National Trade Unions, and by 1960 had dropped all of its religious connections. The other major labour central, the Quebec Federation of Labour, was linked to the international unions and the Canadian Labour Congress. In addition to these two labour centrals there was the Quebec Teachers Union (CEQ).

By the late 1960s and early 1970s, all three had become radicalized, and were calling for fundamental changes in Quebec, including but not only the independence of the Québécois. In 1970 the FLQ crisis led to Prime Minister Trudeau's declaration of the *War Measures Act*, the entry of federal troops into Quebec, and the arrest of 419 Québécois, including more than twenty trade unionists. The following year each of the three major labour bodies published manifestos far more radical than anything seen in the postwar period, and they all expressed their commitment to a socialist Quebec. This turn of affairs represented the re-emergence of a link between militant trade unionism and socialist thought, which had played such an important part in the drive for industrial unionism in the first half of the century.

Public-sector unions were in the forefront of this militant labour outburst in Quebec. In 1972 Quebec's three major labour bodies, having agreed to a Common Front for bargaining with the Quebec government, walked out in a dramatic general strike of public-sector workers — the first

The FLQ Crisis and the War Measures Act:
The *War Measures Act* was a 1914 statute that conferred emergency powers on the federal cabinet, enabling cabinet to govern by decree when it perceived the existence of "war, invasion or insurrection, real or apprehended." The act was proclaimed during each of the two world wars, with detailed regulations placing limits on the freedoms of Canadians. The only domestic use of the *War Measures Act* was during the 1970 FLQ Crisis. Following the kidnapping on October 5, 1970, of British trade commissioner James Cross, and on October 10 of Quebec minister of labour and immigration Pierre Laporte, by separate cells of the Front de Libération du Québec (FLQ), the government of Pierre Trudeau declared, on October 16, 1970, that a state of "apprehended insurrection" existed in Quebec, and it invoked the *War Measures Act*. Federal troops were sent into Quebec, the FLQ was banned, normal individual freedoms were suspended, and the state was authorized to arrest and detain individuals without charge. The next day, October 17, Laporte's body was found in the trunk of a car. Those holding Cross were found in December 1970, and they negotiated safe passage to Cuba in return for his release; those who had murdered Laporte were captured shortly afterward and were tried and imprisoned for kidnapping and murder. The use of emergency powers and the suspension of Canadians' freedoms were, and are, hotly contested. Most Canadians at the time supported Trudeau's strong hand. Some, including civil libertarians and the NDP caucus led by David Lewis and Tommy Douglas, vigorously opposed the denial of Canadians' freedoms occasioned by the peacetime imposition of the *War Measures Act*.

general strike of public-sector workers and the largest strike in Canadian history. The Quebec government imposed back-to-work legislation, only to be defied by the three presidents of the Common Front, Marcel Pepin of the CNTU, Louis Laberge of the QFL, and Yvonne Charbonneau of the CEQ, who were jailed as a consequence. The strike spread: "In some towns complete general strikes erupted, and workers took over radio and television stations" (Heron 1989: 118). One interpretation of the strike is that, with the organizers lacking a clear programmatic direction and the full support of Quebec workers, the strike was defeated, and the consequences were severe: in addition to the leaders of the three major labour bodies, forty-nine local union leaders were jailed or fined or both. Some one-third of the CNTU's members left to form a new, more conservative union central, the CSD (Centrale des syndicats démocratiques). Another interpretation is more positive: the three jailed union leaders were released as the result of a wave of protest strikes in the public and private sectors, and the Common Front won its demand for a minimum pay rate for the lowest-paid public-sector workers, many of them women.

Public-Sector Unionism

Public-sector unionism was emerging elsewhere in Canada in the mid- to late 1960s. Indeed, many of the strikes in this renewed round of industrial militancy were public-sector strikes.

Earlier in the century, associations of public employees served largely as social and recreational clubs, later becoming involved in various non-union consultative mechanisms for discussing wages and working conditions. These associations were relatively weak: at best, they produced non-binding recommendations to cabinet. Public-sector unions had their origins with municipal workers (except for firefighters and police), who were for most of the twentieth century able to unionize under the private-sector labour relations legislation of each jurisdiction. Municipal workers constituted the "thin edge of the wedge" for the growth of public-sector unionism. This thin edge was widened when, in 1944, the newly elected CCF government of Tommy Douglas in Saskatchewan extended collective bargaining rights, including the right to strike, to provincial government employees.

Two decades later, in the context of the social and cultural upheavals of the 1960s and the Quiet Revolution, the Quebec government in 1965 extended collective bargaining rights to its employees. The federal government soon followed, in 1967, with the *Public Service Staff Relations Act*, which extended collective bargaining rights to federal government employees. Other provinces followed suit, so that in the decade 1965–75 provincial government employees in every province were granted bargaining rights of some kind. This was achieved quickly and without the bitter struggle that industrial workers had been forced to wage in the first half of the century. Between 1968 and 1986, union density in the public sector rose from 38.5 percent to 62.4 percent (Robinson 1993: 29–31).

A NEW UNION MOVEMENT

The emergence of public-sector unionism represented a dramatic change in the composition of Canada's trade union movement. It increased not only the proportion of public- versus private-sector unions, but also the proportion of Canadian versus international unions. It also increased both the proportion of union members who were white-collar workers and the proportion who were women.

A new working class was being created. The proportion of the labour force employed in traditional, industrial occupations was in decline; the proportion of white-collar workers — in the service and retail sectors, as well as the public sector — was growing. The trade union movement reflected this shift in the structure of the labour market. By 1980 nearly half (45.8 percent) of all trade union members in Canada were in public-sector unions, and Canada's two largest unions — the Canadian Union of Public Employees (CUPE) and the Public Service Alliance of Canada (PSAC) — were public-sector organizations. In addition, particular occupations always thought to have been "professions" began to be **proletarianized** — teachers and nurses especially. The nature of the labour process for nurses and teachers became more like that of industrial workers, and nurses and teachers came to see themselves less as "professionals" and more as workers, and thus in need of the protections and rights that come with unionization.

The face of the working class was changing rapidly, creating a host of challenges for a trade union movement that was still based on the industrial unionism and the labour relations machinery put in place during and immediately after the Second World War. This mismatch — between the changing character of the labour force and the static structure of the trade union movement — would become, by the end of the twentieth century, one of the most pressing challenges facing organized labour.

Women and Labour

At the same time the proportion of the labour force, and of trade union membership, made up of women was growing rapidly, creating yet another set of challenges to the union movement. Indeed, the structure of the labour force changed dramatically as the result of increasing numbers of women entering paid employment. In 1951, 23.6 percent of women aged fifteen years or more were in the labour force; by 1976 that figure had increased to 42 percent; and by 1999 it had risen to 54.6 percent (Statistics Canada 2000b: Table 5.1). In 2005 the **participation rate** of women — the proportion of women in the labour force, either employed for wages or actively looking for waged work — was 61.8 percent. As a result, women came to constitute a growing share of the paid labour force: 22 percent in 1951; just over 37 percent in 1976; almost 46 percent in 1999; and 49 percent in 2005 (Statistics Canada 2000b: Table 5.1; Statistics Canada 2006b: Table 8).

In the early part of the century most women in the labour force were young and single, but after the Second World War the participation rates of married women and women with children grew significantly. As Katherine Marshall (2006) reported in an article on gender roles: "Canadian women have one of the highest participation rates in the world, a rate that is converging with men's. For example, while the difference in labour force participation rates for men and women aged 25 to 54 was 24 percentage points in 1986 (94 percent for men; 70 percent for women), in 2005 it stood at 10 percentage points (91 percent versus 81 percent)."

In short, a higher proportion of women than ever before joined the paid labour force, and were staying in the paid labour force, even with young children at home. This phenomenon would have major consequences for trade unions.

As for the jobs these women moved into, the biggest increase was in clerical work. In 1901, only 5.3 percent of employed women were in clerical work, while 42 percent were in personal services (working in other people's homes) and almost 30 percent were in manufacturing (especially clothing and textiles). By 1991 the proportion of employed women in clerical work exceeded one-third, while the proportion in personal services and manufacturing had dropped to just over 15 and 10 percent respectively (White 1993: 48, Table 2-2).

The effects of these changes in women's labour-force participation were not felt in union membership until the burst of public-sector unionism from 1965 to 1975. The growth of public-sector unionism is the growth also of women in unions. For example, from the time of CUPE's inception in 1963, 32 percent of its membership consisted of women. From the inception of PSAC in 1966, 28 percent of its membership was made up of women. The unionization of teachers and nurses in the 1965–75 period added still more women to the union movement. The proportion of total union members who were women grew steadily after the mid-1960s: from 16.6 percent in 1965 to 26.0 percent in 1975, 36.2 percent in 1985, 42.7 percent in 1995, and about 50 percent in 2006 (Statistics Canada 2006a: 64–71).

Canadianization

In the 1960s and 1970s the proportion of Canada's total union membership who were in Canadian unions also grew rapidly. In large part this was due to the emergence of the public-sector unions; but a nationalist trend within the private-sector unions was also emerging. There had always, of course, been trade unionists who fought the U.S. control of Canada's union movement — and particularly the control by the conservative AFL — and worked to establish a fully Canadian industrial union movement. The OBU was one such example, as was the All-Canadian Congress of Labour. An interesting example of this trend in the 1970s was the Council (later the Confederation) of Canadian Unions (CCU), established by Kent Rowley and Madeleine Parent.

Rowley and Parent had earned their union credentials by organizing textile workers in Quebec for the United Textile Workers of America (UTWA) and by leading bitter strikes against the Dominion Textile Company in 1946 in Montreal and Valleyfield and in 1947 in Lachute. Despite their success in an industry whose workers were sorely in need of effective union representation, they were expelled by the Washington head office of the UTWA in 1952, in the midst of yet another strike against Dominion Textile. The entire process was corrupt and had little if anything to do with the interests of the textile workers. It was similar in some respects to the case of the Canadian Seamen's Union, and could not help but generate Canadian hostility to U.S.-controlled unions. Rowley and Parent responded by starting their own small Canadian union of textile workers, the Canadian Textile and Chemical Union. In 1969 they founded the Council of Canadian Unions, which in 1973 became the Confederation of Canadian Unions. The CCU was, to some extent, a part of the growing tide of Canadian left nationalism of the late 1960s and 1970s, a tide directed at the U.S. takeover of Canada's economy.

But the CCU was strongly opposed by the Canadian Labour Congress. In part this was because of the CCU's approach to creating Canadian unionism — attempting to lure locals of internationals to break away and join the CCU. Accused of raiding, the CCU became an outcast, and in the end was able to represent only a very small proportion of Canada's workers. Still, a case can be made that Rowley and Parent served as catalysts for the Canadianization of Canada's union movement, which would begin in the 1970s not with locals breaking away from internationals but rather with entire Canadian portions of internationals establishing independent Canadian unions. The creation in 1985 of the Canadian Auto Workers is the best known example. The 1974 creation of the Canadian Paperworkers' Union by the 52,000 Canadian pulpworkers in the United Paperworkers International Union was an important early example of what would become a powerful trend.

After 1965 four changes emerged together in the structure of the labour movement: the rise of public-sector unions; the growth of women in the paid labour force and in unions; the shift of the labour force away from manufacturing to the service sector; and the shift away from international unions to national unions. A new working class and a new trade union movement were in the process of being created, much in the way that a new working class and a new trade union movement had emerged early in the twentieth century. The changes represented, in essence, a third wave of unionism, after the emergence of craft unionism in the nineteenth century and of industrial unionism in the first half of the twentieth century.

THE ECONOMIC CRISIS AND AN ASSAULT ON LABOUR

Just as the third wave began to unfold, the long postwar economic boom came sliding to an end. It was replaced by economic stagnation and a growth in both inflation and unemployment, the combination known as **stagflation**. Corporations reacted to declining profit levels with various forms of restructuring; governments did likewise.

Unions responded to stagflation by seeking wage increases. The struggle for wage increases found expression in an increased level of labour militancy. By 1976, "The country was witnessing a full-scale rank-and-file revolt" (Heron 1989: 105). The government responded with a multifaceted assault on workers and trade unions.

The first step taken by the federal government of Pierre Trudeau was to encourage voluntary wage and price restraint. A Prices and Incomes Commission established in 1969 monitored wage and price increases and encouraged unions and firms to forego "excessive" increases in the public interest. This initiative came to naught. A second step came in October 1975, when the Liberal government, after campaigning in 1974 against such measures, stepped up the attack on labour by imposing a three-year regime of compulsory wage and price controls. Labour condemned the controls because they targeted wages, not prices. But the controls achieved the government's purpose. The rate of increase in wages dropped from over 14 percent in 1975 and 1976 to 6.8 percent in 1978. In that year real wages declined by 2.2 percent, while corporate profits increased. This outcome inspired increased labour hostility, and a renewed effort to make up lost ground.

The federal government responded by abandoning the idea of generalized wage controls, substituting instead changes in monetary policy that would drive up unemployment. A policy document prepared for cabinet by the Department of Finance in late 1980 argued that a policy of higher unemployment would reduce the bargaining power and militancy of unions and workers, driving down the rate of increase in money wages and eventually inflation (Black 1982).

In 1981, consistent with this deliberate use of monetary policy to increase unemployment, the Bank of Canada pushed interest rates to unprecedented levels, in excess of 20 percent. The result was a deep recession: unemployment jumped to 11.0 percent in 1982 and 11.8 percent in 1983, when almost a million and a half Canadian workers were unemployed. The recession achieved what the government wanted: strikes declined and real wages fell, as they had since 1978 and as they would until 1998.

The worst, for workers and their unions, was yet to come. In 1982 the federal government suspended the collective bargaining rights of public-sector workers and imposed wage increases over two years of 6 and 5 percent, in some cases rolling back already negotiated wage increases. Most provinces adopted similar legislation, curtailing the rights of public-sector workers and imposing wage settlements. The "6 and 5" policy of 1982 solidified an anti-union strategy that featured the abandonment of free collective bargaining and its replacement with the use of coercion. Prior to 1982 governments had on occasion used legislation to end strikes (Table 4.1). After 1982 the frequency of such legislative curtailments of free collective bargaining increased steadily.

In the 1950s and 1960s these interventions were justified as exceptions initiated in the public interest. It could be argued that they posed no threat to free collective bargaining. But by the late 1960s the exceptions began to look more like the rule. Governments were saying, in effect, that workers have the right to strike until they strike, and then government retains the power to strip them of that right. Canada had entered a new era in which what had been exceptions in the public interest now became the norm, leading Leo Panitch and Donald Swartz to call this the era of **permanent exceptionalism**. With the notable exception of the Manitoba NDP, every government brought in repressive labour legislation in the 1980s. The legislation was especially sweeping in Quebec, Saskatchewan, Alberta, and British Columbia (Panitch and Swartz 1993: 225–28).

Trade unions launched court actions challenging various of these government actions. Section 2 of the Charter of Rights and Freedoms in the 1982 *Constitution Act* identified "freedom of association" as a fundamental right. Labour argued that, to have meaning, this freedom must encompass the right to bargain collectively and to strike. After judgments in the lower courts produced contradictory rulings, the issue went to the Supreme Court for resolution in April 1987. A majority judgment ruled that workers were not guaranteed those rights under the Constitution. After a century and more of struggling for the right to bargain collectively and to strike, these rights were still not guaranteed.

The ruling merely confirmed what workers with a knowledge of the long history of labour's struggles already knew: many are the occasions when the state has trampled trade union rights to secure the interests of capital.

Table 4.1 Back-to-Work Measures, 1950–2004

	Federal	Provincial	Total	Annual Average
1950–54	1	0	1	.2
1955–59	1	1	2	.4
1960–64	2	1	4	.6
1965–69	2	8	10	2.0
1970–74	4	12	16	3.4
1975–79	6	19	25	5.0
1980–84	1	21	22	4.4
1985–89	5	22	27	5.4
1990–94	5	7	12	2.4
1995–99	4	9	13	2.6
2000–04	0	22	22	4.4

Source: Panitch and Swartz 2003: 184; Canada, Human Resources Development Canada, Labour Program (annual), 2003–04.

Capitalist Solidarity and the Lean State

Big business responded to the economic crisis of the early 1970s by, among other things, working to create a united and public voice. Its efforts culminated in 1976 in the formation of the Business Council on National Issues (BCNI).

The BCNI — now called the Canadian Council of Chief Executives (CCCE) — represented 150 of the largest corporations in Canada, many of them involved in the international economy as either transnational corporations or their subsidiaries. The impact of the BCNI on government policy was dramatic, significantly shifting public policy to the advantage of big business and against workers and unions. The BCNI played a central role not only in the promotion of the Canada–U.S. Free Trade Agreement (FTA) and the North American Free Trade Agreement (NAFTA), but also in championing anti-labour measures such as cutbacks in government expenditures on social programs and the restructuring of unemployment insurance. Through the BCNI and similar institutions, capital was acting as a class, and in distinct opposition to the interests of labour.

An extremely wide gulf in public-policy views existed between capital and labour. The only issue that labour and business seemed to agree upon was the use of wage controls to stop inflation. Big business opposed controls as an encroachment on the decision-making power of firms and out of fear that if the state set wages, other interventions might follow. Union leaders

Table 4.2 Class Cleavages in Canada

Percent Agreeing	**Business**		**Union Leaders**
Issue	**Big**	**Small**	
Prohibit hiring of strikebreakers	26	8	94
Legislation to reduce power of unions	51	69	6
Prohibit postal workers from striking	7	79	13
Employee representation on corporate boards	13	38	60
More government cuts to social programs	71	54	8
Establish guaranteed annual income	10	12	71
More government support for health and medical care	12	29	76
Too much difference between rich and poor	22	31	83
Approve of wage controls to combat inflation	9	29	19
Approve of tight money to combat inflation	84	68	30
Approve of government investments in industry	6	22	67

Source: Ornstein 1985.

Table 4.3 Political Parties Favoured by Corporate and Union Leaders

	Conservative	Liberal	NDP
Corporate leaders	63%	31%	1%
Union leaders	10%	23%	62%

Source: Ornstein 1985.

opposed controls as an encroachment on free collective bargaining and a device to shift income from labour to capital. On all other issues business and union leaders were polarized (see Table 4.2). A survey by Michael Ornstein (1985) revealed similar differences regarding political preferences at the federal level (see Table 4.3).

By the late 1980s–early 1990s, **neo-liberalism** — the reliance upon the forces of the market and the profit motive to make decisions about how society is to be organized, with minimal state intervention except to support corporations — was entrenched as the dominant ideology in Canada. It promoted the downsizing of the state through reduced expenditures and taxes, balanced budgets, and a reliance on market forces, private enterprise, and economic individualism. The federal Conservative government under Brian Mulroney had taken policy measures reflecting this ideology — free trade, privatization, deregulation, government downsizing — starting in 1984. In 1993, 1997, and again in 2000, Canadians voted into office majority Liberal governments led by Jean Chrétien, which only accelerated the neo-liberal strategy of dramatically slashing program spending. By 1997 most governments in Canada had balanced their budgets, and some provincial governments, in a throwback to the days of fiscal orthodoxy preceding the Great Depression, had established compulsory balanced-budget legislation.

Dramatic Cuts in Public Spending:
As economist Jim Stanford observes: "The scale of the spending reductions has been astonishing. At the federal level, program spending declined by $14 billion (or about 12 percent) from fiscal 1994 to fiscal 1996.... The cutbacks were experienced in all areas of the program budget: transfer payments to persons (such as UI benefits), transfers to provincial governments for health and education, and the federal government's own direct staffing and program expenses. Provincial governments have not only passed along federal cuts in transfer payments, but they have also added further cutbacks of their own. Provincial program spending declined by over $5 billion between 1993 and the second quarter of 1997. Taken as a whole, program spending in the total public sector declined from 40 percent of GDP in 1992 to just 33 percent of GDP by the spring of 1997."

Source: Stanford 1998: 44.

Jim Stanford (1998, 1999) and

others involved in the Alternative Federal Budget Project (CCPA and CHO!CES, 1997, 1998) have demonstrated that the achievement of balanced budgets resulted primarily from renewed growth in the economy, which in turn resulted from a relaxation of monetary policy — lower interest rates and an expansion of the money supply. Stanford (1998: 47) estimates that 60 percent of the federal government's deficit reduction from 1995 to 1997 was attributable to economic growth and lower interest rates, which not only stimulated growth but also reduced the costs of servicing the federal debt. Continued economic growth, then, would have eliminated deficits within a short time without the resort to drastic expenditure cuts. Stanford argues that the real purpose of government policies was to create a more "flexible" labour force — that is, to create the conditions that would force workers to be more willing to accept lower wages and benefits.

The net result of thirty years of attacks on labour was that by the early years of the twenty-first century, the seemingly secure place of the trade union movement in Canada's political economy had been severely undermined. The massive restructuring in the wake of the economic crisis of the early 1970s had been largely driven by, and accrued almost exclusively to the benefit of, big business. Labour was on the defensive.

That defensive position was true as well in the workplace, where big business was engaged in a similar process of restructuring, the result of which was to subordinate labour to the imperatives of the global marketplace. In some firms the response to the economic crisis took the form of

The Alternative Federal Budget:
The Alternative Federal Budget (AFB) was pioneered by the Winnipeg-based CHO!CES: A Social Justice Coalition, and an Ottawa-based think tank, the Canadian Centre for Policy Alternatives (CCPA). CHO!CES and the CCPA assembled a decision-making body comprising representatives of most of Canada's leading unions and social movements. This alone was an important achievement. The purpose was to prepare a budget that would serve as an alternative to the one prepared by the federal government. Using publicly available data about revenues and expenditures, they met the federal government's goals for deficit and debt reduction. Operating within these constraints, and thus forced to go through the difficult process of making compromises and tradeoffs when there are more demands than there is money to meet them, they were still able to show that the draconian cuts to public spending imposed upon Canadians were not, as the government and its corporate backers insisted, necessary. Governments' repeated claims that "there is no alternative" to drastic cuts to social programs were shown to be false, the product less of economic necessity than of conscious policy choices designed to advance the interests of some at the expense of others.

Consequences of the Attack on Labour in the United States—Lower Wages: The consequences of the attack on labour over the past thirty years in the United States have been colossal. As *The New York Times* reported: "In the first quarter of 2006, wages and salaries represented 45 percent of gross domestic product, down from almost 50 percent in the first quarter of 2001 and a record 53.6 percent in the first quarter of 1970, according to the Commerce Department. Each percentage point now equals about $132 billion."

Source: Greenhouse and Leonhard 2006.

the traditional **speed-up**: making workers produce more without significantly changing the organization of production or increasing pay. Other firms introduced new technologies: computerized reprogrammable machines, robotics, and computer networks in a wide range of manufacturing plants (Gertler 1991); mini-mills using electric-arc furnaces in the steel industry (Masi 1991); and telecommunications technologies in almost all sectors of the economy (Moody 1997: 72–73).

As well, many firms adopted Japanese methods of production. These involved, among other things, **just-in-time production** methods. In the JIT system, elaborate networks of small firms provide materials and parts to large firms just when needed and on an **outsourcing** or **contracting out** basis — that is, jobs are performed by outside contractors rather than by company employees. Wages and working conditions in the contracted out workplaces are inferior, and unionization rates are lower. Most often, JIT work means that full-time jobs are eliminated and replaced with part-time and casual jobs designed to more closely link labour services to peak-period demands (Morris 1991). Japanese methods also involved painstaking recruitment intended to weed out workers with a history of trade union involvement; concentrated training aimed at indoctrinating workers in the anti-union culture of the enterprise; and various worker participation schemes such as **quality circles** — groups of workers who meet regularly in the workplace, often with management assistance, to improve productivity and quality control — and **team production**, designed to create and sustain the idea that workers and their ideas mattered to the enterprise.

The firms intended the various teamwork schemes to promote worker and union co-operation and collaboration with management. In many plants where teams are introduced, total pay is contingent on output: the more workers exceed their quotas, the bigger is their pay. The company penalizes teams or individuals on teams that fall short of expectations. Workers end up policing each other in the company's interests. Team members absent from work (a woman whose child is sick, for example) may not be replaced; other team members have to push harder to make the quota. The result is that team members put pressure on colleagues who miss shifts or cannot sustain the pace of work. Worker is set against worker. As Michael Yates (1998: 73–74) puts it: "The dangers of the team concept are well documented, since they usually weaken the grievance procedure and eliminate hard-won work rules yet never give the union real *input* into the most fundamental management decisions."

The supposedly new methods of **lean production** — as this management system as a whole is sometimes called (Sears 1999) — were not at all new; they were old methods dressed up in a new guise. At their core was the "scientific management" approach designed by Frederick Taylor a century earlier at the birth of monopoly capitalism — a management system deliberately designed to weaken the power of labour.

Consequences of the Attack on Labour in Canada—Lower Wages:
"While job growth over the past decade has been healthy and has certainly benefitted working families, it is striking that, on average, there were no real wage gains whatsoever for workers in the recovery period from 1993 through 2003. Average weekly and average hourly earnings for all workers just about matched the increase in prices. At the end of 2003, the average hourly wage was $17.48 per hour compared to $17.70 per hour (adjusted for inflation) a decade earlier. Private-sector unionized workers saw a very modest real wage gain of just over 2 percent over the whole period, but real public-sector union wages fell by a bit more than 1 percent. Average annual earnings have increased by about 10 percent more than inflation, but this has been the result of lower unemployment and working more weeks in the year, not because of higher wages per hour."

Source: Jackson 2005: 19.

The 1980s and 1990s were characterized as well by company demands for concessions from workers and unions. Concession bargaining included: wage cuts; the introduction of two-tier wage systems that maintained the wages of existing workers but reduced the wages of new workers; fringe benefit givebacks; the acceptance of involuntary overtime; revised disciplinary procedures detrimental to workers; and the exclusion of casual and part-time employees from bargaining units. In non-unionized firms, employers simply imposed concessions. In unionized firms, employers demonstrated an increased willingness either to take the union on in a strike or lockout, or to shut down and relocate production.

THE CHANGING STRUCTURE OF THE LABOUR FORCE

In addition, two important trends in the 1980s and 1990s were changing the composition of the workforce: the growth of part-time work and self-employment; and the growth of low-wage jobs. The proportion of part-time jobs grew steadily, from under 5 percent in the 1950s to over 18 percent in 2004 (Statistics Canada 2005: Table 8). Over half the jobs created in the 1980s were **non-standard**; that is, other than permanent full-time jobs. In clerical, sales, and service occupations, six of every ten workers were now employed part-time, and they were more likely than full-time workers to be paid low wages and less likely to have access to benefits packages (Silver 2000: 5–9). They were also harder to unionize. Similarly, the numbers and proportion of self-employed workers grew significantly in the last quarter of the twentieth century. From 1977 to 2004 the number of self-employed Canadians doubled, and their share of the total numbers of employed workers grew from 12.8 to 15.4 percent (Statistics Canada 2001: Table 8). By 1995, according to Stanford (1999: 131), "Self-employment exceeded total employment in the public sector of the economy for the first time in Canada's postwar history." This dramatic growth in self-employment was closely connected to the restructuring of the Canadian economy — the downsizing of large corporations, cuts in government spending and the numbers of government employees, and high rates of unemployment. Self-employed workers, like part-time employees, earn lower incomes than do full-time employees, and they are much more difficult to unionize. This is the **"flexible" labour force** that, in the eyes of business and government, makes Canada more competitive in the global economy of free trade.

This flexible labour force also has an increasingly racialized character — that is, composed of workers of colour. The number of workers of colour have grown dramatically in the past thirty years due to changes in immigration laws since 1967 — roughly during the time that the flexible labour force has grown — and these workers, as Grace-Edward Galabuzi points out, have become "ghettoized" in "a racially hierarchical and segmented labour market."

> Canada's racialized groups (and particularly racialized women) bear a disproportionate burden of the demands for labour flexibility. Many end up in precarious employment — insecure and low-paying temporary, casual, contract, and home-based employment — and are often at the mercy of unscrupulous employers and employment agencies. Racialized groups thus provide a subsidy for the booming globalizing economy, drawing parallels to the contribution of... slave labour to the emergence of industrial capitalism. (Galabuzi 2006: xii)

As Canada's labour force rapidly becomes more and more **racialized** as the result of the country's growing reliance upon immigration to meet its labour needs, the recruitment and incorporation of workers of colour by trade unions, and the active pursuit of anti-racist policies by trade unions, will become even more important.

FREE TRADE

The problems of workers were further compounded by the free-trade agreements — FTA and NAFTA. The trade agreements were intended to tie the hands of governments, preventing them from intervening in the economy in a wide variety of ways to advance the interests of Canadians. The FTA and NAFTA opened the Canadian economy to greater competitive pressures, thus intensifying the campaign to drive down wages and harmonize labour-market and social institutions with those in the United States. The agreements have also accentuated a weapon that capital has always been able to use to control workers and unions: the threat of relocating production to right-to-work states and low-wage countries such as Mexico. Free trade, deregulation, and privatization became the three pillars of the neo-liberal era, adding dramatically to the ability of big business to control labour and the trade unions.

By the beginning of the twenty-first century, Canada's political economy had been radically reshaped. Lean governments now cater almost solely to the interests of business and have adopted policies that deregulated markets, weakened the social safety net, promoted greater inequalities in the distribution of income and wealth and a higher incidence of poverty, and dramatically restructured the labour force. The result is a trade union movement under assault.

We have also witnessed a profound change in the mindset and prevailing ideology in Canada. During the postwar boom a prevailing assumption was that economic and social problems could be solved collectively, through timely government interventions; now dominant voices argue that governments must get out of the way of business and entrepreneurs. During the postwar boom a prevailing belief maintained that we had an obligation to share the benefits of economic growth through a strong social safety net and social programs; now dominant voices tell us that such programs do more harm than good by interfering with market forces and destroying incentives. Neo-liberals tell us that we should worry only about ourselves, and leave the disadvantaged and less fortunate to make their own way. These neo-liberal beliefs have found expression in the success of the corporate-driven strategy to reduce taxes. As taxes are cut, so too is the capacity of governments to intervene against the forces of the market, and in favour of the collective interests of Canadian workers. This is the antithesis of the historic trade union culture of mutuality and solidarity.

The new set of institutions and the accompanying mentality that have been entrenched in the last thirty years have been characterized as a "Mean Streets" economy (Houston 1992; Palley 1998). Others have described the process as a transformation from a "Main Street" economy to a "Wall Street/Bay Street" economy (Bluestone and Harrison 2000; Stanford 1999). These authors suggest that not only does this new institutional framework serve the interests of business while being detrimental to the interests of organized labour, but also that it is riddled with contradictions that raise questions about its sustainability over the longer term. For example, Galabuzi (2006:

How Free Trade Works:
Free-trade agreements are not primarily about trade. They are about restricting the role of government.

The FTA and NAFTA place restrictions on the extent to which and the ways in which our democratically elected governments can intervene in the economy. Free trade ties the hands of governments. That is its real purpose.

When governments' hands are tied, more decisions are turned over to the private sector and thus, in practice, to the large transnational corporations that dominate the private sector. This is the real purpose of free trade: to reduce the powers of governments and turn those powers over to corporations.

This practice erodes democracy. Citizens have at least some control over governments — for example, by means of the vote — but we have little or no control over corporations, which are not at all accountable.

Why is free trade called "free"? First, it is not citizens who are made "free" by free trade. On the contrary, our freedom is eroded, because we come to have even less control over the institutions that shape so much of our lives.

Corporations get more control because they are freed from government restrictions. This is where the "free" in free trade comes from — corporations are made more free from government restrictions.

Corporations have increased their demands for these freedoms as they have become bigger and more global in their operations. As they move about the globe, they find various government restrictions burdensome and expensive. They want to be "freed" from these restrictions. Yet what corporations see as burdensome restrictions, most of the rest of us see as hard-won benefits and rights. Environmental protection, labour laws and standards, minimum wages, and health and safety legislation are examples.

It should therefore come as no surprise that the bodies that supported the original Canada–U.S. Free Trade Agreement, and that are pushing now for more of the same through the World Trade Organization, are transnational corporations and business associations. Free trade, then, should be seen as a class issue: it benefits big corporations; it harms working people.

Free trade deals harm working people in two main ways: 1. They prohibit many government initiatives that benefit working people. 2. They open Canada up to more competition from U.S. and other corporations, thereby inducing a "race to the bottom."

The "race to the bottom" means that, in the face of increased competitive pressures, corporations will feel the need to restructure their operations by laying off workers and by driving down wages and social benefits in order to be able to produce at lower costs.

> If corporations cannot force costs down low enough to be competitive, they may move somewhere else in the world where wages and other costs are lower. Free trade makes it easier for them to be mobile in search of maximum profits, because it removes obstacles to their movement.
>
> Therefore, working people will be under even greater pressure to lower wages and benefits and to reduce labour and environmental standards and social programs, or risk companies moving away and jobs being lost.
>
> *Source: Silver and Shaw 1998.*

7) argues that although racialized workers are particularly exploited in this neo-liberal era, "Ironically, the racializing of the division of labour may serve to undermine the neo-liberal project by mobilizing racialized workers in solidaristic formations based in workplaces where they predominate." The obvious question is: how long will working people be prepared to accept diminished rights in labour markets and workplaces, and the denigration of their role as citizens, in exchange for the promise — for now simply a promise — of better times ahead?

This is where we have arrived. The question we now turn to is: what were unions doing during this transformation?

LABOUR'S RESPONSE TO THE TRANSFORMATION OF CANADA

In some important respects, unions in Canada have fared better than unions in the United States during the neo-liberal era. Unionization, after all, has not declined as drastically in Canada. Canadian unions have also demonstrated a greater willingness to oppose concession bargaining.

The differing approaches to concession bargaining by unions in Canada and the United States show themselves clearly in the case of the autoworkers in the two countries. In 1982 in the United States the United Auto Workers (UAW) adopted a strategy of concession bargaining in exchange for promises of greater job security and improved conditions in the future. Their position was "short-term pain for a promise of long-term gain." The Canadian UAW took the opposite stance, saying "No to Giving Up and Giving Back" (Gindin 1995: 185), opting instead to press for wage increases, improved working conditions, and additional benefits. This brought the Canadian UAW into conflict with union leaders in Detroit. The UAW achieved a settlement with automakers in the United States that included concessions; the Canadian UAW fought concessions and was able to make modest gains. The difference in strategies was apparent again in 1984 when the UAW settled peacefully with the automakers, while in Canada autoworkers struck GM to achieve annual gains in wages — a special Canadian adjustment. The tensions arising from the opposing strategies in the United States and

No to Concession Bargaining:
With respect to concession bargaining, labour analyst Donald Swartz states: "With Canadian autoworkers in the lead, the CLC formally rejected concession bargaining and pledged its support for struggles by workers resisting such demands. Concession bargaining was rejected, not just because concessions were seen to be contrary to workers' immediate interests, but because the unions perceived that selling defeats as victories, and cooperation with employers as the way to secure workers' interests, would undermine the very basis of unions as vehicles for collective struggle by workers."

Source: Swartz 1993: 390.

Canada led in 1985 to a "divorce," and the formation of the Canadian Auto Workers Union.

Fighting concessions did not always yield such positive results. In the 1986 case of the Gainer's meat-packing plant in Edmonton, for example, the stage was set for concession demands in Canada by developments in the meat-packing industry south of the border. The United Food and Commercial Workers Union in the United States reversed its policy on concessions in the 1980s from one of opposition to one of compliance, largely because of a reluctance by members in many plants to oppose employers with strike action. Demands for concessions spread to Canada, but encountered opposition from Canadian members of the UFCW. When Gainer's in Edmonton demanded concessions, workers struck the plant and waged a bitter and protracted battle. This strike involved the use of scabs as well as mass arrests and a strong public reaction against both the employer and the anti-union posture and legislation of the Alberta government. The union and workers won the battle, but lost the war: Maple Leaf subsequently bought the plant and again demanded major concessions. Workers struck again; Maple Leaf shut the plant down. Now concessions are pervasive in the meat-packing industry, in Canada as in the United States.

Such battles took place in most sectors of the economy. In many situations workers voluntarily made concessions in bids to save their jobs. This was especially true in the slumps in the early 1980s and early 1990s. In other cases workers fought back but found it difficult to win in the cold climate that had settled over industrial relations in Canada. A recent survey of unions demonstrates that things did not improve appreciably in the late 1990s. When asked about their recent experiences in bargaining, more than three of every four unionists surveyed replied that demands for concessions in wages and benefits, and in work rules, had increased; fewer than 4 percent reported that such demands had decreased (HRDC 1998a: 49).

Neo-liberalism has also taken its toll in the public sector, often in the form of privatization and contracting out to create the "flexible" workforce that is a primary objective of neo-liberalism and the lean state. In British Columbia from 2002 to 2005 a series of struggles pitting the anti-labour, neo-liberal government of Premier Gordon Campbell against public-

> Racialized Women in a Segmented Workforce:
> "Non-English-speaking and racial-minority immigrant women are part of a segregated and marginalized workforce and are employed mainly in three areas: private domestic service, service industries and light manufacturing. Many immigrant racial-minority women working in the public sector are employed as cleaners, cafeteria workers, nurses' aides, and lower-level clerical workers (Vorst et al. 1989). Brand (1987) observed that most Black women work at low-status jobs in homes and institutions and do 'Black women's work'"
>
> *Source: Henry et al. 2000: 106.*

sector unions typified the attacks against public-sector workers, and also demonstrated both a powerful resistance by workers and broadly based support for their cause. One of those struggles, for example, came in the Health Employees' Union (HEU) strike of 2004. Some 85 percent of the members of that union were women, and almost one-third of the members were workers of colour. Most members — as typical in the racialized neo-liberal labour market — were doing food service, laundry, housekeeping, and other support work in hospitals and long-term care facilities. They went on strike against legislation that imposed wage cuts and contracting out, and stayed out in defiance of back-to-work legislation. They did so with a spirit of determined resistance that managed to crystallize the public's anger with a harshly neo-liberal government, and that proved to be the catalyst for a popular mobilization of support from other unions, especially but not only CUPE, and from broad sectors of the general public. The mobilization and degree of support were so strong that calls came for a general strike, reminiscent of the B.C. Solidarity movement in 1983. Similarly reminiscent was the settlement that was eventually reached, negotiated by the union leadership and without a membership ratification vote. It left many thinking that the strike was ended too soon and that continued defiance was warranted.

David Camfield (2006) has posed this debate in a useful way. Did the union leadership agree to a concessionary settlement because they believed that what they were getting was the best that could be achieved and that any further strike action would result in government retaliation that would cause long-term damage to the union and its members? Or did the union leadership settle because they did not want to give the Campbell government grounds for an attack on HEU in the form of "Who is running the province, the elected government or the unions?" which would hurt NDP electoral prospects? Or was a concessionary settlement agreed to because union leaders became socially removed from rank-and-file members and would not push for members' interests outside the legal framework of collective bargaining? As was the case in the province in 1983, union leaders did not push as far as union and other radicals would have liked them to have done, leaving many disappointed. Both struggles, in 1983 and 2004, are worth studying more closely for the lessons that trade union members can draw from them.

Mergers and Canadianization

Under siege and in some cases facing declining memberships, many unions looked to mergers as a way of adding members and money so as to strengthen their capacity to fight back. As well, some Canadian branches of international unions found themselves increasingly constrained by the policies and practices established by their U.S.-based parents, and opted for independence.

The number of union mergers in Canada increased consistently after the 1960s: fifteen in the 1960s; twenty-six in the 1970s; twenty-nine in the 1980s; and nineteen in 1990–93 (Chaison 1996). An increasing proportion of mergers over this period consisted of outright absorption (the takeover of one union by another) as opposed to amalgamations (the formation of a new union out of two or more existing unions). The proportions of total mergers taking the form of outright absorptions are: 53 percent in the 1960s; 81 percent in the 1970s; 79 percent in the 1980s; and 95 percent in 1990–93 (Chaison 1996: 58).

Gary Chaison attributes the increased merger activity to the more difficult conditions facing unions in the last quarter-century and to greater political and economic uncertainties. Chaison (1996: 59) concludes:

> These circumstances are forcing large Canadian unions (for example, CAW, CUPE) to turn to absorptions as alternatives to traditional organizing, while small ones merge to avoid stagnation and decline. The new complexity and higher stakes of bargaining, particularly the need to evaluate and counter employers' proposals for wage moderation, downsizing and work rule modifications have [forced small unions to throw in their lot with larger ones]. Finally, although labour's approach to politics may be in flux, a large, expanding and nationwide membership resulting from merger still provides political clout and a dominant role in coalitions. These are the same factors that union leaders identify in their assessment of the key factors influencing industrial relations. In the HRDC survey, unions cited government budget/spending cuts (74 percent), employer attitudes (63 percent), economic uncertainties (62 percent), industry restructuring (57 percent), and adverse changes in labour legislation (56 percent) as very important determinants of the industrial relations climate. (Chaison 1996: 48)

Another change — the rise in the number of unions previously part of international unions that reconstituted themselves as national unions — has had a great effect on the shape of unionism in Canada. As late as 1977, after the wave of public-sector unionization, 59 percent of union members were still in international unions. By 1994 international membership had declined to 30 percent, which is roughly where it is today. Two of the largest, most powerful, and most diversified unions in Canada now are CAW and CEP. Between them they have more than 400,000 members. Both were built in the same way: separation from international unions and expansion through mergers. What was once just autoworkers now includes workers in airlines, railways, the fishing industry, and other segments of manufacturing. The CEP brought together unions in the chemical, paper, and communications industries. Given the continuing pressure on unions, merger activity will most likely continue to figure prominently in the restructuring of the union movement in Canada, as small unions are driven to the wall and big unions seek to build their memberships and strength.

Interestingly, these developments strike a chord with the drive for industrial unionism that occurred early in the twentieth century and the argument then, by more radical unionists, for one big union. The idea was that in unity was power. Today the merger movement in Canada is creating mini-versions of the one big union — unions that represent large numbers of workers in several crucially important industries. The potential political power of these merged unions is considerable, because they have the capacity to shut down important sectors of the economy.

By the early years of the twenty-first century, following thirty years of unrelenting attacks by capital and the state, the Canadian trade union movement was holding its own, having suffered not nearly as much as U.S. trade unions. Still, many formidable challenges confront the Canadian trade union movement today as the dynamic changes at the heart of capitalism continue to alter the economic world in which trade unions operate.

If they are to effectively defend and advance the interests of their members, unions in Canada are going to have to draw upon, and further develop and refine, the creative militancy that led to so many gains for working people in the twentieth century.

CHAPTER 5

ACTING POLITICALLY

Trade unions get involved in politics in part because political decisions shape the legal and regulatory framework within which unions operate. Are unions to be outlawed or legal? Will employers be required or not required to recognize and bargain with unions that have the support of a majority of employees? Will the law make it more or less difficult to organize? To negotiate first contracts? To strike? The answers to these questions and many more are a function of political decisions.

Unions also get involved in politics because the interests of workers extend beyond the workplace. Should we have strong or weak social programs? Should health care and education be provided on a private, for-profit or a public, not-for-profit basis? These questions and others like them are political matters in which trade unions and their members have a direct interest. To defend these interests, trade unions need to act politically.

But what is the best way of doing that? Is it to influence existing political parties, supporting the ones that are friendly to labour, opposing the ones that are not? Is it to establish a separate political party that would represent labour's interests? Is it to abandon political parties and parliamentary politics altogether and confine efforts to revolutionary industrial unionism and the general strike? Is it to abandon both parliamentary politics and direct action in favour of educating the working class to create the revolutionary consciousness necessary for the socialist revolution and the elimination of the wage system? At various times in the past one or another segment of Canada's labour movement has practised each of these approaches to politics. Indeed, differences over how best to engage in politics have from the beginning helped to keep the union movement in Canada divided. How best to engage in politics continues to be a source of division, and a particularly contentious one, in the first decade of the twenty-first century.

The relationship between capital and labour, between corporations and trade unions, is conflictual, or oppositional. Business and labour oppose each other across the bargaining table over such matters as wages, benefits, and working conditions. Business and labour oppose each other beyond the workplace over a wide range of public policy issues; and Canada's mainstream political parties most often advance the interests of business on these various matters. The Liberals and Progressive Conservatives, and more recently the Reform Party and Canadian Alliance, and now the

Conservative Party of Canada — the neo-conservative result of the takeover by the Canadian Alliance of the former Progressive Conservative Party of Canada — represent the interests of business to a far greater extent than they represent the interests of labour.

But throughout the past century a wide variety of non-mainstream political parties have advanced the interests of labour. None of these parties has ever formed the government at the federal level — although there has been more success at the provincial and territorial levels — and, at least at the federal level, none of these parties has ever won the support of a majority of those they sought to represent — workers and trade union members. Yet the conflictual character of the relationship between capital and labour necessitates that the interests of labour be represented not only at the workplace, by unions, but also beyond the workplace, by political parties committed to the interests of labour.

PARTYISM

In the nineteenth century, most unions, or at least union leaders, supported one of the two main political parties — the Conservatives or the Liberals. In the 1870s it was the Conservatives, the result of Prime Minister John A. Macdonald's introduction of the *Trade Unions Act* in 1872.

By the beginning of the twentieth century the establishment of a federal Department of Labour and introduction of the *Industrial Disputes Investigation Act* were winning trade union support for the Liberals. For most of the twentieth century, and irrespective of the political strategy adopted by their union leaders, more rank-and-file members of Canadian trade unions would support the Liberals than they would any other political party. This support continued to be the case at the federal level even after the establishment in 1961 of the union-supported New Democratic Party.

The political strategy of supporting one or the other of the existing political parties — **partyism** — emerged independently in Canada, but was consistent with the dictum of AFL president Samuel Gompers: "Reward your friends, punish your enemies." Gompers opposed the creation of an independent labour party, and especially opposed socialism. He believed in working within the existing party framework. Most craft-based unions have practised this form of politics. The results, however, have been limited. The existing parties are and have always been dominated by the business community. Labour's interests are an afterthought. As early as the 1870s some trade union leaders, seeing this, sought to elect independent labour candidates.

By the mid-1880s, some labour candidates were running under "Liberal-Labour" or "Labour-Conservative" banners. In some cities this movement was further developed as independent labour organizations emerged — for example, the Workingmen's Political Club of Cape Breton, and the Hamilton Labour Political Association. For the rest of the nineteenth century, however, electoral victories were few and the fledgling labour political associations short-lived.

LABOURISM

Nevertheless, efforts to go beyond partyism to a more independent labour politics continued to be made, and in the first two decades of the twentieth century they enjoyed considerable success. The objective of **labourism** was to elect workers, on the grounds that only workers could adequately represent the interests of labour.

Labourism was not a radical ideology. It was largely the expression of skilled crafts workers seeking to institute reforms that would benefit labour. In the period before the First World War, labourism was, especially at the local level, very successful. Many labour candidates were elected to school boards, municipal councils, and provincial legislatures, and almost every industrial community had an Independent Labour Party — even though these organizations tended to be small and short-lived. Sometimes these local parties federated to establish provincial labour parties. This happened in Ontario and Manitoba, albeit briefly, in 1906–07, and more broadly across the country after 1916, when Independent Labour parties were established in Nova Scotia and Ontario, Dominion Labour parties on the prairies, and the Federated Labour Party in British Columbia.

Yet labourism was highly fragmented and decentralized and somewhat episodic. When industrial conflict swelled up, independent labour organizations would emerge, but when the conflict subsided the organizations would atrophy. Many of the members would drift back to the left wing of the Liberal Party, as happened, for example, with three labour candidates elected federally before the First World War — Ralph Smith, Arthur Puttee, and Alphonse Verville — each of whom quickly slid back into the Liberal caucus. Nevertheless, the numerous local successes, although relatively limited and short-lived, formed part of the foundation upon which a social-democratic party — the Co-operative Commonwealth Federation — would later be built.

SYNDICALISM

While labourism was the dominant form of labour politics east of the Rockies prior to the First World War, syndicalism was an important political variant in British Columbia and Alberta. Labourism was a product of the circumstances and needs of crafts workers; syndicalism emerged in the much rougher working conditions faced by metal miners, loggers, and other, often itinerant and/or immigrant, resource-based workers.

Syndicalists eschewed political parties and legislative bodies, preferring direct action at the workplace. For the syndicalists, revolutionary industrial unionism and the general strike were what independent labour candidates and labour parties were to labourism. The Industrial Workers of the World was an especially prominent syndicalist organization. Established in 1905 in Chicago, and openly hostile to the Trade and Labour Congress and its U.S. parent — the "American Separation of Labor" to the IWW — the Wobblies were committed to revolutionary industrial unionism. For them, the final battle against capitalism would come in the form of the general strike, although exactly how this might happen was never fully clear.

The Wobblies organized the itinerant, often immigrant workers — loggers, miners, railway navvies, construction workers, harvest hands — who were ignored by the crafts unions. Packing their blankets for beds as they tramped the country and rode the rails in search of work, these workers — few of whom met the citizenship or residency requirements to vote — were the targets of the Wobblies' often multilingual organizing efforts. Wobbly organizers worked the street corners in the urban skid rows where itinerant workers returned between jobs, and led the struggle for 'free speech' when local police tossed them in jail for their efforts. In remote logging and railway and mining camps the Wobblies used music, and especially the songs of Joe Hill, to do their organizing. Many who rode the rails came to carry the Wobblies' red organizing card. According to Wobbly

Joe Hill:
I dreamed I saw Joe Hill last night
Alive as you and me
Says I,
"But Joe, you're ten years dead"
"I never died," says he
"I never died," says he.
"In Salt Lake City Joe, by God,"
says I
Him standing by my bed
"They framed you on
a murder charge"
Says Joe, "But I ain't dead"
Says Joe, "But I ain't dead."
"The copper bosses killed you Joe"
They shot you Joe," says I
"Takes more than guns
to kill a man"
Says Joe, "I didn't die"
Says Joe, "I didn't die."
And standing there as big as life
And smiling with his eyes
Joe says, "What they forgot to kill
Went on to organize
Went on to organize,"
"From San Diego up to Maine
In every mine and mill
Where workers start to organize"
Says he, "You'll find Joe Hill"
Says he, "You'll find Joe Hill."
I dreamed I saw Joe Hill last night
Alive as you and me
Says I,
"But Joe, you're ten years dead"
"I never died," says he
"I never died," says he.

Lyrics by Alfred Hayes
Music by Earl Robinson.

legend the last words of Joe Hill, the Wobbly singer/songwriter who was executed in Salt Lake City in 1915, were "don't mourn for me, organize!"

But it was the campaign for industrial unionism and the use of the general strike that constituted the real challenge to the political establishment. Although the IWW was in decline by 1913–14, the Wobbly ideas found expression in the great wartime labour revolt that led to the One Big Union and the Winnipeg General Strike.

SOCIALISM

Alongside labourism and syndicalism there emerged in Canada in the late nineteenth and early twentieth centuries a Marxist-inspired, worker-based socialism. Its first important expression, arising out of the amalgamation in 1904 of several smaller socialist parties, was the Socialist Party of Canada.

In its early years, the SPC promoted the "uncompromising principles of revolutionary socialism" and adopted a form of politics sometimes called by some **impossibilism**. The official view of the SPC was that it was impossible to reform capitalism and the pursuit of reform was therefore futile, as was the election of labour candidates. Socialist education, in preparation for the workers' revolutionary overthrow of capitalism and the wages system, took precedence over the parliamentary struggle for immediate reforms of the labourists, or the direct action of the syndicalists.

Members of the SPC were leading figures in what was a rich political culture — a culture of ideas and public debate — in early twentieth-century Canada. Worker-intellectuals of the SPC were remarkably well-read, especially but not only in the Marxist classics, and "were willing to debate anyone of any political persuasion, anytime, anywhere" (Campbell 1999: 247). Many SPC locals held weekly educational meetings, and SPC members were leading participants in Sunday evening open forums that attracted thousands of people each week, in major cities across the country, to debate all manner of political issues and ideas.

The party's official refusal — its more than occasional practice to the contrary notwithstanding — to support the struggle for immediate reforms led to a split. The result was the creation in 1911 of the Social Democratic Party of Canada (SDPC), whose members, while still Marxists, were as a matter of principle more prepared to contest elections in pursuit of immediate reforms. But a second generation of SPC leaders, including R.B. Russell, was more closely linked to the union movement and more committed to radical political action, and it was this renewed SPC that played a key role in the founding of the One Big Union and the 1919 Winnipeg General Strike.

Women were involved with the Socialist Party of Canada, but they comprised less than 10 percent of the party's membership and were confined largely to subordinate roles. The party adhered to the notion of the "male breadwinner" and the "family wage." It frowned upon the formation of autonomous women's committees. The editor of the SPC paper, the *Western Clarion*, opposed demands for a women's column, leading B.O. Robinson of Toronto to write, "Women with spirit of revolt aroused in them can never be encouraged to join such an obvious men's movement" (L. Kealey 1984: 89).

The SDPC was somewhat more open than the impossibilist SPC to women's involvement and the promotion of women's issues, and it did encourage the establishment of separate women's committees. In British Columbia these were numerous enough "to require a provincial secretary to organize them" (L. Kealey 1984: 95), and in 1913 the party established a Women's Social Democratic League in Ontario.

Nevertheless, the role and concerns of women were secondary to the male-dominated class struggle in early twentieth-century Canadian socialist parties, as in trade unions more generally. The struggle by women for an equal role in the politics of unions, and of political parties, including socialist parties, seeking to represent the interests of unions, would be long and bitter.

Even longer has been the struggle by racialized workers who have usually, with some important exceptions, been confined to the most precarious and unattractive forms of employment, and kept outside the ranks of unions and pro-labour political parties.

THE 1919 STRIKES

The Winnipeg General Strike and the sympathy strikes all across Canada can be viewed as the culmination of the radical, worker-based, Marxist-inspired, syndicalist and socialist strands that had for two decades struggled against employers, the state, and the crafts-based unions to emerge as significant elements of Canada's labour politics. Other strands — labourism, and the cautious partyism of the Trades and Labour Congress — were pushed to the side; thousands of workers in TLC unions abandoned their cautious approach and were swept up in the radical, even revolutionary, mood of the times.

But the 1919 strikes were defeated; the rising wave of revolutionary militancy was stopped in its tracks (see chapter 4). The consequences for trade union politics were momentous: the virtual elimination, as a viable political option for Canadian trade unions, of both syndicalism and the independent, Canadian-controlled, Marxist-inspired socialism of the century's first two decades; and a dramatic realignment of the politics of organized labour.

THE COMMUNIST PARTY OF CANADA: 1921–35

A majority of the Socialist Party of Canada, a minority of the Social Democratic Party of Canada, and almost all of the even more impossibilist Socialist Party of North America (formed in 1915 in Southern Ontario as another breakaway from the SPC) joined the Communist Party of Canada (CPC), formed in 1921. These Canadian-based, independent, Marxist-inspired parties were replaced by a party that, although worker-based in both its leadership and its membership, took its ideology and direction from Moscow. It was the Communist Party of Canada's relationship with Moscow, and the resultant twists and turns in policy that were the product of that relationship, that would be the party's central weakness.

> Lenin:
> Vladimir Lenin was the leader of the Bolshevik Party, which overthrew the Russian Tsar in October 1917, ushering into existence the world's first socialist state, the Union of Soviet Socialist Republics. Lenin was forced to step down in 1923, the result of a second, crippling stroke, and he died in 1924. A brilliant political thinker and tactician, he was almost certainly the most influential political leader and theorist of Marxism in the twentieth century. His ideas, forged in the particular circumstances of early twentieth-century Russia, came to be at least a part of the basis of the operation of communist parties throughout the world. Lenin's ideas were seriously distorted, however, by his successor, Stalin. Stalinism bore little if any resemblance to the political thought of Karl Marx.

In the early 1920s the CPC, relying upon instructions provided by Lenin in his pamphlet *Left-Wing Communism: An Infantile Disorder*, worked within the TLC to build a left-wing current. But by 1926 the CPC was shifting its strategy, acting outside the TLC to organize industrial unions; for example, the Mine Workers Union of Canada headed by the great Cape Breton union leader J.B. McLachlan (Frank 1999), and the Lumber Workers Industrial Union in Northern Ontario. The CPC initially supported the establishment of a new, Canadian trade union central, the All-Canadian Congress of Labour, only to abandon it by the late 1920s, clearing the way for the creation in 1930 of the Workers' Unity League. The WUL was the source of almost all the union and unemployed organizing that occurred in the first half of the 1930s, culminating, symbolically, in the dramatic On-to-Ottawa Trek of 1935. But then, in yet another of its Moscow-directed reversals, the WUL was dissolved and its unions instructed, a decade after leaving it, to rejoin the TLC.

Its constant reversals of strategy and obvious subservience to Moscow undermined the party's credibility, and eroded the possibility of labour-left unity. Nevertheless, many of the outstanding Communist trade union organizers, whose skills had been honed in the militant and often highly creative WUL, went on, under the banner of the CIO, to build the industrial union movement in Canada in the decade after 1935. Clearly, any evaluation of the Communist Party's work with trade unions must recognize these many contradictions.

THE EMERGENCE OF THE CCF

In the immediate aftermath of the 1919 Winnipeg General Strike, Canada's traditional two-party system broke down, the result in part of electoral victories by labour representatives, but even more the result of the massive electoral success of the "Farmers' Revolt." Between 1919 and 1922, farmer-based governments were formed in Ontario, Alberta, and Manitoba, while at the national level sixty-five members of the farmer-based Progressive Party were elected in 1921, along with two labour representatives. The farmers' revolt not only broke apart the national two-party system, opening the door for the rise, mostly in Western Canada, of relatively radical third parties, but also shaped the character of the **social democracy** that would struggle to emerge over the next decade.

What Canadian social democracy would look like was the subject of considerable debate and conflict throughout the 1920s. A great many organizations and ideological currents were part of a complex political landscape. Independent, provincially based labour parties had emerged or re-emerged in the immediate aftermath of the 1919 Winnipeg General Strike. So too had the farmers' movements. How best could these political

Social Democracy:
Social democracy has its intellectual origins in the political thought of Eduard Bernstein, a leading German Marxist who, at the turn of the century, advanced significant revisions to Marxist theory. Bernstein, who was influenced by the British Fabian socialists, laid the intellectual groundwork for a shift from a revolutionary to a gradualist and reformist socialism, which eventually became transformed into the still more moderate social democracy.

Social democracy accepts, and seeks to gain office by means of, the existing electoral system, and seeks then to use the state to reform, rather than to replace, capitalism. Central features of social democracy include an increased degree of state intervention in the economy, usually including at least some state ownership, and the development of the range of social programs that constitute the welfare state, together with the maintenance of a multiparty system and the civil liberties intrinsic to liberal thought.

The Cooperative Commonwealth Federation was a social-democratic party. Whether its successor, the New Democratic Party, remains a social-democratic party or has moved further to the centre of the ideological spectrum so that it is now indistinguishable from reform liberalism is open to question.

forces be brought together? Some participants advocated the establishment of a British-style labour party. Others called for a farmer-labour party; still others called for a people's party. The central figure in navigating these complex political waters and creating a distinctive Canadian form of social democracy was J.S. Woodsworth.

Woodsworth was among those charged for his involvement in the 1919 Winnipeg General Strike. He was also, along with William Irvine of Alberta, one of the two labour representatives elected to the House of Commons in 1921. Irvine informed the Speaker of the House of Commons: "The honourable member for Winnipeg Centre [Woodsworth] is the leader of the labour group — and I am the group" (Avakumovic 1978: 42). In 1924 Woodsworth and Irvine were joined in the House of Commons by eleven members of the Progressives to form the "Ginger Group," which by 1929 had grown to twenty-one. The Ginger Group was one of the strands that would come together in 1932 to form the Co-operative Commonwealth Federation.

Throughout the 1920s and into the mid-1930s, Woodsworth was subjected to relentless and often vicious attacks by the Communist Party. In 1929, for example, the executive report to the sixth convention of the CPC stated:

> Woodsworth is one of the most dangerous elements in the working class. The fact is that he is the main representative of the bourgeoisie in the ranks of the working class, yet a large number of workers look upon him as a real champion of the workers. (Penner 1977: 148)

These attacks were part of the CPC's determined effort to defeat the forces of social democracy in the struggle for the allegiance of the Canadian trade union movement. That battle would rage right throughout the 1930s and 1940s.

Woodsworth was a determined opponent of the Communist Party, but was equally determined that any new party established would be a socialist party. It would not, however, be a socialist *labour* party like the British Labour Party, because it was Woodsworth's position that, unlike the case in Britain, the working class in a less industrialized Canada was too small to support, on its own, an electorally viable labour party. What Canada needed, he believed, was a people's party that included labour, farmers, the middle class, and socialists. This was a vision distinctive not only from that of Britain, but also from that of the CPC and the pre-war Marxist-inspired Canadian socialist parties, all of which were almost exclusively labour parties.

Two other ideological strands contributed to shaping what would become the CCF. The first, the **social gospel**, was the set of ideas advanced by a radical group of Protestant ministers who left or were pushed out of the church and sought to build the kingdom of heaven, of social and economic justice, here on Earth. Woodsworth was one of these — he left the church in 1918 — as was William Irvine. This strain of morally based, social-justice-oriented socialism became an important part of Canadian social democracy.

The League for Social Reconstruction (LSR) was established in 1932 by a group of Eastern university professors, including Frank Scott, Frank Underhill, Eugene Forsey, and, although still then a student, David Lewis. The LSR brought to Canadian social democracy the second other ideological strand, **Fabian socialism**, with its origins in the British Labour Party. This was a gradualist form of socialism (social democracy, really) characterized by a strong emphasis on central planning and the role of technical experts. The LSR, significantly, represented the first time that intellectuals played a significant role in Canadian socialism, which up to then had been largely the preserve of workers.

The CCF, which Woodsworth would guide to formation, would include these many non-labour strands — farmers, Fabianism, the Ginger Group, the social gospel — even while seeing itself as the party of labour.

Women, too, played a significant role in the early development of the CCF, but their efforts were often undervalued, in part because so much of their contribution was "support work." Women did administrative and organizational work at the constituency level and in election campaigns, played a key role in the party's educational work, and in numerous instances worked as local and regional organizers. Much of this invaluable work was done through semi-autonomous women's committees of various kinds, even while women remained under-represented in the party's leadership.

Indeed, the party encouraged women, sometimes in a patronizing tone, to play what we would now see as stereotypical roles. Describing "How to Organize a Successful CCF Unit," one CCFer noted, "The social committee, an essential unit of the party, should be at least two-thirds women because they were 'perfect jewels' at raising funds and loved 'playing amateur salesladies at bake sales'" (Sangster 1985: 77). Women generally were not supported in their efforts to win party nominations, and when party stalwart Beatrice Brigden reported to the 1936 CCF national convention on the activities of Winnipeg women members, and particularly on the establishment of women's groups to discuss birth control, "her report was greeted with 'chortles' of amusement by the assembly" (Sangster 1985: 87). Some forty years later, in the 1970s, when women trade unionists fought at union and NDP conventions to advance "women's issues," the response would be little changed.

The Co-operative Commonwealth Federation was formally established at a conference in Calgary in 1932, the result of more than a decade of hard work, with a mandate to meet in Regina in 1933 to finalize and adopt a program. The result was the 1933 Regina Manifesto, famous less for its detailed listing of fourteen immediate demands than for its ringing declaration: "No CCF government will rest content until it has eradicated capitalism and put into operation the full program of socialized planning which will lead to the establishment in Canada of the Cooperative Commonwealth."

The establishment of the CCF crystallized the political landscape of Canada's trade union movement. First there was the Communist Party of Canada, acting through the Workers' Unity League, which had put down deep and meaningful roots in the trade union movement as the champion of militant industrial unionism. Then there was the CCF, a people's party with, at the time of its establishment, only minimal labour representation — the TLC was still committed to a Gompers-style "partyism." Finally, there was the Liberal Party under the leadership of the wily Mackenzie King, engineer earlier in the century of the IDIA, author in 1918 of *Industry and Humanity*, a virtual blueprint for the welfare state in Canada, and fully prepared, in response to the creation of the CCF, to move the Liberals to the left in order to hold the labour vote in the Liberal camp, where it would remain for most of the twentieth century. Thus the newly established CCF found itself attacked from the left by the CPC and from the right by the Liberal Party, both attempting to prevent the CCF from becoming the party of organized labour.

By the mid-1930s the CCF was most certainly *not* the party of organized labour. However, certain key figures in the CCF, led by National Secretary David Lewis, saw the need to make a concerted effort to win the allegiance of the trade union movement, thus setting the stage for a monumental battle between the Communist Party and the CCF for the hearts and minds of Canadian trade unionists.

Given the energetic organizing efforts of the WUL, the CCF was far behind in this regard in 1935. Moreover, the CCF's distinctive social character — its farmer–social gospel–LSR–worker alliance — placed it at a disadvantage relative to the more purely proletarian CPC. Lewis and others in the CCF — Woodsworth much less so, given his commitment to a people's party — saw that it was imperative, therefore, for the CCF to establish a much closer link with organized labour. To achieve this goal, the CCF would have to squeeze out the Communist Party of Canada, just as the CPC had been attempting, since its establishment in 1921, to squeeze out the social democrats. This great battle, in which Lewis would play a central role, would not end until the early 1950s, by which time the CCF had largely vanquished the CPC.

CPC VERSUS CCF: THE BATTLE FOR LABOUR'S ALLEGIANCE

From 1935 to 1940 two simultaneous struggles, the one superimposed upon the other, shaped the politics of Canadian labour. The first was the drive for industrial unionism, under the banner of the CIO but driven almost exclusively by Canadian organizers. The second was the battle between the Communist Party and the CCF to win the allegiance of organized labour by controlling labour's central institutions.

For most of this period the CCF had only a tenuous presence in the labour movement. Graham Spry wrote to David Lewis in 1937 to say: "Everywhere there is the demand for union organizers, everywhere there is the cry 'labour party,' everywhere there is a new attitude, a new public opinion, and everywhere the CCF is almost totally ineffective" (Abella 1973: 24).

The Communist Party, by contrast, was leading the charge for industrial unionism, as a consequence of the party's cadre of experienced and talented ex-WUL organizers, directed by J.B. Salsberg, "the commissar of trade unions." By 1939 the Steel Workers Organizing Committee (SWOC), established in 1936 at the direction of CIO leader John L. Lewis, was dominated by Communist Party organizers. According to Abella (1973: 55), "There was a direct pipeline from the CIO offices to Communist headquarters."

Then, in September 1939, just prior to the declaration of war, Stalin and Hitler signed a non-aggression pact, as a result of which the Communist Party — until then strongly anti-fascist — did yet another of its Moscow-determined policy shifts and attacked Canada's war effort as merely another conflict between capitalist countries. As historian Norman Penner (1988: 164) has described it, of all the party's shifts in strategy, "None were more incredible than this decision to oppose the war against fascism. In all the countries of the West, an exodus of Party members and supporters took place, in an angry and confused response to this sudden change." On June 6, 1940, the Communist Party was declared illegal, and leading members of the CPC, including many who were active union organizers, were interned, thus further weakening their efforts to control the Canadian labour movement.

When Hitler invaded the Soviet Union on June 23, 1941, the CPC again reversed its stance, becoming the labour movement's most patriotic supporter of the war effort, enforcing a no-strike pledge, and promoting wartime production targets. The CCF became the more militant party. In 1940 the CCF engineered a merger of the ACCL with the CIO to form the Canadian Congress of Labour. At least in part because of his efforts at the founding convention, the CCF's Lewis was able to say that the constitution of the CCL "establishes the relation between our office and their work on a much more direct basis" (Abella 1973: 51–52).

This growing CCF control was reinforced when Charles Millard — a

The RCMP Spied on Tommy Douglas: We now know that for more than thirty years, starting in 1939, the RCMP spied on Tommy Douglas: when he was the CCF premier of Saskatchewan from 1944 to 1961; and while he was leader of the federal NDP from 1961 to 1971. We know this because, as the result of a request under the *Access to Information Act*, the Canadian Press obtained a 1,142-page, nine-volume dossier on Douglas from Library and Archives Canada. The documents revealed in detail the RCMP's spying on a democratically elected leader of the CCF and NDP.

Source: Globe and Mail, December 18, 2006.

staunch CCFer appointed CIO representative for Ontario by John L. Lewis in 1939 — appointed talented young CCF organizers to important positions in CIO unions. As Gad Horowitz (1968: 68) noted, "To claim that ... staffs of the new industrial unions at this time were hired solely on the basis of their political affiliations would not be an exaggeration." Millard soon had a staff of ten active CCFers at the SWOC headquarters, which only recently had been dominated by the CPC. Thus, by the end of 1940 the CCF had dramatically improved its position in the labour movement. In 1943 its efforts were capped when the Canadian Congress of Labour passed a resolution recognizing the CCF as the "political arm of labour in Canada."

These gains were replicated at the polls: from 1941 to 1944 electoral support for the CCF boomed. In 1941 the CCF formed the official opposition in British Columbia, winning a plurality of votes. In February 1942, CCF candidate Joe Nosworthy defeated federal Conservative leader Arthur Meighan in a by-election, picking up the first-ever CCF seat in Ontario. In the Ontario provincial election of August 1943 the CCF narrowly missed forming the government. Its share of the vote jumped from 5 to 31 percent, and the party formed the official opposition, going from zero to thirty-four seats, nineteen of them won by active trade unionists. A month later, in September 1943, a federal Gallup poll showed the CCF running just ahead of the Liberals and Conservatives in Canada-wide popularity. In 1944, under the leadership of Tommy Douglas, the CCF formed the provincial government in Saskatchewan, the first social-democratic government ever in North America. The CCF, it appeared, was on a roll.

In 1945, though, the party was stopped in its tracks. In the 1945 Ontario provincial election the CCF share of the vote dropped by 10 percent; its seats plummeted from thirty-four to eight. A week later in the federal election the CCF almost doubled its share of the federal vote, going from 8.5 percent to 15.6 percent, and electing a record twenty-eight CCF Members of Parliament, putting the party in third place for the first time ever. But relative to its hopes, the results were disappointing: the party was unable to win a single seat in Ontario and Quebec. It was confined, still, to its original Western stronghold. These results were the best the CCF would ever achieve. The 1945 federal election was the beginning of the end for the party.

What happened, for one thing, was that Mackenzie King's Liberals had appropriated part of the CCF program. Immediately after the September 1943 Gallup poll that showed the CCF ahead of the Liberals, King had taken steps to move the Liberals to the left, adopting a far-reaching program of reform. He established a Committee on Reconstruction, whose research director was LSR member Leonard Marsh, to plan a Canadian version of the welfare state, and before the 1945 federal election he introduced the family allowance. King wrote in his diary: "I think I have cut the ground in large part from under the CCF" (Horowitz 1968: 38). Indeed, this would become the pattern for the next quarter-century: when the CCF/NDP threatened to make electoral gains, the Liberals moved to the left to appropriate its program and electoral support.

At the same time a brutal propaganda attack, financed by big business, was directed at the CCF. In Ontario, in 1943–45, Premier George Drew led the attack:

> using advertisements in the daily press and the mails, spreading the most blatant slanders to convince the Ontario electorate that the CCF was a Communist party, planning to subvert and destroy the democratic way of life which Canadians had enjoyed up to that time. Anti-semitic attacks on David Lewis were included in this barrage. (Penner 1992: 82)

The CCF's disappointing electoral results in the 1945 Ontario provincial election and the federal election followed. The CCF never recovered.

COMMUNIST PURGE

After the Second World War the struggle between the CCF and the Communist Party for dominance of the industrial union movement raged on, and by 1951 the CCF was victorious. The International Woodworkers of America, which was strongest in British Columbia, where "the BC labour movement was, at least until 1948, almost a personal fiefdom of the Communist Party" (Abella 1973: 111), and the United Electrical Workers, which had been "completely and consistently dominated by the party in both Canada and the US" (Abella 1973: 139), had been ousted from the Canadian Congress of Labour. The 1950 CCL convention adopted a resolution permitting the expulsion of unions "following the principles and policies of the Communist Party." The result was that by 1951, no large Communist-influenced union remained in the Congress. The battle had been rough; the tactics not always admirable. The purging of Communists from the Canadian Seamen's Union, for example, had been achieved by the use of hired thugs under the direction of the infamous Hal Banks. The interests of the maritime workers were, in some cases literally, trampled underfoot.

Given the enormous role played by Communist organizers in making possible the long-sought success of industrial unionism in Canada, the purge carried a brutal irony:

> There seems little doubt that the contribution of the Communists to the creation of the CIO in Canada was invaluable. They were activists in a period that cried for activity; they were energetic, zealous and dedicated, in a period when organizing workers required these attributes.... It was Communists under the able guidance of J.B. Salsberg who helped organize most of the CIO unions in Canada in the 1930s. The large CIO unions, Steel, Auto, Electric, Woodworkers, Mine-Mill, and Textile, were organized at the beginning by Communists and were all, at one time or another in their history, dominated by the party. (Abella 1973: 221–22)

However crucial the party's role in building Canada's industrial union movement, the CPC's Moscow-inspired twists and turns eroded its credibility, and the anti-communist hysteria of the Cold War in the late 1940s and the 1950s finished it off as a viable political force in Canada's labour movement. The Communist Party of Canada continued to exist throughout the second half of the twentieth century, but it never again attained the influence that it had exerted in the 1930s and 1940s.

MERGER AND THE NEW PARTY

With the Communists largely removed from the major industrial unions, the ground was prepared, finally, for a merger of the industrial and crafts unions. Joint meetings in 1954, and the 1955 merger in the United States of the AFL and CIO, began the process that led to the merger in 1956 of the industrial CCL and the crafts-based TLC, creating the Canadian Labour Congress (CLC).

But in the postwar period the CCF suffered electorally. Its share of the national popular vote declined steadily: 1945, 15.6 percent; 1949, 13.4 percent; 1953, 11.3 percent; 1957, 10.7 percent; 1958, 9.5 percent. In the 1957 federal election, CCF candidates lost their deposit in 112 of 162 ridings (69 percent), and the party elected no members in Southern Ontario or east of the Ontario-Quebec border. Following the 1958 election, a sweep by the Progressive Conservatives led by John Diefenbaker, the CCF was reduced to only eight seats, its worst showing since 1940. Its 9.5 percent of the popular vote was just marginally above the 8.7 percent the party had won in its first federal election campaign more than twenty years earlier in 1935. The CCF was finished.

During the party's period of decline, it turned increasingly to the trade union movement. CCF members, particularly its leftists, had long been wary of the party's links to labour. The fear was that labour would come to dominate the party, and would water down its left-wing policies, moving the CCF in a more moderate and pragmatic direction. But according to Horowitz (1968: 151), "By 1951 there could no longer be any doubt, even among those suspicious of 'labour domination,' that salvation could come only from the unions."

Accordingly, the 1956 Winnipeg Declaration made the party's ideology more compatible with the newly created CLC. It removed the radical rhetoric of the Regina Manifesto, making the party, as the *United Auto Worker* put it, "much more acceptable to union voters" (Horowitz 1968: 174–75). Following the CCF's resounding electoral defeat in 1958, the deliberations of the National Committee for the New Party, with ten representatives from each of the CCF and the CLC, led to the 1961 founding of the New Democratic Party. The convention elected Tommy Douglas, former CCF premier of Saskatchewan, as the party's first leader.

The NDP, unlike its predecessor, was a party that had, in its very formation, the labour movement playing a central and direct role. The link with organized labour provided money and organizers for NDP campaigns, and the new party soon reversed the electoral decline of the CCF. By the mid-1960s the NDP was winning 17–18 percent of the popular vote at the national level; by the late 1970s it was at 20 percent — more than double what the CCF had won in its last federal election in 1958.

But what was the impact on rank-and-file union members of the trade union's links with the NDP? The answer is complex. First, trade union membership does apparently influence individual voting behaviour. Studies of the 1965, 1968, 1974, and 1979 federal elections (Archer 1985: 357) show that union members were *twice* as likely as non-union members to vote NDP. Members of unions affiliated with the NDP — and less than 10 percent are affiliated — were *three* times as likely to vote NDP.

Still, even though union membership increased the likelihood of an NDP vote, more union members continued to vote Liberal than NDP, and this was the case even for unions affiliated to the NDP. Canadian unions, despite their linkage to the NDP, proved unable to deliver their memberships' vote to the party. As was the case throughout the twentieth century, it was for many years the Liberals, not the NDP, who proved best able to win the votes of rank-and-file trade union members. More recently it has been the Reform/Canadian Alliance/Conservative Party of Canada that has been relatively successful in securing the union vote. Elizabeth Gidengil (2002: 282–83) found that in "the 1997 federal election, union members were more likely to vote for the Reform Party (20 percent) than for the NDP (15 percent)." In the 2000 federal election, "The Alliance had outpolled the NDP by more than two to one among union households." In 2004 the NDP "doubled its share of the union vote, drawing almost as much support from union households (28 percent) as the Conservatives (30 percent) did" (Gidengil et al. 2006: 9). Nevertheless, in 2004, despite the doubling of the NDP's share of the union vote, more union members voted for the very right-wing Conservative Party than for the NDP.

That this is so is most likely a product, at least in part, of the postwar compromise: the industrial relations machinery that regulated union-management relations, bringing economic benefits to trade unions and their members but at the cost of bureaucratizing the movement and increasing the distance between union leaders and their members. Union members became consumers of services delivered by unions and paid for with their union dues. Efforts to create a distinctive working-class culture, so important in the development of trade unionism earlier in the century, gave way in the postwar period to the day-to-day tasks of negotiating and servicing contracts.

The NDP, too, became in the course of time an electoral machine, increasingly indistinguishable from other political parties. Efforts to create a socialist or social-democratic culture, so important earlier in the century, gave way to the more technical tasks of polling and image-making aimed at winning elections. Meanwhile, throughout the postwar period, the culture of individualism and consumerism was relentlessly conveyed in a myriad of ways by the corporate media — newspapers, television, movies, magazines. Politically, union members, swept up in the powerful culture of capitalism, became increasingly indistinguishable from their non-union neighbours.

THE WAFFLE

Within a decade of the NDP's formation the drift to the right was challenged by a left-wing faction emerging from within the party. The Waffle Manifesto, *For an Independent Socialist Canada,* was first presented and debated at the NDP's 1969 federal convention. While a cross-section of the NDP membership was represented in the faction, which became known as the Waffle, the driving forces were disproportionately young, affiliated with universities as professors or students, and shaped by the radical ideals of the 1960s. Few of the Waffle leaders had any first-hand experience in political organizing or with trade unions. But their policy positions represented a significant challenge to the now more moderate and labour-based New Democratic Party, and to the leadership of the union movement.

The heart of the Waffle's position was its members' claim that Canada was becoming an economic colony of the United States. As Bob Hackett (1980: 7) put it: "Canadian independence is not now possible without socialism: and socialism cannot be achieved without independence, because American-dominated corporate capitalism is the main obstacle."

The attempt to transform the NDP into a socialist and anti-imperialist party was, in some important respects, an attempt to reverse what had only recently been achieved with the creation in 1961 of the NDP. To make the new party possible, the Regina Manifesto had been replaced by the less radical-sounding Winnipeg Declaration, and the Communist Party had been purged from the industrial unions, making possible both the merger of the TLC and the CCL to create the Canadian Labour Congress, followed by the CLC's commitment to the NDP. For party veterans like David Lewis, who had worked tirelessly for thirty-five years to build the closer links between the CCF and the trade union movement, which had finally been achieved with the creation of the NDP, the Waffle and its left-wing policies were especially dangerous.

Thus the 1971 NDP convention, when Lewis faced graduate student and Waffle candidate Jim Laxer for the leadership of the party, took on a particular importance. Trade union leaders were at the heart of the battle for the party leadership: "A steering committee of 25 key union leaders was established under the aegis of the CLC to coordinate the assertion of labour's position at the Convention, particularly in opposition to the Waffle's policy position" (Hackett 1980: 40). Lewis finally prevailed, but only after Laxer had pushed him to a humiliating fourth ballot. Lewis won in the end because 80 percent of trade union delegates cast their ballots for him.

Relations between the trade union movement and the Waffle went rapidly downhill. For the November 1971 convention of the Ontario Federation of Labour the Waffle Labour Committee, formed out of the April 1971 federal convention, produced another manifesto. *A Socialist Program for Canadian Trade Unionists* denounced the "right-wing establishment" of the trade union movement and called for "completely independent Canadian unions" as a long-term goal. These were fighting words to the heads of the international unions, especially the United Steelworkers and United Autoworkers.

In March 1972, in a speech to the NDP provincial council, Stephen Lewis, leader of the Ontario provincial NDP and son of David Lewis, accused the Waffle of "a sneering, contemptuous attitude towards official trade unionism and the labour leadership" (Hackett 1980: 55). This attack was followed by a June 1972 ultimatum that made no concessions whatever to the Waffle: its members could stay in the NDP only if they complied with party rules. Most Waffle members left, forming the Movement for an Independent Socialist Canada, which lasted only two years.

The purge of the Waffle was largely the work of organized labour. It was, as trade unionist Ed Finn described it, "mainly a response to pressure from the Steelworkers, the United Auto Workers and other American unions ... the internationals have, in effect, given the NDP an ultimatum: Either the Waffle goes, or we go" (Penner 1992: 102).

Stephen Lewis later confirmed this view:

> There was an unstated ultimatum from the trade union movement, which weighed very heavily on the party leadership.... For some people... it was terrifying that the trade union movement should be threatening to tell the party to shove it, that they weren't going to continue to be a part as long as people like [University of Toronto economist and Waffle leader Mel] Watkins and Laxer called the shots. (Hackett 1980: 55)

Although the Waffle soon died out as a force, on many of the issues its members proved more right than wrong. For example, they saw the dangers of U.S. control of Canada's economy two decades before the Canada–U.S. Free Trade Agreement, and accurately identified the source of many of the problems that would come to confront Canada's labour movement. With respect to women's issues the Waffle was also, in some important respects, ahead of its time. Although, in a glaring omission, the Waffle Manifesto made no mention of women's liberation, many of the Waffle's most creative and active leaders were women, and they energetically forced their issues, despite considerable opposition, onto the agenda at the April 1971 federal convention, and onto the NDP's agenda more generally.

But politically the Waffle members were naive, and perhaps worse. To build a base of support in the labour movement takes time, and patience, particularly for a group that tended to have young leaders with no trade union experience. The sociological and generational differences between the leaders of the Waffle and the leaders of the NDP and the union movement were wide to begin with. They could only widen when the Waffle Labour Committee took direct aim at the leadership of the major international unions without first having built a significant base of support among rank-and-file unionists. Seen as aggressive and brash, as arrogant and contemptuous, the Waffle — despite the undeniable merits of so many of its policy positions — was destined to fail politically.

Unfortunately, the price of that failure, the price of the purging of the Waffle, was high. The price includes the loss from the party of many young people with ideas and vision. The early CCF was a party of ideas; the post-Waffle NDP lacked imagination and vision. As two observers put it: "After the overt or covert Communist Party members were got rid of, it became time to eliminate people who espoused ideas that sounded 'communist.' Soon it became suspect to have socialist or radical ideas. And eventually it became unacceptable to have any ideas at all" (Ehring and Roberts 1993: 6). When the NDP ceased to be a party of ideas and vision, it ceased to be attractive to many bright and energetic young people. Many potential supporters ended up not in the NDP but in the new social movements that emerged in the latter part of the century.

UNION POLITICS IN THE NEO-LIBERAL ERA

The purge of the Waffle coincided with the onset of economic crisis. But when the crisis took root in the early 1970s, it was the pro-corporate political right, not the pro-labour political left, that seized the moment. The right successfully advanced its anti-labour, neo-liberal prescriptions — privatization, deregulation, expenditure cutbacks, concession bargaining, layoffs. By the mid-1970s the political right and its corporate backers had established the Business Council on National Issues (now called the Canadian Council of Chief Executives) and the Fraser Institute. In 1979 Margaret Thatcher was elected in Britain; in 1980 Ronald Reagan became president of the United States of America. The computer revolution and the increased globalization of the economy put additional constraints on pro-labour governments and political parties, pushing them further to the right.

Nevertheless, in the 1970s the NDP elected provincial governments in Manitoba (1969–77), Saskatchewan (1971–82), and British Columbia (1971–75). These administrations were not the "transmission belts between new ideas and the Canadian political system" (Ehring and Roberts 1993: 5) that the CCF in Saskatchewan had been from 1944 to 1960. In Saskatchewan, under the leadership of Premier Tommy Douglas, the CCF government was a pioneer: collective bargaining rights, including the right to strike, for public-sector employees; public auto insurance; and public hospital and medical insurance, later extended to create Canada's medicare system. But, although not quite so innovative, the 1970s-era NDP governments in Western Canada introduced relatively strong labour legislation, including significant gains in health and safety legislation as well as social legislation, and it would be reasonable to argue that these governments served Canada's trade unions relatively well, and justified union support of the NDP.

At the federal level, in the wake of the Waffle purge the NDP gradually began to succumb to the economic and ideological forces pushing to the right. Despite a brilliant federal campaign in 1972, when David Lewis attacked the "corporate welfare bums," and despite the relative success of the provincial NDP governments in Western Canada in the 1970s, the federal NDP slid gradually to the right. As it did so, a host of popular movements arose, each promoting politically progressive positions on specific issues. In the 1980s and 1990s, the trade union movement would gradually learn how to do politics with these organizations, but that learning experience was fraught with difficulties.

POPULAR MOVEMENTS

The origins of the popular movements were in the cultural upheaval of the 1960s. The civil rights, student, and anti–Vietnam War movements demonstrated the capacity for social change embodied in broadly based, non-party movements. Others followed: the second wave of the women's movement, and the environmental, peace, and gay and lesbian rights movements.

At the same time, international social democracy, of which the NDP was the Canadian variant, was having difficulty responding effectively to the new economic crisis. Social democracy is committed to the parliamentary process, and thus to winning elections, but the industrial working class — historically the core of its political support — has never been large enough on its own to secure election victories. Therefore, social-democratic parties have broadened their appeal and watered down their programs to win the electoral support of the middle class. Mobilization and education of members have gradually been abandoned because they might threaten and thus lose middle-class voters. Such parties were able to effect some useful changes when capitalism was booming in the postwar period, because they were able to redistribute the "**fiscal dividend**," the bulging government coffers that were the consequence of rapid economic growth. But when the boom ended in the early 1970s, the fiscal dividend disappeared, to be replaced by growing deficits and debt loads. With mobilization and education of the membership long since abandoned in the interests of short-term electoral gain, social-democratic parties had little by way of creative energy, ideas, and imagination and vision to fashion a response to the crisis. They drifted, becoming increasingly ineffectual as the 1970s turned into the 1980s and 1990s.

The social movements that had emerged from the turmoil of the 1960s became a new source of political energy and creativity. Occasional attempts were made to bring the many movements together in the form of broadly based coalitions linked to the labour movement. Such attempts met with difficulty, as the experience of British Columbia in the early 1980s demonstrated. There, a host of regressive and anti-labour bills introduced in 1983 by the Social Credit government of Bill Bennett — "a legislative menu that could only have been dreamed up by the business-funded Fraser Institute" (Morton 1990: 322) — led to the mobilization of a large, broadly based, energetic, and creative movement. This "Operation Solidarity" included teachers, human rights workers, seniors' organizations, a host of other social movements, and the labour movement. Massive demonstrations and teach-ins mobilized tens of thousands and culminated in a staged general strike that step by step shut down government offices, then schools, and threatened to shut the province down completely. Within hours of the kind of challenge posed by the 1919 Winnipeg General Strike or the 1972 Quebec Common Front, union leaders headed by Jack Munro of the Woodworkers met with Premier Bennett and fashioned a settlement. The social movements were excluded, and Solidarity militants were outraged. After taking part in and helping to build an impressive campaign that involved a broadly based coalition that reached far beyond organized labour, the trade union leaders had abandoned their allies.

This decision confirmed in the minds of many social movement activists the belief that the trade union movement had become conservative and bureaucratic, and that it would not work constructively with progressive forces in the community unless labour called the shots. Many labour leaders, for their part, distrusted the predominantly middle-class leadership of the social movements and were convinced that only organized labour had the right to vote on whether union members were to strike. As Jack Munro put it: "They were all well-meaning, all dedicated to their causes... but with all due respect to their organizations, they shouldn't have been voting on whether our members were going to be out of work" (Munro and O'Hara 1988: 6). The result was tension and division.

WOMEN AND LABOUR

The difficulties that unions had in learning to work with the popular movements in the 1980s had already been experienced with the women's movement in the 1970s. Women's struggle for equality in the trade union

Women Rise:
"At a 1910 union rally in Montreal an anonymous, dark-haired young woman climbed onto a makeshift stage and read out a poem to the assembled audience:

Do we live for those who love us
For the work they make us do?
For the middleman above us?
For the employer, landlord too?
Do we live to rise each morning
Work and slave till eventide?
Oh yes, we live for others
In the saddest sense of the phrase
We live that they may exploit us
In a thousand various ways.

In 1910 that poem — a clear call not just for economic justice but for recognition of ruthlessly skewed relationships — created a sensation, as did the sight of women on strike, marching in the streets. But by 1940 women's voices calling for equality in the workplace had grown faint indeed — and it would not be until the late 1960s and early 1970s, with the push of the second wave of feminism and a renewed labour movement, that those voices would be heard so strongly and sharply once again."

Source: Steedman 1997: 259–60

movement heated up in the late 1960s–70s. The **second wave of feminism** — the "first wave" is usually considered to have been the suffragists' struggle early in the twentieth century for women's right to vote — took the world by storm, with its demands for women's equality and economic independence in all realms of society. Its effects resounded throughout the union movement.

One form it took was wives' strike support committees. For example, Wives Supporting the Strike, which emerged during the 1978 Steelworkers' strike against Inco in Sudbury, evolved out of a women's group established in Sudbury in 1971 called Women Helping Women. Their rationale was that homemakers bear the brunt of a strike because there is less money to run the household, and the resulting pressure at home can harm the strike effort. The women involved with Wives Supporting the Strike undertook a host of activities. Some of the actions were politically challenging, especially given that most of the group had little or no prior political experience: plant-gating, theatre performances, public speaking, press releases. These new roles, these tangible expressions of women's liberation, threatened many men in the union, including the local union leadership. They opposed the efforts of Wives Supporting the Strike in many ways — a reflection of the antagonism that had historically characterized the relations between trade unions and women and wives' groups.

But for many of the women it was a defining experience. "As women we 'came out' in many ways," said one. As a result of their involvement, of their actively engaging in the struggle for social change, she added, "Women who had been involved in the strike committee will never be the same again" (Luxton 1983: 342–43). The women's movement had an effect on the lives of many union wives, who in turn contributed to the long struggle for women's equality in the labour movement.

Women Have Had to Fight—Judy Darcy: I remember my first CLC convention in 1974 when any female felt she was taking her life in her hands if she walked through certain sections of the convention. Those were the days when women only merited a few short paragraphs in a policy paper on human rights. Any woman who spoke felt she had to bend over backwards by saying, "I'm not one of those women's libbers, but...." I remember being told by a higher-up male trade union official that when I cried a little in a very emotional strike meeting, I wasn't displaying "tough leadership qualities." When I took my four-month-old son to a union convention I was told, "Get your priorities straight."

Source: Darcy 1985: 32.

But it was women trade unionists who bore the brunt of the burden in bringing women's liberation to Canada's trade union movement. In meeting after meeting, women struggled to be taken seriously. In the early 1970s, for example, verbal sexual harassment was common at union meetings —

The Most Dangerous Songs in the World, by Loa Henry:
Music has always been used to further the struggle to build a better world. Music is the voice that cannot be silenced. We have seen this over and over, throughout history and across the world.

A strike at the woollen mills in Lawrence, Massachusetts, in 1912, became the inspiration for the song *Bread and Roses,* which has become the anthem for International Women's Day and is synonymous with the women's movement.

Music became a powerful unifying force in the civil rights movement, with people linked arm-in-arm singing *We Shall Overcome.*

The song *Nkosi Sikelel'i-Afrika* was a powerful weapon against the Apartheid regime in South Africa. It is now the anthem of a liberated South Africa.

In Chile, the Pinochet dictatorship smashed the hands of musician Victor Jara with the butt of a machine-gun. Pinochet's henchman knew the power of music to sustain, to uplift, to spread the message of resistance to tyrants. They feared Victor Jara's music. Here, I think of the song *El Pueblo Unido Hamas Sera Vencido.*

Hay Una Mujer calls out the names of eight women, missing in Chile, "disappeared" by the junta. They symbolize the many thousands of political prisoners and others who have been "disappeared" by dictatorships around the world.

The song I have chosen for the most dangerous song in the world is *Warrior,* written in 1993 by Kim Baryluk of the Wyrd Sisters. I chose this song because it is the one that I relate to on a personal level because of my work in feminist theatre. *Warrior* has a powerful message: it calls upon women to break out of the mould set for them by a patriarchal society, to stand up, to be warriors against violence and oppression.

It also is about aging, and about becoming strong women — women joined in sisterhood, each responsible for the other, warriors for a better world.

Loa Henry is the director of the Winnipeg Labour Choir and was for many years a member of and artistic director of Canada's oldest feminist theatre group, Nellie McClung Theatre. This is the full version of her November 2, 2006, comments on *Canadian Dimension's* radio show, *Alert Radio,* at 101.5 UMFM.

as women in Manitoba found when they raised the issue of child care at a 1975 convention (see chapter 2, sidebar 2-19). But women fought back: supporting each other; caucusing at conventions; networking between conventions; establishing women's committees; demanding representation in union decision-making bodies. At conventions and in collective bargaining

Warrior:
I was a shy and lonely girl
With the heavens in my eyes
And as I walked along the lane
I heard the echo of her cries.

Chorus
I cannot fight
I cannot a warrior be
It's not my nature or my teaching
It is the womanhood in me.

I was a lost and angry youth
There were no tears in my eyes
I saw no justice in my world
Only the echoes of her cries.

Chorus
I cannot fight
I cannot a warrior be
It's not my nature or my teaching
It is the womanhood in me.

I am an older woman now
And I will heed my own cries
And I will a fierce warrior be
Til not another woman dies.

I can and will fight
I can and will a warrior be
It is my nature and my duty
It is the womanhood in me.

I can and will fight
I can and will a warrior be
It is my nature and my duty
It is the womanhood in me.

they insisted upon advancing what had earlier been seen as personal issues — violence against women, for example — giving tangible expression to the slogan "the personal is political." As Bryan Palmer (1992: 333) notes, "They fought their way into the labour movement and redefined the very notion of collectivity." Although many struggles remained to be won before women could achieve equality in the union movement, the impact of the feminist movement on trade unions, and the determined efforts of women to secure their rights in unions, resulted in important gains.

Among the struggles yet to be won was equality for immigrant women and women of colour. It has been argued (Ng 1995; Das Gupta 1998) that the second wave of feminism implicitly defined women as white women and did not include women of colour or recognize their multiple oppressions. Winnie Ng, a union organizer with the International Ladies Garment Workers Union in the late 1970s, describes working at that time with a Toronto group called Women Working With Immigrant Women, and attending her first International Women's Day march in 1978. "But I didn't feel part of the women's movement at the time. We saw it as separate, because there was never any effort to include us" (Rebick 2005: 133). If women have had to fight their way into the labour movement, women of colour have faced an even longer and tougher fight.

THE STRUGGLE AGAINST FREE TRADE

By the late 1980s, despite the disappointing outcome of British Columbia's Operation Solidarity, trade unions and social movements were working together more effectively. Nowhere was this more evident than in the fight against the Canada–U.S. Free Trade Agreement. In April 1987 the Canadian Labour Congress, the National Action Committee on the Status of Women, the National Farmers Union, and other social movement organizations joined to form the Pro-Canada Network (PCN).

Over the next year and a half leading to the 1988 federal election, the PCN did a superb job of political education and mobilization, producing a myriad of publications about the dangers of the FTA, including two million copies of the cartoon booklet *What's the Big Deal?* distributed in major centres across Canada. The campaign was a roaring success: as more and more Canadians became aware of the details and likely implications of the FTA, opposition grew rapidly. On election day, more people voted for parties opposed to FTA than in favour of it. The deal was implemented because the anti-FTA vote was split between the Liberals and the NDP, allowing Mulroney's Conservatives to be re-elected.

The fight against free trade revealed with remarkable clarity the class basis of Canadian politics. Corporate Canada spent millions promoting the FTA, just as it had worked to stop the surging CCF in 1945. Labour and a host of people-based organizations opposed the deal, relying less on money than on creativity and imagination to make their case. (Table 5.1, showing who fought on which side of the FTA battle, makes the class character of the issue crystal clear.)

The fight against free trade also exposed the growing weakness of the NDP. The party failed to identify the FTA as the all-encompassing, pro-corporate, and anti-labour initiative that it was, and failed to lead the effort to mobilize and educate Canadians about its massive dangers. The bulk of the mobilization and education that took place was the result of the direct efforts of the labour and social movements, working together effectively in the PCN. In the wake of the 1988 election, Bob White, president of the recently created Canadian Auto Workers, wrote a public letter to the NDP criticizing the party for its failure on this all-important issue. The link between labour and the NDP, the product of decades of work from the mid-1930s to 1961, was under pressure.

The fight against free trade and the neo-liberalism that it embodies was also manifested in the late-1999 Battle of Seattle, the mass street protests by the so-called anti-globalization movement against the World Trade Organization (WTO), and in the April 2001 demonstrations at the Summit of the Americas in Quebec City, which were protesting the proposed Free Trade Area of the Americas (FTAA), an attempt to extend the FTA and NAFTA to the entire Western hemisphere. The FTAA has since been slowed

Table 5.1 Political Alignments on the Free Trade Issue

Groups Supporting Free Trade	Groups Opposing Free Trade
Business Council on National Issues	Canadian Labour Congress
Canadian Chamber of Commerce	Quebec Federation of Labour (FTQ)
Canadian Manufacturers' Association	Quebec Teachers' Federation (CEQ)
Canadian Bankers' Association	Canadian Teachers' Federation
Canadian Federation of Independent Business	National Farmers' Union
Mining Association of Canada	National Action Committee on the Status of Women (NAC)
Canadian Pulp and Paper Association	Congress of Canadian Women
Pharmaceutical Manufacturers Association	National Anti-Poverty Organization
Investment Dealers Association of Canada	Council of Canadians
Canadian Export Association	United Church of Canada
International Business Council of Canada	Assembly of First Nations
The C.C. Howe Institute	Toronto Disarmament Network
Canada West Foundation	Law Union of Canada
The Fraser Institute	Coalition of Senior Citizens' Organizations
The Financial Post	Canadian Council of Retirees
The Financial Times	Pollution Probe
The Globe and Mail (Toronto)	Playwrights' Union of Canada
The Southam Press	ACTRA
The Thomson Newspapers	Writers' Union of Canada

Source: Warnock 1988: 116–17.

by the rise of politically progressive governments in Latin America — in Venezuela and Bolivia, for example — while the anti-globalization movement was slowed by the marked shift to the right in the United States and Canada in the wake of the events of September 11, 2001. But the Seattle and Quebec City events were dramatic forms of political protest — tens of thousands of demonstrators marching, using various forms of creative political theatre, and engaging in civil disobedience — that revealed and rekindled a remarkable anti-capitalist sentiment.

These protests also revealed underlying tensions between organized labour and popular movements. Labour participated at both Seattle and Quebec City, as did the NDP. But generally speaking this participation took a less radical and creative form than did the activities of some others who were involved. At Quebec City, for example, labour was widely criticized for its decision to route its march away from the despised security fence erected around the site of the talks. One commentator observed, "Much of the conflict between labour and newer social movement groups can be attributed to the conservative, bureaucratized structure of unions" (MacKay 2003). Nevertheless, the street protests of Seattle and Quebec City represent an important form of left politics that may arise again, creating tactical and strategic questions for unions and their members.

THE RAE GOVERNMENT AND THE SOCIAL CONTRACT

In the 1990s the relationship between unions and the NDP would create the most immediate challenge for the labour movement. The decade initially brought new possibilities. NDP governments were elected in Saskatchewan and British Columbia in 1991, in Yukon in 1992, and, most important by far, in Ontario in September 1990. The unexpected election of Bob Rae's NDP government in Ontario seemed to represent the pinnacle of NDP success and promise. Finally, a provincial NDP government had been elected in Canada's industrial and commercial heartland, almost half a century after the bitter disappointment of 1945. More than half of Canada's population was now governed by the NDP. This was a genuinely exciting prospect.

But despite introducing some pro-labour legislation, all of the NDP governments were disappointing. Rather than challenging capitalism in the interests of working people, they accommodated their policies to its demands, practising restraint and implementing cutbacks that made provincial NDP governments little different, in practice, from governments led by other parties. Nowhere was this more apparent than in Ontario.

In the first part of its term the Rae government amended industrial relations legislation to the advantage of labour. The changes included anti-scab provisions restricting the ability of employers to maintain production during a strike or lockout. As well, the government brought in pay equity legislation and improvements in social programs. But for labour these gains paled into insignificance when weighed against a later measure: the 1993 imposition on public-sector unions of the Social Contract, which removed the right of free collective bargaining for public-sector workers. It did this by forcing the reopening of existing public-sector collective agreements, and imposing unpaid days off — "Rae days" — to cut costs. The unions that fought the proposal suffered deeper cuts than did the ones that acquiesced. Union members, feeling betrayed by their political ally, were outraged. In the 1995 Ontario provincial election — in which the Rae government ran a campaign virtually devoid of social-democratic content or vision — most unions offered only tepid support to the NDP. Some unions, the CAW for example, stood on the sidelines.

The relationship between the trade union movement and the NDP, forged in 1961 after so many years of struggle, now became the subject of open debate. At the federal level the NDP had taken its distance from trade union struggles in the 1980s and had failed to provide leadership in the fight against the FTA. At the provincial level the NDP governments of the early 1990s were largely indistinguishable from their non-NDP counterparts. In Ontario the failures of the Rae government shattered the great hopes of 1990.

But when much of the trade union movement pulled back its support for the NDP in the 1995 Ontario election, the result was the election of a particularly regressive, pro-corporate, anti-labour government — the Conservatives led by Mike Harris. Almost immediately, in 1996, Harris introduced his Omnibus Bill, which consisted of a range of attacks on labour, the public sector, and the poor. Thus was established the quandary with which the labour movement continues to grapple. Should labour refuse to support the NDP when that party's governments let them down, on the grounds that nothing is to be gained from supporting a party that does not defend labour's interests? Or should labour continue to support the NDP, even when the party lets labour down, on the grounds that even a weak NDP is better than the alternative as represented by the likes of the Harris government?

This quandary is a live issue in Manitoba and Saskatchewan. The NDP have most recently formed provincial governments in Manitoba since 1999 and — if we include a brief period when they governed as a minority with the support of three Liberal MLAS — in Saskatchewan since 1991, until their defeat in 2007. In both provinces the party developed ways of governing that are, at least in the short run, electorally successful, but at the price of moving still further to the ideological middle.

The strategy used by the NDP in Manitoba has been clearly laid out by Flanagan (2003), who uses the analogy of "inoculation" to describe how the governments of Premier Gary Doer have made policy decisions. They "inoculate" themselves by giving their traditional enemies at least a bit of what they demand, much as we inoculate ourselves against a disease by injecting into our bodies a bit of the disease. In recent years the business community and their various associations — Chambers of Commerce, the Canadian Taxpayers Federation, the Canadian Federation of Independent Business, the corporate-funded think tanks such as the Fraser Institute — have aggressively demanded tax cuts. Their purpose is to reduce the role of government, and turn more powers over to the private sector. The response of NDP governments in Manitoba and Saskatchewan has been to

Tax Cuts in Manitoba and Saskatchewan:
The *Manitoba Alternative Budget 2006* estimated that NDP governments in Manitoba had cut personal and property taxes by $391 million since 1999, and the *Manitoba Budget 2007* announced a further cut of $35.3 million in 2007. Business taxes had been cut by $128 million since 1999, with a further cut of $24.9 million announced in the 2007 provincial budget. One recent estimate suggests that by 2010, combined tax cuts by Doer-led governments will approximate $900 million (MacKinnon and Hudson 2007). Tax cuts have saved $150 per year for a family of four earning $20,000 per year; they have saved $1,700 per year — more than ten times as much — for a family of four earning $100,000 per year (MacKinnon and Hudson 2007).

The record of the Calvert governments in Saskatchewan is similar. An examination of various Canadian Centre for Policy Alternatives–Saskatchewan documents, plus Province of Saskatchewan budgets, reveals that between 2000 and 2006 income tax rates were cut by close to one-third, and, as in Manitoba, the higher one's income, the greater the benefit from the cuts. The Calvert government, in its 2007/08 budget, committed to cutting the Provincial Sales Tax from 7 to 5 percent, at an estimated cost of $340 million; pledged to eliminate the Corporate Capital Tax, thereby removing an additional $480 million from government coffers; and responded positively to the Saskatchewan Business Tax Review Committee's recommendation to reduce the Corporate Income Tax rate from 17 to 12 percent — it is expected to reach the 12 percent target by July 2008. These tax cuts, directly benefiting business, are being undertaken despite evidence that Saskatchewan's business costs, including taxes, are already among the lowest in North America.

A similar pattern — ensuring that corporate needs are met — prevails respecting natural resource royalties. The Saskatchewan Department of Industry and Resources reports that for natural resources, it has a "competitive royalty structure developed in partnership with industry." Between 1982 and 1991 Conservative governments in Saskatchewan reduced oil and gas royalties dramatically. During the 1991 provincial election the NDP pledged to reverse this policy, but it has since chosen not to do so. CCPA-Saskatchewan estimates that maintaining the Conservative government's lowered oil and gas royalty rates cost the Saskatchewan government some $2 billion in 2003 alone. Royalties on potash, uranium, and coal have also fallen in recent years under NDP governments. In Manitoba, the Fraser Institute has described the provincial government as having the "best policy environment in the world for mining investment."

The approach of the Manitoba and Saskatchewan NDP governments to these two policy areas — taxation and natural resource royalties — is consistent with Flanagan's description of the "inoculation" strategy — give traditional opponents much of what they ask for, in order to mute their opposition.

Source: Silver 2008.

acquiesce to these demands. That is, they give the business community at least some of what it wants — tax cuts — in order to dampen the opposition and thus increase their chances of re-election. To date this approach has worked, at least electorally.

The problem with this strategy is that NDP governments end up *defining* their governing strategy by the demands of their traditional enemies. They boast of their tax cuts: the Saskatchewan government of Premier Lorne Calvert cut the Provincial Sales Tax by 2 percent in 2006; Manitoba's Doer government cut taxes in budget after budget after 1999. These cuts reduce the funds available to governments to invest in initiatives aimed at creating greater equality; and the administrations exercise exceptional caution in governing. They do not want to offend the business community. Thus their improvements to labour legislation are meek. Their efforts to address the rapidly growing problems of racialized poverty in Manitoba and Saskatchewan are, at best, half-hearted. Some five or ten years or more of this kind of governance makes them increasingly indistinguishable from other parties. As they move to the ideological centre, they run the risk of losing many of their traditional supporters — those who do the work in election campaigns, who knock on doors and pull out the vote.

The Doer and Calvert NDP governments argue to their traditional supporters that they are better than the right-wing alternatives that would replace them if they were to be defeated. And this is true: they *are* better for working people than their right-wing alternatives. The enormous damage caused by the Harris government in Ontario after it defeated Rae's NDP government is a cruel testimony to that truth. But the logic of such a strategy is that as time passes, the amount by which they are better diminishes, until many former supporters argue that there *is* no difference, or that the difference is so minimal that it is not worth working for or even supporting. Such governments spend so much time and money placating their electoral enemies that they have little time and money left for building what, for their supporters, would be a better world. In Manitoba and Saskatchewan in particular the quandary created by "today's NDP" is: At what point do people stop supporting a party that is increasingly indistinguishable from the parties that have historically been anti-labour? Is it always the case that for labour a middle of the road NDP is better than any alternative?

POLITICAL QUANDARY

The decline of the NDP and the rise of social movements have generated a crucially important debate in the trade union movement about how organized labour ought to do politics. This debate goes back to the 1870s and earlier. Since then trade unionists have advanced and promoted a variety of political strategies — partyism, labourism, syndicalism, socialism, communism, social democracy, a labour party. The debate appeared, for a while, to be settled with the 1961 establishment of the NDP. But the failure of that party, and social democracy more generally, to respond adequately to changing economic circumstances has once again thrown the issue open to debate, and has once again split the labour movement.

Many — perhaps most — unions, at least at the leadership and activist level, want to continue to support the NDP. They reason that the NDP, with all its failings, is better than the alternatives. This position has been advanced most strongly in Ontario by the Steelworkers. But the federal election in November 2000 reduced the NDP to only thirteen seats, one more than needed to form an official party in the House of Commons, and to only 8.5 percent of the popular vote, which is about where the CCF was when it decided that a new party had to be created. Although the NDP share of the vote subsequently returned to its more traditional levels — 15.7 percent in the 2004 federal election and 17.5 percent in 2006 — the November 2000 result once again led to a general reconsideration of the future of the party and its relationship to the labour movement. Indeed, by December 2000 the Canadian Labour Congress had launched a review of its relationship with the NDP.

The issue arose again in the 2006 federal election campaign, when CAW leader Buzz Hargrove called for **tactical voting** — for supporting NDP candidates only in those seats where they had a chance of winning and, in seats where they were unlikely to win, supporting the Liberal Party — in an attempt to prevent a victory by the aggressively neo-conservative Conservative Party led by Stephen Harper. Hargrove went so far as to publicly present a CAW jacket to Liberal Prime Minister Paul Martin. The executive of the Ontario wing of the NDP retaliated by voting, in February 2006, to revoke Hargrove's party membership. The CAW responded by withdrawing support for the NDP at all levels, citing as its reason, "The continuing rightward drift of the NDP's own policies" (CAW 2006: 16). A similar dilemma may well occur in forthcoming federal elections. The question will again be: Should trade union members and working-class people generally support a Liberal Party that seems more likely to defeat a hard-line neo-conservative government? Or should they vote NDP on the grounds that in the long run working people need a healthy pro-labour party in Ottawa?

As part of this difficult but crucial rethinking, it is important to recognize the serious limitations of the social movements. Despite their significant achievements — among which might be counted the dramatic growth in awareness of environmental dangers — they do not seek to exercise power, and of late they have become primarily defensive organizations fighting against corporate-inspired initiatives. The exercise of power, and the use of power to shift social and economic relationships to the advantage of trade unions and people generally, require a political party. Is that party the NDP? If so, what can be done to make the party once again "a transmission belt for new ideas to the political system"? If not the NDP, then what? How might any other new party avoid the failings of the New Democrats? What role, if any, should social movements play? What role should and can organized labour play? Can labour rise above what we consider to be the recent limitations of its political vision, and contribute in a meaningful way to the kind of progressive, left-of-centre politics that would be in the interests not only of the labour movement, but also of Canadians more generally?

The answers to these questions will unfold in the years to come. Organized labour will play a significant role in this debate, and the strength and effectiveness of the labour movement in the twenty-first century will depend, at least in part, on the outcome of that debate.

CHAPTER 6

FACING THE TWENTY-FIRST CENTURY

Capitalism generates change — the constant, never-ending, "creative destruction" that is the inevitable consequence of its competitive search for profit. In recent decades change has become so rapid and so dramatic that it would be foolhardy to try to predict the challenges that trade unions might be facing by the middle of the twenty-first century.

Some of the challenges that unions will have to grapple with in the immediate future are clear enough, however. These include: working internationally, not just domestically, to counter the increasingly global reach of transnational corporations (TNCs); organizing in the new labour force created by the turn-of-the-century restructuring of capitalism; educating and mobilizing members and democratizing unions to create a stronger and more effective trade union movement; meeting the needs of the growing numbers of women and workers of colour in the labour force and in trade unions; working at the local level, through labour councils, to build progressive alliances and promote community economic development in response to such challenges as persistent poverty, racism, and the destruction of our environment; and determining how best to promote labour's political interests.

This is a formidable set of challenges — but the trade union movement has always had to overcome formidable challenges. At the beginning of the twentieth century, when monopoly capitalism was dramatically changing the structure of industry and the labour force, the movement needed to take up new forms of organization. Efforts to build an industrial unionism were met with unrelenting opposition. Early attempts failed. Workers experimented with different organizational forms. The struggle was bitter and long-lasting. But in the end the desire of working people to come together to protect and advance their common interests in the face of the unrelenting demands of competitive capitalism prevailed. In the coming century we are likely to see similar patterns: formidable challenges posed by capitalism; determined and creative organizing by labour, with success coming only after creative experimentation with different forms and styles of organizing; and similar experimentation with forms of political representation.

All of this will occur despite the predictable and continuing claims that trade unions are the product of earlier times and circumstances and have now "outlived their usefulness." Such claims were advanced by anti-union advocates throughout the twentieth century, and even more of them will no doubt come in the face of the rapid changes that will characterize the twenty-first century. Claims that they have "outlived their usefulness" are an inevitable part of the anti-union ideology that is a constant feature of capitalism. The truth is that far from having outlived their usefulness, trade unions are now more needed than ever.

THE CHALLENGES OF GLOBALIZATION

Huge transnational corporations scour the globe in search of lower wages, larger markets, and cheaper raw materials, in order to maximize their profits — a process of capitalist expansion that has lately become known as globalization.

Globalization is not new. It is an accentuation of the drive to expand that is intrinsic to capitalism. But globalization did increase dramatically in the last quarter of the twentieth century. Companies increasingly set up production anywhere in the world, playing one jurisdiction off against another by moving to wherever labour costs are lowest and regulations are least restrictive. International trade agreements such as the FTA and NAFTA accelerated this trend; and the WTO, among other bodies, works to expand these agreements. These international treaties significantly reduce the capacity of elected governments to interfere with the profit-seeking activities of transnational corporations. That is their purpose. They *free* these corporations from many of the obstacles placed in their way by governments — obstacles that working people see as benefits: labour laws, labour standards, and environmental regulations, for example. They free the corporations to move about the globe without restrictions, leaving plant closures, job loss, and community devastation in their wake.

But an anti-globalization movement has also emerged, sufficiently powerful, at least for a time, that it harkened back to the days of the civil rights and anti–Vietnam War movements. Global in character, it comprised a loose alliance of trade unions and a host of popular movements opposed to the process of corporate-driven globalization and the international agreements that facilitate it. Its strength became evident in the Battle of Seattle in 1999 and at the Summit of the Americas in Quebec City in April 2001. If the WTO has become the visible symbol of corporate-driven globalization, the Battle of Seattle and the mass mobilization in Quebec City became, at the turn of the twenty-first century, the symbol of the growing mass movement against corporate-driven globalization.

In November–December 1999 the workings of a previously obscure international organization, the WTO, were suddenly being debated all across the world, as was the proposed FTAA in April 2001. Organized labour and the popular movements, working together in the extra-parliamentary fashion developed over the last two decades of the twentieth century, were highly successful in both cases in what amounted to a global consciousness-raising effort. Information about Seattle and the WTO, Quebec City and the FTAA, spread like wildfire via the Internet and the alternative media, adding still further to the building of this global movement.

For most of those opposing globalization, their efforts are not a matter of being anti-internationalist. The world is becoming more global, and this is a process that cannot be stopped. The issue is: Who will make the rules that guide this globalization of economic activity, and in whose interests will those rules be made? Will they be corporate-friendly, or people/labour-friendly? Will it be globalization from above, or globalization from below (Brecher, Costello, and Smith 2000)? The transnational corporations want corporate-friendly rules developed in a process of globalization from above. For instance, they seek to extend the WTO's General Agreement on Trade in Services to public services such as health and education. The result of that shift would be the eventual privatization of much of the public health and education systems, and huge profits for corporations. The interests of most people, and certainly of working people, would be jeopardized.

The trade union movement has opposed this approach and will continue to do so, but how is this best done? Should labour and the anti-WTO movement seek to replace the corporate-driven international arrangements? If so, what should they be replaced with? What is the alternative? Extra-parliamentary movements have proved to be effective in *opposing* initiatives, but less so in proposing alternatives. Or should labour and its allies seek to *modify* the international deals, for example, by the implementation of side agreements like the ones that already exist in the NAFTA, whose wording seeks to offer protections for labour and the environment?

The answers to these questions are not clear from a tactical point of view, although there can be no doubt at all that corporate-driven trade deals are destructive to working people and trade unions and need to be opposed. Nor is it fully clear how labour and the popular movements that comprise this loosely structured mass global movement can build on their campaign in order to keep it moving forward. After mass demonstrations in the streets, what is the next political step, besides still more and bigger demonstrations?

In addition, the events of September 11, 2001, set back the anti-globalization movement and became the excuse for intensified U.S. military aggression abroad — especially in Afghanistan, and then Iraq — and the restriction of civil liberties in most of the world's advanced capitalist countries, including Canada. This has made the rallying cry of the anti-globalization movement — "a different world is possible" — all the more relevant, but it

> The Use of Child Labour to Maximize Profits:
>
> "An estimated 200 children, some 11 years old or even younger, are sewing clothing for Hanes, Wal-Mart, J.C. Penney and Puma at the Harvest Rich factory in Bangladesh.
>
> The children report being routinely slapped and beaten, sometimes falling down from exhaustion, forced to work 12 to 14 hours a day, even some all-night, 19 to 20 hour shifts, often seven days a week, for wages as low as six and a half cents an hour....
>
> In the month of September [2006], the children had just one day off, and before clothing shipments had to leave for the US, the workers were often kept at the factory 95 to 110 hours a week. After being forced to work a grueling all-night 19 to 20 hour shift, from 8 a.m. to 3 or 4 a.m. the following day, the children sleep on the factory floor for two or three hours before being woken to start their next shift at 8 a.m. that same morning."
>
> *Source: National Labor Committee 2006.*

has also, at least for now, seriously weakened the movement.

One important response to the increased capital mobility that is at the heart of globalization is the effort to promote union organizing in the low-wage jurisdictions to which corporations are moving. The establishment of effective unions in these low-wage jurisdictions would benefit workers there by improving their wages and working conditions. But it would also benefit workers in Canada and other higher-wage jurisdictions by reducing the incentive for TNCs to relocate in pursuit of low-cost labour.

TNCs, though, use their ability to relocate to low-cost jurisdictions as a lever against all union efforts. For example, one study found that in the United States between 1993 and 1995, "Employers threatened to close the plant in 50 percent of all union certification elections," and carried out the threat in 15 percent of cases — three times the pre-NAFTA level (Bronfenbrenner, cited in Klein 2000: 223). Corporations regularly make similar threats to relocate as a tactic in response to union efforts to secure higher wages and more favourable labour legislation. By this means, worker is set against worker, on a global scale.

Organizing unions in low-wage jurisdictions will not be easy. Because they derive enormous benefits from the existence of these reserves of cheap labour, TNCs are determined to oppose unionization attempts. They are generally supported in these objectives by local governments. In the export zones in the Philippines, for example, anti-union signs shout: *Do Not Listen to Agitators and Trouble Makers* (Klein 2000: 212). Union organizers are subject to intimidation; workers seeking unions are subject to dismissal and blacklisting and even physical violence. States help out by using the police and the armed forces to prevent unionization, not only in the Philippines but also in Mexico, Guatemala, South Korea, and most jurisdictions where low wages and poor working conditions prevail.

The working conditions in most of these jurisdictions are appalling. In the export zones in Asia, for example, forced overtime is common. "Regular shifts last from 7 a.m. to 10 p.m., but on a few nights a week employees must work 'late' — until 2 a.m. During peak periods, it is not uncommon to work two 2 a.m. shifts in a row, leaving many women only a couple of hours of sleep before they have to start their commute back to the factory" (Klein 2000: 215). In a March 1999 report on twelve Chinese toy factories, the Asia Monitor Resource Centre found: "During the peak season, not a single worker can leave the workplace after eight hours work. Most workers in these toy factories work 10 to 16 hours a day, 6 or 7 days a week.... They never receive overtime pay" (Greider 2000). In many cases, refusal to work overtime is punishable with dismissal. As long as such working conditions exist anywhere in the world, they directly hurt Canadian workers by eroding the bargaining strength of Canadian unions.

Unions in Canada and other higher-wage jurisdictions are beginning to develop ways of responding to these challenges. Canadian unions are now involved in many tangible expressions of cross-border labour solidarity. For example, since 1985 at least five Canadian unions have established international solidarity funds, to which each Canadian member of the union contributes one cent per hour via payroll deduction. The CAW is a member of the North America Ford Workers' Solidarity Network, which, for example, has "supported Ford workers in Cuautitlán, Mexico, where thugs from the state-dominated labour federation killed a union activist" (Wells 1998: 34). Many Canadian unions work closely with sister unions in the United States and Mexico to promote both information-sharing and continental collective bargaining. The Inter-American Council of the Postal, Telegraph and Telephone International is a federation co-ordinating telecommunications unions in 115 countries. The Teamsters were involved in setting up the UPS (United Postal Service) World Trade Union Council, composed of unions representing UPS workers in eleven countries in Europe and North America. The Steelworkers organize "linkage visits" that bring together union activists from Canada and countries of the South. Teachers' unions in Quebec, English-speaking Canada, the United States, and Mexico have formed a coalition to monitor the impact of the NAFTA on public education. These international efforts, despite the many obstacles, are beginning to bear fruit.

All of these embryonic attempts at global labour solidarity, and more, will have to be nourished if Canadian unions are to successfully meet the challenge of globalization. Rank-and-file trade unionists, not just union leaders and staff, will need to become directly involved; if they don't, the result will be not only resentment of leaders' international travels but also fears about the neglect of local concerns. It is essential that union members see that global concerns *are* local concerns.

ORGANIZING A NEW LABOUR FORCE

The structure of the labour market has changed significantly in the last quarter of the twentieth and first decade of the twenty-first centuries. Corporations have sought to move to what they call a more flexible labour force, one increasingly characterized by the use of part-time or non-permanent and lower-waged work. Many new jobs are non-union, in relatively small units in the retail or service sector, and are staffed by women and/or workers of colour. In other words, a high proportion of new jobs have been and are being created in areas in which unions have traditionally faced the greatest difficulties in organizing. In the 1980s and 1990s attempts to unionize such companies as McDonald's and Wal-Mart have been met with exceptionally aggressive anti-union efforts by employers, and most of the union efforts have met with failure.

U.S. Workers Want to Be in a Union:
"In 2002 Harvard University and University of Wisconsin researchers found at least 42 million workers want to be organized into a bargaining unit — more than double the 16 million unionized workers in America. A 2005 nationwide survey by respected pollster Peter Hart found 53 percent of nonunion workers — that's more than 50 million people — want to join a union, if given the choice.

Increasingly, however, workers have no real choice. According to Cornell University experts, 1 in 4 employers illegally fires at least one worker during a union drive, 3 in 4 hire anti-union consultants, and 8 in 10 force workers to attend anti-union meetings."

Source: Sirota 2006.

In the case of McDonald's, for instance, repeated attempts to unionize the restaurants have fallen short of the goal. In 1997, following four earlier failed attempts to unionize outlets in Quebec and a similar failed attempt in Orangeville, Ontario, in 1993–94, the Teamsters signed 82 percent of the sixty-two employees at a McDonald's in St.-Hubert, a suburb of Montreal. Success seemed imminent. Then management pulled out its well-worn bag of anti-union tactics. According to writer Christian Huot (1998: 25):

> First, they tried the classic methods of harassment and reduction of working hours of union sympathisers. They also started giving special gifts and privileges to the 'soft' elements of the staff to try to rally their support.... The owners of the franchise also tried to argue that the union had to recruit a majority in the four other restaurants they owned, since all of these restaurants had to be considered together as one business.

After a year-long fight the workers did win accreditation, "and became the only McDonald's employees in either Canada or the US to be unionised workers" (Huot 1998: 25). But two weeks before, knowing what was coming, the owners had shut the restaurant down — permanently. Better, McDonald's believes, to sacrifice one restaurant than to let unionization get a foot in the door.

Anti-union efforts now include an entire industry of consultants who advise management on how to keep companies "union-free." A 1997 study done for the labour ministries of Canada, the United States, and Mexico found that in the 1992–95 period:

> More than one-third of US employers faced with NLRB (National Labor Relations Board) representation elections discharged workers for union activity, more than half threatened a full or partial shutdown of the company if the union succeeded in organizing the facility, and between 15 and 40 percent made illegal changes in wages, benefits, and working conditions, gave bribes or special favors to those who opposed the union, or used electronic surveillance of union activists during organizing campaigns. (Bronfenbrenner and Juravich 1998: 5)

But the problem is not just employer opposition. Part of the problem, as Craig Heron (1989: 144) observes, is:

> The modern labour movement has inherited a model of organizing based on the large mass-production factory with a fairly stable, semi-skilled, male workforce.... This model is not helpful for signing up the thousands of highly transient, part-time workers in the booming service industries, where most of the new jobs are now being created.

New union strategies are being tried now, especially in the United States. Some are proving successful. Recent research shows:

> Campaigns in which the union focussed on person-to-person contact, house calls, and small-group meetings to develop leadership and union consciousness and to inoculate the workers against the employers' anti-union campaigns were associated with win rates that were 10 to 30 percent higher than traditional campaigns that primarily used gate leafleting, mass meetings and glossy mailings to contact unorganized workers. (Bronfenbrenner and Juravich 1998: 24)

This same research found that organizing success also depends upon the issues that organizers focus upon. "Unions that focussed on issues such as dignity, justice, discrimination, fairness, or service quality were associated with win rates that were nearly 20 percentage points higher than those that focused on more traditional bread-and-butter issues, such as wages, benefits and job security" (Bronfenbrenner and Juravich 1998: 24). In short, the experimentation with new organizing techniques for the new labour force can yield positive results.

This has been the case, for example, in the successful organizing of the mostly female support staff in U.S. universities. The organizing of Harvard University support staff involved what its advocates call "the feminist model of organizing," which includes different kinds of literature, emphasis on different issues, and smaller, one-on-one meetings with workers:

> The heart and soul of the campaign were these "one on ones." Instead of relying on leaflets and big meetings, Harvard organizers persistently met with co-workers, usually at work or lunch. These meetings set out to establish beneath-the-surface supportive networks which sustained people through the long drive. (Leary and Alonso 1997: 4)

With the 1995 election of John Sweeney as president of the AFL-CIO, organizing became a priority for the U.S. labour movement. The AFL-CIO has attempted industry organizing — attempts to reach all the plants/branches in a particular industry and geographical area, as opposed to organizing on a shop-by-shop basis. Its "Justice for Janitors" campaigns used this approach with success, targeting all the building owners and cleaning contractors in a given city. The AFL-CIO also promoted joint organizing efforts, involving more than one union working co-operatively, and set up an organizing fund for such initiatives. It established an Organizing Institute as well as a Union Summer program that introduces talented and idealistic young people to the excitement and challenge of organizing. Union Summer brings them "into the streets and neighborhoods for a four-week educational internship to participate in and develop skills useful for union organizing drives and other campaigns for workers' rights and social justice" (AFL-CIO website).

These organizing efforts were less than successful to date. By 2004 the union density rate among private-sector workers in the United States had declined further, to 7.9 percent from 10.4 percent in 1995, and the sense of optimism raised initially by Sweeney's election in 1995 and his commitment to union organizing "proved fleeting" (Masters, Gibney, and Zagenczyk 2006: 484, 479).

Claiming dissatisfaction with the AFL-CIO's organizing efforts, seven unions representing more than 40 percent of AFL-CIO membership broke away and formed a new group, Change to Win, whose founding convention was held in September 2005. Change to Win argues that it will be more committed to organizing than the AFL-CIO was, and that it will organize aggressively in the growing service sector. It promised to experiment with different organizing and union models and to promote structural changes — for instance, mergers to create stronger unions, and more centralized decision-making and control over resource flows in order to better co-ordinate organizing activities in particular industries. Critics argue that this new formation will undermine union solidarity while promoting more of the same old business unionism (Estreicher 2006; Greer 2006), and they may, for the most part, be proven correct. Within the next few years, at least, change to Win had *not* brought to the U.S. labour movement the kinds of changes so desperately needed; neither it nor the AFL-CIO had yet found the key to unleashing a successful mass unionization drive where it is most needed — the precarious and increasingly racialized sectors of the labour market that are growing most rapidly in the neo-liberal era.

Members of Change to Win:
Service Employees International Union (SEIU); Union of Needle, Industrial and Textile Employees — Hotel and Restaurant Employees (INITE-HERE); International Brotherhood of Teamsters (IBT); United Food and Commercial Workers (UFCW); United Brotherhood of Carpenters and Joiners (IBCJ); Laborers International Union of North America (LIUNA); and United Farm Workers (UFW).

A second ingredient for success in organizing the new labour force is legislative change. In Canada the labour movement has discussed broader-based or sectoral bargaining. Current labour law facilitates organizing at single work sites — it presumes bargaining on a workplace by workplace basis — thus effectively discriminating in favour of the unionization of large industrial workplaces, where workers are disproportionately male. This legal bias makes organizing especially difficult and prohibitively expensive in industries in which each small workplace has to be separately organized and serviced, where employees are disproportionately female and/or youth and/or workers of colour, and where jobs are part-time or non-permanent or otherwise "non-standard." Unions have advanced several proposals for such broader-based bargaining. An interesting example of a proposal for a shift in the bargaining approach came in recommendations made by John Baigent, Vince Ready, and Tom Roper for labour law reform in British Columbia.

Unfortunately, far from making legislative gains, the trade union movement in Canada has struggled and is struggling against provincial right-wing governments that are dismantling many of the legislative gains of the postwar compromise. In Ontario, for instance, the former Mike Harris government amended the *Labour Relations Act* in December 2000 to further curtail union rights. As a result of these amendments, unions were restricted to one certification drive a year in any given workplace, and what was previously an unfair labour practice — namely, the provision by employ-

Sectoral Bargaining:
"It is simply impractical and unacceptably expensive for unions to organize and negotiate collective agreements for small groups of workers if their dues cannot begin to cover the costs involved in developing separate collective agreements for each of their work sites. As a result, persons employed as clerical support staff in small business, farm workers or service station attendants do not have any realistic prospect of ever being represented by a trade union under present labour legislation.

Yet these are the very workers who are most in need of trade union representation. Put simply, for these persons certification and collective bargaining rights are illusory. The options are stark: either maintain a status quo in which many workers will seldom achieve collective bargaining rights, or fashion a model which allows employees in these sectors the option of banding together for the purpose of collective bargaining with other employees performing the same types of jobs.

The model we recommend would be available only in sectors which are determined by the Labour Relations Board to be historically underrepresented by trade unions and where the average number of employees at work locations within the sector is less than 50. A sector has two characteristics: a defined geographic area... and similar enterprises within the area where employees perform similar tasks (e.g., preparing fast food, child care, picking fruit).

For example, a sector could consist of 'employees working in fast food outlets in Burnaby.' We recommend that a union that has the requisite support of more than one work location within a sector could apply for certification of the employees at those locations. In addition to demonstrating support at each location, the union would have to prevail in a vote amongst all the employees at the work locations where certification was sought.

If successful the union would be granted certification for a bargaining unit within the sector. Collective bargaining would then take place between the union and the various employers whose employees had become certified. A standard collective agreement would be settled and subsequently, if the union could demonstrate sufficient support at additional locations within the sector, it would be entitled to a variance of its bargaining certificate to encompass the new employees.

As a matter of principle we believe certification should be made available to workers in these areas unless doing so would impose unacceptable restrictions on the rights of others. The model we propose rejects the notion of 'sweeping in' employees at a particular location against their will."

Source: Baigent, Ready, and Roper 1992.

ers to employees of information on how to decertify their union — became required by law. The Ontario Harris government justified these changes on the grounds that they would "strengthen workplace democracy, promote workplace stability and encourage investment" (*Lancaster's Labour Law News* 2000: 3–4). Even pro-labour provincial governments, like the NDP in Manitoba, have failed to take the steps needed to facilitate organizing. Although research confirms that workers are more likely to be successful in achieving certification in jurisdictions with a 50 percent plus one threshold for automatic certification, the threshold for automatic certification in Manitoba remains at 65 percent of the members of a bargaining unit, a proportion set in the 1990s by the previous Conservative government and which has not been changed by subsequent NDP governments (Black and Silver 2007).

Still, government anti-union efforts have prompted an interest in new organizing strategies. In April 1997, for example, the OFL hosted a conference, New Organizing Strategies, at which Kate Bronfenbrenner, Director of Labour Education Research at Cornell University and a leading researcher on the new organizing strategies in the United States, was a keynote speaker. Many Canadian unions are actively organizing members of the new labour force. Although Canadian union density rates have not plummeted like those in the United States, thanks in large part to the high rates of unionization in the Canadian public sector, organizing drives targeting those sectors and workers created by the restructuring of capitalism in the late twentieth century are essential.

Whether those organizing drives will be successful, despite the many obstacles, remains to be seen. Certainly, though, similar, and in some respects perhaps even tougher, conditions prevailed in the 1930s, yet during those earlier years skilled and dedicated union organizers were eventually successful, as a result of their militancy and creativity, in building the new industrial unionism. Unions make gains when they are militant and creative.

As part of the promotion of militancy and creativity, unions must mobilize their members as part of a broader movement for social change. This poses yet another challenge for the trade union movement: the need to actively involve the membership in the many aspects of their unions' work.

EDUCATION, MOBILIZATION, AND DEMOCRATIZATION

The vast majority of union members are not actively involved in their union or in the NDP. Most members see the union as a distant organization that delivers services to them in exchange for their union dues, but over whose decisions and direction they have little control. As for the NDP, most union members are not only not involved with the party, but also do not even vote for it. Some union members are even supporters of Canada's right-wing parties.

In CAW Local 222 in Oshawa in the early 1990s, for example, a movement emerged from within the membership to disaffiliate from the NDP. The Movement Against Political Affiliation (MAPA) was led by well-off, conservative, skilled trades workers, many of whom owned rental properties or other investments and who, as a result, identified less with their fellow workers than with business interests (Casey 1993: 13). Their politics reflected a desire to protect their relatively privileged positions as well-paid skilled workers and investors.

Although unsuccessful in its drive for disaffiliation, MAPA was able to appeal to some members of the local on the grounds that the union was a distant force that made political decisions about which most members had no say. If unions are to be a powerful force for advancing the interests of workers, they must be open and democratic institutions in which members feel they are genuinely involved. They must be organizations committed to educating and mobilizing members to create an alternative culture to the one established by the wealthy and powerful few who control our society's sources of information and entertainment. As Leo Panitch and Donald Swartz (1988: 114) put it, this means "opening the way for unions to become, as far as possible, centres of working class life and culture." Unions should be striving towards this goal. But in the postwar period, this was not the direction taken by most unions in Canada. The education and mobilization of the membership were for the most part replaced by the negotiation and servicing of collective agreements. Union leaders became bureaucratic; administration replaced mobilization and broadly based education.

The same process was taking place in the NDP: a separation of leaders from members; a narrow focus on winning elections rather than educating and mobilizing and developing the capacities of people. This was a world away from the early years of the NDP's predecessor, the CCF, when:

> As a movement, the focus was on educating, organizing, mobilizing. Newspapers were established to disseminate information and analysis; during the thirties, the CCF had six newspapers in six different provinces supported by a central news co-op. Educational activity was paramount as reading lists were distributed, study groups formed, and leaders travelled the country not to get a sound-bite on the news, but to teach and debate the issues. New people were constantly brought into "politics" by creating new institutions for fighting back — like councils of the unemployed. (CAW 1994)

These initiatives were part of a broader movement for social and economic change, out of which emerged the final, successful, CIO drive for industrial

Reinventing Labour Councils:
"There are formidable obstacles facing unions seeking to organize in the private sector. Recent efforts to unionize Wal-Mart, for example, have met with some success, but Wal-Mart is a ruthless employer, comparable to the coal barons and the Eatons and chartered banks of previous eras. Wal-Mart will stop at nothing to thwart efforts to unionize, including cutting off its own parts to prevent the spread of unionization.

To organize workers in the Wal-Marts of this world, organized labour has to build grassroots support in the communities where Wal-Mart and other such reactionary employers are located.

Historically, local labour councils mobilized support for workers involved in industrial disputes with employers; organized educational activities on political, social and economic issues for workers; and supported efforts to elect working people to city council, school boards and federal and provincial legislatures.

These activities were inspired by the belief that the labour movement represented all working people, and was committed not only to improving conditions in the workplace, but also to building better communities. Labour councils led the fights for public libraries, for universal suffrage in local, provincial and federal elections, for parks and recreation, for public utilities to provide sewer and water, public transit and public health services. Labour councils fought in national campaigns in support of universal pensions, Medicare, unemployment insurance and a social safety net for the poor.

But in recent decades, labour councils have been battered by relentless attacks on working people and their organizations by employers and governments. Labour councils have had to fight defensive campaigns to block the GST, stop cuts to Unemployment Insurance, oppose privatization, protect Medicare, and block anti-union legislation. At the same time, many trade unions that had historically encouraged their members to get active in labour councils, withdrew their support to pursue more narrowly-focused agendas.

If we are to breathe new life into the labour movement, and reverse the long-term decline in union density, we need once again to look to local labour councils as a catalyst in building a culture supportive of trade unionism and progressive social change. It is labour councils that can, through their active campaigns to support communities, promote a vision that embraces all working people.

To achieve these results, three things need to happen immediately. First, the Canadian Labour Congress must direct more resources to local labour councils to support them in expanding their range of activities and initiatives in local communities. The CLC has previously considered, but backed away from, requiring affiliates to contribute per capita dues to labour councils. Perhaps the time has come to revisit this idea.

Second, while money is important, so is active participation by unions in support of labour councils. The CLC and its affiliates must encourage local unions to elect/ appoint delegates to labour councils, and support and promote the initiatives of labour councils, including, for example, information pickets directed at anti-union employers, and election campaigns in support of progressive labour candidates.

Third, labour councils must build coalitions with other progressive organizations in their communities to unite on issues of common concern, for example, degradation of the environment, poverty and affordable housing, and the building of community through support for improved public transit, and local library and recreational facilities.

This rejuvenation at the bottom that arises from involvement in local communities will contribute significantly to building social solidarity, expanding the ranks of unionized workers, and promoting democracy and social justice."

Source: Black and Silver 2005.

unionism. Union organizing success was clearly a product of a broader movement for social change.

Labour can build that kind of movement by developing the capacities of individual workers. This means creating unions that are democratic, and in which members feel they have a say; promoting more broadly based education, by which workers come to understand their position in the broader political economy; and involving workers in struggles for social change, both within and beyond their unions, so that they gain organizational skills and self-confidence. It means consciously setting about to increase the number of activists within the union — and especially the number of those actively involved in the running of the union. As Gindin (1995: 275) argues:

> Building that cadre of activists and activists-to-be is achieved by expanding educational opportunities, by establishing the widest range of forums and conferences, and, above all, by maintaining the union's constant involvement in campaigns and struggles. Activism creates activists.

BUILDING INCLUSIVE AND REPRESENTATIVE UNIONS

The exclusion or marginalization of certain types of workers also weakens the labour movement. The crafts unions excluded industrial workers; most unions excluded or marginalized women; and newly arrived immigrants and workers of colour have historically been excluded or marginalized.

A central challenge will be to create a labour movement that is inclusive and representative and that responds to the needs of *all* its members and *all* workers. Building a labour movement by creating trade union activists

Immigrant Workers Organize:
"Immigrant workers who have arrived in Canada in the past 20 years — mainly people of colour and from the South — face disappointment.... Racial and other barriers in the labour market push many immigrants to the bottom, where they work in the worst jobs. Some, like domestic and farm workers, are recruited through special immigration programs to do specific kinds of work that Canadians are unwilling to do for the wages and work conditions offered.... [Unions'] ability to organize recent arrivals to Canada has been limited. It is difficult to organize workers in small factories and in unstable jobs with high turnover.

New strategies to organize have been devised.... For example, in the U.S., immigrant workers and their allies have founded... "community unions," a new form of labour organizing that provides direct services, organizes immigrant workers and advocates for policy changes. In the US there are 133 such centres in more than 80 communities.

The Immigrant Workers Centre (IWC) in Montreal is an example of the community labour approach being put into action in Canada. The IWC was founded in 2000 by a small group of Filipino-Canadian union and former union organizers and their activist and academic allies.... They observed that much of their recruitment and education to support a union drive had to take place outside of the workplace, and, apart from personal homes, there were few places where this could happen. The idea of the Centre was to provide a safe place outside the workplace where workers could discuss their situations. Further, they forwarded a critique of the unions themselves, arguing that once they got a majority to sign cards and thus join the union, the processes of education and solidarity built into the organizing process were lost as union "bureaucrats" came in to manage the collective agreement.

In its first year, the organization was able to secure a grant from the social-justice fund of the Canadian Auto Workers to intervene on labour issues in the community. The IWC then got to work providing ongoing education and critical analysis beyond the specific role of unions, and finding ways to address worker issues outside the traditional union structures.

IWC activities cover individual-rights counseling, popular education and political campaigns that reflect issues facing immigrant workers, like dismissal, problems with employers, or, sometimes, inadequate representation by their unions. Labour education is a priority.... Workshops on themes like the history of the labour movement, the Labour Standards Act and collective-organizing processes have been presented.... In addition, the IWC supports union organizing in workplaces where there is a high concentration of immigrant workers.

Campaigns are viewed not only as ways to make specific gains for immigrant workers but also as means to educate the wider community....

For example, the first campaign, in 2000, was to defend Melca Salvador, a domestic worker admitted to Canada under the Live-in Caregiver Program, against deportation. Besides winning the campaign, the IWC was able to bring into the public sphere the issue of importing immigrant labourers as "indentured servants," and many community organizations and unions became involved.

As the IWC has become better known, workers come for advice and support on specific problems and issues. The Centre sees this as a way to encourage and support people in standing up against their bosses, but also as a basis upon which to build wider campaigns....

Another aspect of the IWC's work has been its contribution to organizing cultural events with political content. The first was an International Women's Day event organized in 2001. A coalition of immigrant women of diverse origins organized a cultural event, panels and a march to emphasize the concerns of immigrant women and international solidarity. This has become an annual event, and, through its success, has increased the profile and the issues faced by immigrant women within the wider women's movement in Quebec....

New forms of labour organizing are required in the current context that includes support both for and from the trade-union movement.... The IWC has become a meeting place for many groups of social activists. The core of the organization is a group comprised of immigrant union and labour organizers and allies who have been active in both labour and community issues for many years. The IWC is also connected to student and anti-globalization activists.... Many of these students have been involved in student organizing, and this has helped to connect students to the issues raised by the IWC. In addition, students at the Quebec Public Interest Research Groups (QPIRG) have found the IWC to be an opportunity to combine radical politics with local work. At the same time, the IWC's connections with these groups have pushed its own positions on broader social issues. The IWC is a place that brings together union, community and student activists, people of different ages, ethnic, cultural and class backgrounds, to work together for social justice for immigrant workers."

Source: Hanley and Shragge 2006.

who are prepared and able to play leadership roles around issues of exclusion and marginalization — not only with respect to women, but also as regards gay and lesbian workers, Aboriginal workers and workers of colour, and workers with disabilities — is a matter of great importance.

A major challenge for the trade union movement in the twenty-first century will be to overcome the divisions among workers, the exclusion and marginalization of particular groups of workers that is so much a part of capitalist profit-making. It is not in workers' interests to go along with capital's desire for cheap labour justified by racist or sexist ideologies. As Galabuzi (2006: 235) pus it:

> Perhaps no institution represents as much promise in empowering racialized workers to overcome their oppression in the labour market as does organized labour. The role of unions in improving the lives of working people is well documented. The major improvements in the lives of workers in the post-war period were not a gift from employers or capital, but rather the outcome of workplace and political struggles waged by organized workers in Canada. For Canada's racialized group members to make significant progress in the labour market, they need the union advantage — the power of collective bargaining. The leadership and members of Canada's organized labour must seize the opportunity to meet the challenge of empowering an increasingly marginalized and socially excluded segment of our society. Unions can bargain employment equity provisions as well as organize drives in the sectors of the economy in which racialized groups are overrepresented. They can improve the lives of racialized workers in precarious environments by organizing part-time and temporary workers.

It is in organized labour's interests to do this, to improve the wages and working conditions of *all* workers, so that one group of workers cannot be used against another. If an important challenge for labour is to educate and mobilize workers and democratize unions so that working people themselves build the capacities and self-confidence to become the agents for social change, it follows that this process must be inclusive. It must include all workers — women as well as men, non-white as well as white, gay and lesbian as well as heterosexual, less-abled as well as more-abled. Unions have made considerable gains in these areas in recent decades — in the form of union education programs, clauses in collective agreements, constitutional requirements for the representation of women and workers of colour in executive positions, for example — thanks largely to the hard work of dedicated union activists. Much more remains to be done, for a divided union movement is a weakened union movement.

LABOUR IN POLITICS

An immediate political challenge facing Canada's trade union movement is how to relate to the NDP. Trade unions have always seen the need to play a role in broader political struggles beyond the immediate workplace, and various factions of the labour movement, over a long period of time, have advanced many different political strategies. When the NDP was established

Giving the Ontario NDP Thumbs Down
by Ed Finn:
The sad fact is that, as a party of the Left, the NDP has self-destructed. It is a spent force....

Those in the labour movement who seek to save the NDP from extinction are doing no one a favour. If the party survives its self-inflicted wounds, it will be a political zombie with no real life or credibility. Far better to disconnect its life support system and let it go....

Perhaps the demise of the NDP will clear the way for the emergence of a party that will not shrink from testing the limits of fair and progressive governance in Canada. If it fails, it will at least be a noble failure, not the NDP's ignoble retreat.

For more than 30 years, I supported and helped build the NDP. I pleaded with Canadians hungry for social and economic justice to give the NDP a chance. They did. The NDP let them down.

Before 1991, the NDP's setbacks came because it stuck to its principles, not because it had repudiated them. And so, even after its worst electoral defeats, it retained the trust and support of the party faithful. Now much of that strong core support has been lost, and the loss is irretrievable.

The sooner the unions and other progressive organizations and individuals accept that grim reality, the sooner we can regroup and try again.

Ed Finn is a former provincial leader of the NDP in Newfoundland and was an NDP candidate in two provincial and two federal elections.

Giving the Ontario NDP Thumbs Up
by Hugh Mackenzie:
Despite a rabid response from business, despite having to govern in the teeth of the worst recession since the 1930s, and despite having to cope with central bank and federal government policies that deepened and prolonged the economic collapse, the Ontario NDP can point to significant gains for working people.

Ontario's labour legislation is, by far, the most favourable to organizing and collective bargaining in North America. Ontario has the highest minimum wage in Canada. Social assistance benefits are the highest in Canada. Under the NDP, more progress has been made on equity issues in four years than in the previous 20 years. In health care, it has shifted resources away from big, centralized institutions towards community-based facilities. It has increased Ontario's support for child care significantly....

So where does that leave trade unionists in Ontario in the 1995 election? With four good reasons for supporting the New Democratic Party. First, in the face of implacable opposition and an economic meltdown, the government delivered progressive change. Second, in the real world situation in which we find ourselves, the choices are not Bob Rae and the NDP on one hand and the Ontario Federation of Labour Policy Book on the other. The options are Bob Rae, Mike Harris or Lyn McLeod. The choice should be obvious. Third, a retreat from involvement in electoral politics at this point, amounts to an endorsement of the 'reward your friends and punish your enemies' philosophy of Samuel Gompers that was a disaster for the labour movement in the US.

Finally, with the Right in ascendancy and the Left essentially shut out of the public debate in much of North America, nothing could be more self-destructive than to hasten the obliteration of the one electorally successful social democratic movement in the history of this continent.

Hugh Mackenzie was, at the time of writing, assistant to the national director of the United Steelworkers of America in Toronto.
Source: Canadian Dimension, June/July, 1995: 12/13.

in 1961 it seemed that the problem of labour's political strategy was solved: labour would support the NDP; the NDP would act in labour's interests.

Developments in the last two decades of the twentieth century cast doubt on this political strategy. These doubts remain, in the minds of many trade unionists, in the first decade of the twenty-first century. It was the Social Contract of Bob Rae's Ontario NDP government that really opened up the debate about labour's relationship to the party. The Social Contract clawed back the right of free collective bargaining from Ontario's public-sector workers. The labour movement in Ontario was dramatically split on the issue: most of the private-sector unions advocated continued electoral support, despite the Social Contract, for the NDP; most of the public-sector unions plus the Canadian Auto Workers believed that the Social Contract effectively severed labour's historic relationship with the party.

While the NDP has been, at least in the view of some trade unionists, drifting, the social movements have been providing new sources of political energy and creativity. Particularly from the time of the anti-FTA battle in the mid-1980s, the trade union movement has learned, through practice, to work collaboratively and effectively with the social movements. In the mid-1990s this collaboration found expression in the Alternative Federal Budget (AFB). Funded largely by the trade union movement and the voluntary contributions of highly skilled labour by hundreds of community activists across the country, and involving almost all of Canada's major unions and major social movement organizations, the AFB showed that the huge cuts to public spending of the Mulroney and Chrétien governments were not necessary, and it set out a range of fiscally achievable and often creative policy alternatives (see CCPA and CHO!CES 1997). The Alternative Federal Budget met the government's deficit and debt reduction targets, but did so without destructive expenditure reductions. The AFB has been important because it has proved that, contrary to the insistence of governments and the corporate sector, *alternatives* to the neo-liberal agenda are possible; and it showed that labour and the social movements can work together constructively in a highly creative and sophisticated political exercise that goes beyond simply opposing government and corporate policies. The Alternative Federal Budget continues to be produced by a broadly based coalition of unions and social movement organizations headed by the Canadian Centre for Policy Alternatives, and it continues to demonstrate clearly that labour-friendly and people-friendly alternatives are possible.

Despite their energy and creativity, the alliance of labour and the social movements around particular issues still leaves open the question of power. The limitations of the alliance became obvious both in the dramatic Days of Action campaign directed at the Ontario Conservative government of Mike Harris, and in the Battle of Seattle and the mass mobilization against the Free Trade Area of the Americas in Quebec City in 2001. In both cases, massive numbers of people demonstrated. In the Days of Action, eleven separate Ontario cities were the sites of a sequential series of labour/community strikes/protests, including the virtual shutdown of Toronto on October 26, 1996, in what may well have been the largest demonstration in Canadian history. Similarly, in Seattle and Quebec City tens of thousands of trade unionists and environmentalists and community activists of every imaginable kind came together in a dramatic mobilization and confrontation.

But in each of these cases the dilemma became: "What do we do next? How do we translate this energy and creativity and anger at injustice into the political power needed to implement policies that benefit people?" In the case of Ontario, for instance, the labour movement was deeply split around future direction. The so-called "Pink Group" of private-sector unions insisted that the vast energy exhibited in the Days of Action had to be diverted into electoral support for the NDP. In the other camp at least some activists were calling for an escalation to a general strike. In the end, the Days of Action withered away in dissension and confusion in the face of the absence of consensus on political direction.

Early in the twenty-first century, Canada's trade union movement is going through the kind of reassessment of its politics that it last went through almost half a century earlier, when the CCF, then in the final stages of a fifteen-year decline, was folded up and a new party was created. In the wake of the sad results of the November 2000 federal election, many voices in the labour movement called for a review of its members' commitment to the NDP. The 2006 federal election, which led to a minority Conservative government with a particularly harsh neo-conservative approach, also occasioned much debate within labour's ranks. The outcome of these and other such efforts at rethinking the politics of the labour movement remains to be seen.

However, what can be seen, based on the historical experience of the labour movement in Canada, is the importance of union activism, especially when that activism and militancy are part of a broader social movement in making political and other gains. After all, corporate power is based on money; union power is based on people. But people power is only a *potential* power until those people are mobilized into active involvement in the struggle for a greater good.

Perhaps the *prior* question, therefore, is not "what shall labour do about the NDP?" but, rather, how can labour and a political party create activists — the activists who build movements for social and political change? The creation of more activists, by means of a greater focus on education and mobilization and action, will generate the broadly based debate that the trade union movement now needs to meet the challenge of determining a political strategy for the twenty-first century. The struggle for trade unionism has always been most effective when unions have focused their efforts on educating and mobilizing their own members, on creating activists — members who apply their activist skills within their own unions and as part of a broader-based political movement for social and economic justice.

Meanwhile, the accentuated mobility of capital undermines union efforts at home, and necessitates the building of tangible forms of international worker solidarity, while the intensive restructuring of capital has created a new and especially difficult set of union organizing challenges. To build strong and effective unions in this difficult environment requires an intensified effort to involve rank-and-file members, including those traditionally marginalized and excluded. A union's power is its membership, but only if that membership sees itself not as passive recipients of union services but as active creators of better working and living conditions. This in turn requires that unions act not only at the workplace, but also in local communities and on the broader political stage.

It is important for all of us, trade unionists or not, that unions are successful in meeting the challenges, because unions are a positive force in a liberal-democratic society. They increase wages, improve benefits and working conditions, promote social and economic equality, reduce the arbitrary power of owners and managers by bringing the rule of law to the workplace, and increase the sense of dignity and self-respect of working people. In these ways they are a force for democracy, which, again, is not merely a matter of casting ballots in general elections from time to time, important though that is. In complex liberal-democratic societies, democracy is advanced by a host of institutional arrangements and practices that protect and extend our rights and freedoms. Trade unions are one of those institutions. They protect and extend the rights of working people. They are an *essential* element of democracy. This is especially so in the early twenty-first century, an era of unparalleled corporate power that threatens union rights and democracy everywhere on the globe.

Despite, or perhaps because of, their essential role in the health of democracy, trade unions have always been opposed by those with power. It is no coincidence that one of the first actions of fascist governments is always the crushing of trade unions. Even in non-fascist liberal-democratic societies, increasingly powerful TNCs exert enormous pressure on governments to erode trade union rights and weaken labour laws, and they threaten to move their capital and associated jobs if governments do not accede to their demands. TNCs have enormous advantages in this conflict between the classes because of their ownership of the means of production as well as of almost all of the media. As a result, unions are consistently portrayed in a negative light — "relics of an earlier age," as so frequently and erroneously claimed.

Meeting the new challenges will not be easy. Indeed, trade unionism has *never* come easily. Trade union gains are always the result of the hard work and militancy and creativity of trade unions, and especially of skilled and dedicated trade union activists. Not all unions are open and democratic: some are; some are not. But the *idea* of a union — the idea that the people who do the work should have a voice in how the work is to be done and what they are to be paid for that work — is intrinsically a democratic idea. Those struggling to overcome the challenges to the building of strong and effective unions in the twenty-first century are working not only to advance social and economic justice, but also to build democracy. They are working together to build a better world.

REFERENCES

Abella, Irving. *Nationalism, Communism and Canadian Labour: The CIO, the Communist Party, and the Canadian Congress of Labour, 1935–1956* (Toronto: University of Toronto Press, 1973).

Adams, Roy J. "Voice for All: Why the Right to Refrain from Collective Bargaining is No Right At All." In James A. Gross (ed.), *Workers' Rights as Human Rights* (Ithaca: Cornell University Press 2003).

AFL-CIO. Website. www.aflcio.org/unionsummer.

Akyeampong, Ernest B. "Unionization — An Update." *Perspectives on Labour and Income* (Ottawa: Statistics Canada, Catalogue No. 75-001-XPE, Autumn 1999).

_____. "The Rise of Unionization among Women." *Perspectives on Labour and Income* (Ottawa: Statistics Canada, Catalogue No. 75-001-XPE, Winter 1998).

_____. "A statistical portrait of the trade union movement." *Perspectives on Labour and Income* (Ottawa: Statistics Canada, Catalogue No.75-001-XPE, Winter 1997).

Alberta Economic Development Authority. *Final Report Joint Review Committee Right- to-Work Study* (Edmonton: Alberta Economic Development Authority, 1995).

Archer, Keith. *Political Choices and Electoral Consequences: A Study of Organized Labour and the New Democratic Party* (Montreal/Kingston: McGill-Queen's University Press, 1990).

_____. "Canadian Unions, the New Democratic Party and the Problems of Collective Action." *Labour/Le Travail* 20, 1987.

_____. "The Failure of the New Democratic Party: Unions, Unionists and Politics in Canada." *Canadian Journal of Political Science* 18 (2), 1985.

Avakumovic, I. *Socialism in Canada: A Study of the CCF-NDP in Federal and Provincial Politics* (Toronto: McClelland and Stewart, 1978).

Babcock, Robert H. *Gompers in Canada: A Study in American Continentalism before the First World War* (Toronto: University of Toronto Press, 1974).

Baigent, J., V. Ready and T. Roper. *Recommendations for Labour Law Reform: A Report to the Honourable Moe Sihota, Minister of Labour* (Submitted by the Sub-Committee of Special Advisors, Victoria, B.C., 1992).

Baker, Patricia. "Reflections on Life Stories: Women's Bank Union Activism." In Linda Briskin and Patricia McDermott (eds.), *Women Challenging Unions* (Toronto: University of Toronto Press, 1993).

Benjamin, Dwayne, Morley Gunderson and W. Craig Riddell. *Labour Market Economics: Theory, Evidence, and Policy in Canada (4th Edition)* (Toronto:

McGraw-Hill Ryerson, 1998).

Bercuson, David. *Confrontation at Winnipeg: Labour, Industrial Relations and the General Strike* (Kingston and Montreal: McGill-Queen's University Press, 1973).

Black, Errol. "The 'New' Crisis Of Unemployment: Restoring Profits and Controlling Labour." In Les Samuelson and Wayne Antony (eds.), *Power and Resistance: Critical Thinking about Canadian Social Issues (2nd Edition)* (Toronto: Fernwood Publishing, 1998).

_____. "Labour in Manitoba: A Refuge in Social Democracy." In Jim Silver and Jeremy Hull (eds.), *The Political Economy of Manitoba* (Regina: Canadian Plains Research Centre, 1990).

_____. "Canada's Economy, the Canadian Labour Movement, and the Catholic Bishops" (mimeo, 1984).

_____. "Just a Few More Notches." *Canadian Dimension* 16 (2), 1982.

Black, Errol, with Brian Campbell. *Strength in Solidarity: The Brandon and District Labour Council at 50* (Brandon, MB: Brandon and District Labour Council, September, 2006).

Black, Errol, and Robert Chernomas. "What Kind of Capitalism? The Revival of Class Struggle in Canada." *Monthly Review* 48 (1), 1996.

Black, Errol, and Jim Silver. "Automatic Certification at Fifty Percent Plus One: Now is the Time" (Winnipeg: Canadian Centre for Policy Alternatives–Manitoba *Fast Facts*, July 2007).

_____. "Strategies for Reversing the Long-Term Decline in the Unionization Rate" (Winnipeg: Canadian Centre for Policy Alternatives–Manitoba *Fast Facts*, January 2006).

_____. "The Way Forward for Labour" (Winnipeg: Canadian Centre for Policy Alternatives–Manitoba *Fast Facts*, May 2005).

Black, Errol, and Jim Silver (eds.). *Hard Bargains: The Manitoba Labour Movement Confronts the 1990s* (Winnipeg: Committee on Manitoba's Labour History, 1991).

Bluestone, Barry, and Bennett Harrison. *Growing Prosperity: The Battle for Growth with Equity in the 21st Century* (New York: Houghton Mifflin, 2000).

Boivin, Jean, and Ester Deom. "Labour-Management Relations in Quebec." In Morley Gunderson and Allen Ponak (eds.), *Union-Management Relations in Canada (3rd Edition)* (Toronto: Addison-Wesley, 1995).

Boyer, Richard O., and Herbert M. Morais. *Labor's Untold Story* (New York: United Electrical, Radio & Machine Workers of America, 1955).

Brand, Dionne. "Black Women and Work: The Impact of Racially Constructed Gender Roles on the Sexual Division of Labour." *Fireweed* 25, 1987.

Brandon and District Labour Council. *By-Laws*. 1979.

Brecher, Jeremy, Tim Costello and Brendan Smith. *Globalization from Below: The Power of Solidarity* (Cambridge, MA: South End Press, 2000).

Briskin, Linda, and Lynda Yanz (eds.). *Union Sisters: Women in the Labour Movement* (Toronto: Women's Press, 1983).

Broad, Dave. *Hollow Work, Hollow Society: Globalization and the Casual Labour Problem* (Halifax: Fernwood Publishing, 1999).

Bronfenbrenner, Kate, and Tom Juravich. "It Takes More than House Calls:

Organizing to Win with a Comprehensive Union-Building Strategy." In Kate Bronfenbrenner et al., *Organizing to Win: New Research on Union Strategies* (Ithaca, NY: Cornell University Press, 1998).

Brown, Lorne. *When Freedom Was Lost: The Unemployed, the Agitator and the State* (Montreal: Black Rose Books, 1987).

Camfield, David. "Neoliberalism and Working Class Resistance in British Columbia: The Hospital Employees' Union Struggle, 2002–2004." *Labour/Le Travail* 57, 2006.

_____. "Public Sector 'Reform' and the Future of Public Sector Unions" (Winnipeg: Canadian Centre for Policy Alternatives-Manitoba, December 2005).

Campbell, Peter. *Canadian Marxism and the Search for a Third Way* (Montreal and Kingston: McGill-Queen's University Press, 1999).

Canadian Auto Workers (CAW). *In the Eye of the Storm: The CAW and the Re-Making of Canadian Politics* (Vancouver: CAW 8th Constitutional Convention, August 15–18, 2006).

_____. *Rethinking, Redefining and Rebuilding: A CAW Discussion Paper* (Toronto: Canadian Auto Workers, 1994).

Canadian Centre for Policy Alternatives (CCPA). "Canadian Workers' Paycheques in 30-Year Holding Pattern: Study." (Ottawa: CCPA press release, June 28, 2007).

Canadian Centre for Policy Alternatives (CCPA) and CHO!CES. *Alternative Federal Budget Papers, 1997* (Ottawa: Canadian Centre for Policy Alternatives, 1997).

Canadian Labour Congress. May Day 2000: Demanding Our Rights! Celebrating Our Struggles (Pamphlet) (Ottawa: CLC 2000).

Carter, Donald D. "Collective Bargaining Legislation." In Morley Gunderson and Allen Ponak (eds.), *Union-Management Relations in Canada (3rd Edition)* (Toronto: Addison-Wesley, 1995).

Casey, Jay. "Why CAW Local 222 Dumped the NDP." *Canadian Dimension* 1993.

Chaboyer, Jan, and Errol Black. "Conspiracy in Winnipeg: How the 1919 General Strike Leaders Were Railroaded Into Prison and What We Must Now Do To Make Amends." *CCPA Review: Labour Notes* (Winnipeg: Canadian Centre for Policy Alternatives–Manitoba, March, 2006).

_____. "Day Marks True Start of Labour Movement." *Brandon Sun*, April 29, 2000.

Chaison, Gary N. "Union Mergers in the U.S. and Beyond." *Journal of Labor Research* 25, 1, 2004.

_____. *Union Mergers in Hard Times: The View from Five Countries* (Ithaca, NY: Cornell University Press, 1996).

Chamberlain, Neil. *The Labor Sector* (New York: McGraw-Hill, 1965).

Chaykowski, Richard P. "The Structure and Process of Collective Bargaining." In Morley Gunderson and Allen Ponak (eds.), *Union-Management Relations in Canada (3rd Edition)* (Don Mills: Addison-Wesley, 1995).

Citizenship and Immigration Canada. "Facts and Figures." 2005.

Clemens, Jason, Niels Veldhuis, and Amila Karabegovic. "Explaining Canada's High Unionization Rates." *Fraser Alert*, 2005.

Conway, J.F. "Calvert Outflanks His Opponents on the Right." *Winnipeg Free*

Press, November 5, 2006.

Craig, Alton W.J., and Norman A. Solomon. *The System of Industrial Relations in Canada (3rd Edition)* (Scarborough, ON: Prentice-Hall, 1993).

Darcy, Judy. "Foreword." In Linda Briskin and Patricia McDermott (eds.), *Women Challenging Unions: Feminism, Democracy and Militancy* (Toronto: University of Toronto Press, 1993).

Das Gupta, Tania. "Anti-Racism and the Organized Labour Movement." In Vic Satzewich (ed.), *Racism and Social Inequality in Canada* (Toronto: Thompson Educational Publishing Inc., 1998).

Davis, M. "Why the U.S. Working Class Is Different." *New Left Review* 123 (3), 1980.

Draper, Hal. *Karl Marx's Theory of Revolution Vol 2: The Politics of Social Classes* (New York and London: Monthly Review, 1978).

Ehring, George, and Wayne Roberts. *Giving away a Miracle: Lost Dreams, Broken Promises and the Ontario NDP* (Oakville, ON: Mosaic Press, 1993).

Episcopal Commission for Social Affairs. *Ethical Reflections on the Economic Crisis* (Ottawa: Canadian Conference of Catholic Bishops, 1983).

Estreicher, Samuel. "Disunity Within the House of Labor: Change to Win or to Stay the Course?" *Journal of Labor Research* XXVII, (Fall) 2006.

Fantasia, Rick. *Cultures of Solidarity: Consciousness, Action, and Contemporary American Workers* (Berkley: University of California Press, 1988).

Flanagan, Donne. "Inoculating Traditional NDP Weaknesses Key to Doer's Success" (paper in authors' possession, June, 2003).

Foner, Philip S. *May Day: A Short History of the International Workers' Holiday 1886–1986* (New York: International Publishers, 1986.)

Forrest, Anne. "Securing the Male Breadwinner: A Feminist Interpretation of PC 1003." In Cy Gonick, Paul Phillips and Jesse Vorst (eds.), *Labour Gains, Labour Pains: 50 Years of PC 1003* (Winnipeg/Halifax: Society for Socialist Studies/Fernwood Publishing, 1995).

Forsey, Eugene. *Trade Unions in Canada: 1812–1902* (Toronto: University of Toronto Press, 1982).

Frager, Ruth. "Women Workers and the Canadian Labour Movement." In Linda Briskin and Lynda Yanz (eds.), *Union Sisters: Women in the Labour Movement* (Toronto: Women's Press, 1983).

Frager, Ruth, and Carmela Patrias. *Discounted Labour: Women Workers in Canada, 1870–1939* (Toronto: University of Toronto Press, 2005).

Frank, David. *J.B. MacLachlan: A Biography* (Toronto: James Lorimer, 1999).

Freeman, R., and J. Medoff. *What Do Unions Do?* (New York: Basic Books, 1984).

Friesen, Gerald. "Bob Russell's Political Thought: Socialism and Industrial Unionism in Winnipeg, 1914–1919." In Gerald Friesen, *River Road: Essays on Manitoba and Prairie History* (Winnipeg: University of Manitoba Press, 1996).

_____. "'Yours in Revolt': The Socialist Party of Canada and the Western Canadian Labour Movement." *Labour/Le Travail* 1, 1976.

Galabuzi, Grace-Edward. *Canada's Economic Apartheid: The Social Exclusion of Racialized Groups in the New Century* (Toronto: New Scholars' Press,

2006).

Gertler, Meric S. "Canada in a High-Tech World: Options for Industrial Policy." In Daniel Drache and Meric S. Gertler (eds.), *The New Era of Global Competition: State Policy and Market Power* (Montreal and Kingston: McGill-Queen's University Press, 1991).

Gidengil, Elizabeth. "The Class Voting Conundrum." In Douglas Baer (ed.), *Political Sociology: Canadian Perspectives* (Don Mills: Oxford University Press, 2002).

Gidengil, Elizabeth, Andre Blais, Joanna Everitt, Patrick Fournier and Neil Nevitte. "Back to the Future? Making Sense of the 2004 Canadian Election Outside Quebec." *Canadian Journal of Political Science* 39, 1, 2006.

Giles, Antony, and Akivah Starkman. "The Collective Agreement." In Morley Gunderson and Allen Ponak (eds.), *Union-Management Relations in Canada (3rd Edition)* (Toronto: Addison-Wesley, 1995).

Gindin, Sam. *The Canadian Auto Workers: The Birth and Transformation of a Union* (Toronto: James Lorimer, 1995).

Goddard, John. "Beliefs about Unions and What They Should Do: A Survey of Employed Canadians." *Industrial & Labor Relations Review* 50 (3), 1997.

_____. *Industrial Relations, Economy and Society* (Toronto: McGraw-Hill Ryerson, 1994).

Godin, Keith, and Milagros Palacios. "Comparing Labour Relations Laws in Canada and the United States." *Fraser Alert*, 2006.

Goldfield, Michael. *The Decline of Organized Labor in the United States* (Chicago: University of Chicago Press, 1987).

Gordon, David. *Fat and Mean: The Corporate Squeeze of Working Americans and the Myth of Managerial 'Downsizing'* (New York: Free Press, 1996).

Greenhouse, Stephen and David Leonhard. "Real Wages Fail to Match a Rise in Productivity." *New York Times*, August 28, 2006.

Greer, Ian. "Business Union vs. Business Union? Understanding the Split in the US Labor Movement." *Capital & Class* 90, Autumn, 2006.

Greider, William. "Global Agenda: After the WTO Protest in Seattle, It's Time to Go on the Offensive. Here's How." *The Nation*, January 31, 2000.

Hackett, Robert. "Waffle." *Canadian Dimension* 15 (1–2), 1980.

Hackett, Robert, and Richard Gruneau. *The Missing News: Filters and Blind Spots in Canada's Press* (Toronto: Canadian Centre for Policy Alternatives and Garamond Press, 1999).

Haiven, Larry. "PC 1003 and the (Non) Right to Strike: A Sorry Legacy." In Cy Gonick, Paul Phillips and Jesse Vorst (eds.), *Labour Gains, Labour Pains: 50 Years of PC 1003* (Winnipeg/Halifax: Society for Socialist Studies/Fernwood Publishing, 1995).

Hall, Dave. "Rights of Migrant Workers Recognized." *Fast Facts* (Winnipeg, Canadian Centre of Policy Alternatives, July 2007).

Hanley, Jill, and Eric Shragge. "Justice for Immigrant Workers." *Canadian Dimension* May–June, 2006.

Henry, Frances, Carol Tator, Winston Mattis and Tim Rees. *The Colour of Democracy: Racism in Canadian Society, Second Edition* (Toronto: Harcourt Brace Canada, 2000).

Heron, Craig. *The Workers' Revolt in Canada: 1917–1925* (Toronto: University of Toronto Press, 1998).

_____. *The Canadian Labour Movement: A Short History* (Toronto: Lorimer, 1996).

_____. *The Canadian Labour Movement: A Short History* (Toronto: Lorimer, 1989).

_____. "Labourism and the Canadian Working Class." *Labour/Le Travail* 13, 1984.

Horowitz, Gad. *Canadian Labour and Politics* (Toronto: University of Toronto Press, 1968).

Houston, D. "Is There a New Social Structure of Accumulation?" *Review of Radical Political Economics* 24, 1992.

Human Resources Development Canada (HRDC). *Directory of Labour Organizations in Canada* (Ottawa: HRDC, 2006).

_____. "The 1997 HRDC Survey of Innovations and Change in Labour Organizations." In *Directory of Labour Organizations in Canada, 1998* (Ottawa: Minister of Public Works and Government Services Canada, 1998a).

______. *Directory of Labour Organizations* (Ottawa: Human Resources Development Canada, 1998b).

Huot, Christian. "Unionizing the Impossible." *Canadian Dimension* 1998.

Hyman, Richard. *Strikes (2nd Edition)* (Glasgow: Fontana-Collins, 1977).

Iacovetta, Franca, Michael Quinlan and Ian Radforth. "Immigration and Labour: Australia and Canada Compared." *Labour/Le Travail* 38, 1996.

"Immigration Overview: Permanent and Temporary Residents." Available at <www.cic.gc.ca/english/resources/statistics/facts2005/index.asp> accessed on October 23. 2007.

Jackson, Andrew. *Work and Labour in Canada: Critical Issues* (Toronto: Canadian Scholars' Press, 2005).

Jackson, Andrew, and David Robinson. *Falling Behind: The State of Working Canada, 2000* (Ottawa: Canadian Centre for Policy Alternatives, 2000).

Jackson, Andrew, and Sylvian Schetagne. *Solidarity Forever: An Analysis of Changes in Union Density* (Ottawa: Canadian Labour Congress, 2003).

Jamieson, Stuart Marshall. *Times of Trouble: Labour Unrest and Industrial Conflict in Canada, 1900–66* (Ottawa: Supply and Services, 1968).

Kealey, Gregory S. "1919: The Canadian Labour Revolt." *Labour/Le Travail* 13, 1984.

Kealey, Gregory S., and Bryan D. Palmer. *Dreaming of What Might Be: The Knights of Labour in Ontario, 1800–1900* (New York: Cambridge University Press, 1982).

Kealey, Linda. *Enlisting Women for the Cause: Women, Labour, and the Left in Canada, 1890–1920* (Toronto: University of Toronto Press, 1998).

_____. "Canadian Socialism and the Woman Question, 1900–1914." *Labour/Le Travail* 13, 1984.

Klein, Naomi. *No Logo: Taking Aim at the Brand Bullies* (Toronto: Alfred A. Knopf, 2000).

Kumar, Pradeep. *From Uniformity to Divergence: Industrial Relations in Canada and the United States* (Kingston: IRC Press, 1993).

Lancaster's Labour Law News. "Legislation in Opposite Directions: Unionization Promoted in Manitoba, Curtailed in Ontario." November/December 2000.

Leary, Elly, and Jean Alonso, "The Women Who Organized Harvard: A Feminist Model of Labor Organization?" *Monthly Review* 49 (7), 1997.

Lenin, Vladimir Ilyich. *On Trade Unions* (Moscow: Progress Publishers, 1970).

Li, Peter. *Ethnic Inequality in a Class Society* (Toronto: Wall and Thompson, 1988).

Lipton, Charles. *The Trade Union Movement of Canada 1827–1959 (4th Edition)* (Toronto: NC Press, 1978).

Luxton, Meg. "From Ladies' Auxiliaries to Wives' Committees." In Linda Briskin and Lynda Yanz (eds.), *Union Sisters: Women in the Labour Movement* (Toronto: Women's Press, 1983).

MacKay, Kevin. "Solidarity and Symbolic Protest: Lessons for Labour From the Quebec City Summit of the Americas." *Labour/Le Travail* 50, 2002.

MacKinnon, Shauna, and Pete Hudson. "Manitoba Budget 2007: A Budget Without Courage." *Fast Facts* (Winnipeg: Canadian Centre for Policy Alternatives–Manitoba, April, 2007).

Mainville, Diane, and Carey Olineck. *Unionization in Canada* (Ottawa: Statistics Canada, Catalogue No. 75-001-SPE, 1999).

Marshall, Katherine. "Converging Gender Roles." *Perspectives on Labour and Income* 18, 3, (Autumn), 2006.

Martinello, Felice. "Mr. Harris, Mr. Rae and Union Activity in Ontario." *Canadian Public Policy* XXVI (1), 2000.

Marx, Karl. *Capital, Volume 1* (Moscow: Progress Publishers, 1965).

_____. *Wages, Price and Profit* (Moscow: Progress Publishers, 1947).

Masi, Anthony C. "Structural Change in the Canadian Steel Industry, 1970–1986." In Daniel Drache and Meric S. Gertler (eds.), *The New Era of Global Competition: State Policy and Market Power* (Montreal and Kingston: McGill-Queen's University Press, 1991).

Masters, Marick F., Ray Gibney and Tom Zagenczyk. "The AFL-CIO vs. CTW: The Competing Visions, Strategies, and Structures." *Journal of Labor Research* XXVII, 4 (Fall), 2006.

McDermott, Patricia. "The Eaton's Strike: We Wouldn't Have Missed It for the World!" In Linda Briskin and Patricia McDermott (eds.). *Women Challenging Unions* (Toronto: University of Toronto Press, 1993).

Mendelson, Michael. *Aboriginal People in Canada's Labour Market: Work and Employment, Today and Tomorrow* (Ottawa: Caledon Institute of Social Policy, 2004).

Mitchell, Tom, and James Naylor. "The Prairies: In the Eye of the Storm." In Craig Heron (ed.). *The Workers' Revolt in Canada: 1917–1925*. (Toronto: University of Toronto Press, 1998).

Moody, Kim. *An Injury to All: The Decline of American Unionism* (New York/London: Verso, 1998).

_____. *Workers in a Lean World: Unions in the International Economy* (London: Verso, 1997).

Morissette, Rene, Grant Schellenberg and Anick Johnson. "Diverging Trends in Unionization." *Perspectives on Labour and Income* (Ottawa: Statistics Canada,

Catalogue No. 75-001-XPE, Summer 2005).

Morris, Jonathan. "A Japanization of Canadian Industry?" In Daniel Drache and Meric S. Gertler (eds.), *The New Era of Global Competition: State Policy and Market Power* (Montreal and Kingston: McGill-Queen's University Press, 1991).

Morton, Desmond. *Working People: An Illustrated History of the Canadian Labour Movement* (Toronto: Summerhill Press, 1990).

Morton, Desmond, with Terry Copp. *Working People: An Illustrated History of the Canadian Labour Movement* (Ottawa: Deneau, 1984).

Munro, Jack, and Jane O'Hara. *Union Jack: Labour Leader Jack Munro* (Vancouver: Douglas and McIntyre, 1988).

Murray, Gregor. "Unions: Membership, Structures, and Action." In Morley Gunderson and Allen Ponak (eds.), *Union-Management Relations in Canada (3rd Edition)* (Don Mills, Ont.: Addison-Wesley, 1995).

National Child Labor Committee. *Child Labor is Back: Children Are Again Sewing Clothing for Major U.S. Companies*. (New York: National Child Labor Committee, 2006). Available at www.nlcnet.org/article.php?id=147, accessed on November 30, 2007.

Ng, Roxanna. "Sexism, Racism and Canadian Nationalism." In Jesse Vorst (ed.), *Race, Class, Gender: Bonds and Barriers* (Toronto: Garamond 1995).

Ornstein, Michael. "Canadian Capital and the Canadian State: Ideology in an Era of Crisis." In Robert J. Brym (ed.), *The Structure of the Canadian Capitalist Class* (Toronto: Garamond Press, 1985).

Ostry, Bernard. "Conservatives, Liberals and Labour in the 1880s." *Canadian Journal of Economics and Political Science* 18, 1961.

_____. "Conservatives, Liberals and Labour in the 1870s." *Canadian Historical Review* 41, 1960.

Palley, Thomas I. *Plenty of Nothing: The Downsizing of the American Dream and the Case for Structural Keynesianism* (Princeton, NJ: Princeton University Press, 1998).

Palmer, Bryan D. *Working-Class Experience: Rethinking the History of Canadian Labour, 1880–1991* (Toronto: McClelland and Stewart, 1992).

_____. *Solidarity: The Rise and Fall of an Opposition in British Columbia* (Vancouver: New Star Books, 1986).

_____. *Working-Class Experience: The Rise and Reconstitution of Canadian Labour, 1800–1980* (Toronto: Butterworth, 1983).

Panitch, Leo, and Donald Swartz. *The Assault on Trade Union Freedoms: From Consent to Coercion (3rd edition)* (Toronto: Garamond Press, 2003).

______. *The Assault on Trade Union Freedoms: From Wage Controls to Social Contract (2nd edition)* (Toronto: Garamond Press, 1993).

Parker, Mike, and Martha Gruelle. *Democracy Is Power: Rebuilding Unions from the Bottom Up* (Detroit: Labor Notes, 1993).

Penner, Norman. *From Protest to Power: Social Democracy in Canada 1900–Present* (Toronto: Lorimer, 1992).

_____. *Canadian Communism: The Stalin Years and Beyond* (Toronto: Methuen, 1988).

_____. *The Canadian Left: A Critical Analysis* (Toronto: Prentice Hall, 1977).

Pope John Paul II. *Laborem Exercens* (Rome: Papal Encyclical, 1981).

Pope Leo XIII. *Rerum Novarum* (Rome: Papal Encyclical, 1891).

Rebick, Judy. *Ten Thousand Roses: The Making of a Feminist Revolution* (Toronto: Penguin Canada, 2005).

Riddell, W. Craig. "Unionization in Canada and the United States: A Tale of Two Countries." In David Card and Richard B. Freeman (eds.), *Small Differences That Matter: Labor Markets and Income Maintenance in Canada and the United States* (Chicago: University of Chicago Press, 1993).

Robinson, Ian. "Economistic Unionism in Crisis: The Origins, Consequences and Prospects of Divergence in Labor Movement Characteristics." In Jane Jenson and Rianne Mahon (eds.), *The Challenge of Restructuring: North American Labor Movements Respond* (Philadelphia: Temple University Press, 1993).

Roediger, David. *The Wages of Whiteness: Race and the Making of the American Working Class, Revised Edition* (London: Verso, 1999).

Salutin, Rick. *Kent Rowley, the Organizer: A Canadian Life* (Toronto: Lorimer, 1980).

Sangster, Joan. "The Communist Party and the Woman Question, 1922–1929." *Labour/Le Travail* 15, 1985.

Sears, Alan. "The 'Lean' State and Capitalist Restructuring: Towards a Theoretical Account." *Studies in Political Economy* 59, 1999.

Silver, Jim. *The Inner Cities of Winnipeg and Saskatoon: A New Form of Development* (Winnipeg and Saskatoon: Canadian Centre for Policy Alternatives-Manitoba and Canadian Centre for Policy Alternatives-Saskatchewan, 2008).

Silver, Jim (ed.). *Solutions That Work: Fighting Poverty in Winnipeg* (Winnipeg/Halifax: Canadian Centre for Policy Alternatives–Manitoba and Fernwood Publishing, 2000).

Silver, Jim, and Lisa Shaw. *The MAI Primer* (Winnipeg: Canadian Centre for Policy Alternatives–Manitoba, 1998).

Sirota, David. "The War on Workers." *The San Francisco Chronicle*, September 4, 2006.

Smith, Doug. *Let Us Rise: An Illustrated History of the Manitoba Labour Movement* (Vancouver: New Star Books, 1985).

Stanford, Jim. *Paper Boom: Why Real Prosperity Requires a New Approach to Canada's Economy* (Toronto: Lorimer and Canadian Centre for Policy Alternatives, 1999).

_____. "The Rise and Fall of Deficit-Mania: Public-Sector Finances and the Attack on Social Canada." In Les Samuelson and Wayne Antony (eds.), *Power and Resistance: Critical Thinking about Canadian Social Issues (2nd Edition)* (Halifax: Fernwood Publishing, 1998).

Statistics Canada. "Unionization." *Perspectives on Labour and Income* Catalogue No. 75-001-XPE, 2006a.

_____. *Canadian Economic Observer* Catalogue No. 11-010, November 2006b.

_____. "Full-time and Part-time Employment by Sex and Age Group, 2006." CANSIM, table 282-0002 (2006c). Available at <http://www40.statcan.ca/l01/cst01/labor12.htm> accessed on October 23, 2007.

_____. *Canadian Economic Observer, Historical Supplement 2004/05* Catalogue No. 11-210-XIB, 2005.

_____. *Canadian Economic Observer, Historical Supplement 2000/01* Catalogue No. 11-210-XPB, 2001.

_____. *Labour Force Update: An Overview of the 1999 Labour Market* (Ottawa: Catalogue No. 71-005-XPB. Winter 2000a).

_____. *Women in Canada 2000* (Ottawa: Statistics Canada, Catalogue No. 89-503-XPE, 2000b).

Steedman, Mercedes. *Angels of the Workplace: Women and the Construction of Gender Relations in the Canadian Clothing Industry, 1890–1940* (Toronto: Oxford University Press, 1997).

Sufrin, Eileen. *The Eaton Drive: The Campaign to Organize Canada's Largest Department Store 1948 to 1952* (Toronto: Fitzhenry and Whiteside, 1982).

Swartz, Donald. "Capitalist Restructuring and the Canadian Labour Movement." In Jane Jenson and Rianne Mahon (eds.), *The Challenge of Restructuring: North American Labour Movements Respond* (Philadelphia: Temple University Press, 1993).

United States Department of Labor. "Union Members Summary." Available at <www.bls.gov/news.release/union2.nr0.htm> accessed on October 23, 2007.

Visser, Jelle. "Union Membership in 24 Countries." *Monthly Labor Review*, 129 (1), 2006.

Vorst, Jesse, et al. *Race, Class, Gender: Bonds and Barriers* (Toronto: Between the Lines, 1989).

Walkom, Thomas. *Rae Days: The Rise and Follies of the NDP* (Toronto: Key Porter, 1994).

Warnock, John. *Free Trade and the New Right Agenda* (Vancouver: New Star Books, 1988).

Weinberg, Paul. "Showdown in Uniontown." *This Magazine* 34 (1), 2000.

Wells, Donald. "Labour Solidarity Goes Global." Canadian *Dimension* 13 (2), 1998.

White, Julie. *Sisters & Solidarity: Women and Unions in Canada* (Toronto: Thompson Educational Publishers, 1993).

_____. *Mail & Female: Women and the Canadian Union of Postal Workers* (Toronto: Thompson Educational Publishers, 1990).

Whitehorn, Alan. *Canadian Socialism: Essays on the CCF-NDP* (Toronto: Oxford University Press, 1992).

Yates, Michael. *Why Unions Matter* (New York: Monthly Review Press, 1998).